ISLAM IN CENTRAL ASIA AND THE CAUCASUS SINCE THE FALL OF THE SOVIET UNION

COMPARATIVE POLITICS
AND INTERNATIONAL STUDIES SERIES

Series editors, Christophe Jaffrelot and Alain Dieckhoff
Series managing editor, Miriam Perier

The series consists of original manuscripts and translations of noteworthy manuscripts and publications in the social sciences emanating from the foremost French researchers.

The focus of the series is the transformation of politics and society by transnational and domestic factors—globalisation, migration and religion. States are more permeable to external influence than ever before and this phenomenon is accelerating processes of social and political change the world over. In seeking to understand and interpret these transformations, this series gives priority to social trends from below as much as to the interventions of state and nonstate actors.

BAYRAM BALCI

Islam in Central Asia and the Caucasus Since the Fall of the Soviet Union

Translated by
Gregory Elliott

OXFORD
UNIVERSITY PRESS

OXFORD
UNIVERSITY PRESS

Oxford University Press is a department of the
University of Oxford. It furthers the University's objective
of excellence in research, scholarship, and education
by publishing worldwide.

Oxford New York
Auckland Cape Town Dar es Salaam Hong Kong Karachi
Kuala Lumpur Madrid Melbourne Mexico City Nairobi
New Delhi Shanghai Taipei Toronto

With offices in
Argentina Austria Brazil Chile Czech Republic France Greece
Guatemala Hungary Italy Japan Poland Portugal Singapore
South Korea Switzerland Thailand Turkey Ukraine Vietnam

Oxford is a registered trade mark of Oxford University Press
in the UK and certain other countries.

Published in the United States of America by
Oxford University Press
198 Madison Avenue, New York, NY 10016

Copyright © Bayram Balci 2018

All rights reserved. No part of this publication may be reproduced,
stored in a retrieval system, or transmitted, in any form or by any means,
without the prior permission in writing of Oxford University Press,
or as expressly permitted by law, by license, or under terms agreed with
the appropriate reproduction rights organization. Inquiries concerning
reproduction outside the scope of the above should be sent to the
Rights Department, Oxford University Press, at the address above.

You must not circulate this work in any other form
and you must impose this same condition on any acquirer.

Library of Congress Cataloging-in-Publication Data is available
Bayram Balci.
Islam in Central Asia and the Caucasus Since the Fall of the Soviet Union.
ISBN: 9780190917272

Printed in India on acid-free paper

CONTENTS

Preface   vii

Introduction: The End of the USSR and a New Perception of Religion   1

1. Inherited Islam: An Islam Marked by Russian and Soviet Domination   11
2. Turkey as an Islamic Actor in Central Asia and the Caucasus   35
3. Iran: A Minor Religious Actor in Central Asia and the Caucasus   69
4. Influences from the Arabian Peninsula on the Revival of Islam in Central Asia and the Caucasus   103
5. South Asia's Influence on the Revival of Islam in Central Asia   131
6. The Administration of Religion in the Newly Independent Republics   157

Conclusion: The End of Islam in the Singular   183

Notes   191
Bibliography   219
Index   239

PREFACE

Olivier Roy[1]

We hardly speak about Central Asia nowadays, and only slightly more of the Caucasus. Yet when these new spaces opened up in the early 1990s, there was a mad rush: travellers, researchers, experts and missionaries of all kinds streamed into the famous Silk Road. Embassies, research institutes, international missions, mosques, churches and shops began to proliferate, each trying to shape this 'new Asia' to its own image of globalisation.

History finally opened its old drawers—but each drawer told a different version of the past and left an impression of a contradictory future: Islamisation seemed as likely as democracy and nationalism. The oilman and the jihadist, the preacher and the tourist, the diplomat and the researcher rubbed shoulders at Intourist hotels (whose main modernisation was to shift from the ruble to the dollar, well before the arrival of the Sheraton and the Hilton).

Close cooperation between the French Ministry of Foreign Affairs and university researchers enabled the establishment of a research network centered around the IFEA in Tashkent and its several campuses, in addition to an office in Baku. As early as 1995, France had an unrivalled research network covering all of the new republics (with the exception of its Turkmenistan office, which would soon close). The Quai d'Orsay had no difficulty attracting the interest of experienced and passionate diplomats, drawing from its pool of Russian-speaking cadres, who were suddenly mourning the passage of the Soviet Union, flanked by young secretaries who had just joined the diplomatic service.

The opening of these diplomatic missions demonstrated great initiative and curiosity. Local administrations were still taking shape. Some bad Soviet habits still persisted, and the new elites did not know what the future held. Anything and everything seemed possible. Gradually, borders were established and closed, languages changed alphabets and nations changed flags, while a whole string of new initials and stamps saturated the passport pages of those passing through.

At a time when local initiatives were desperately needed, no one in the ministries in Paris had the time either to develop a grand policy or to settle in a new routine. The only hope was that a dynamic ambassador or an enterprising individual would take new initiatives and activate his or her networks to make things happen. No one knew where we were going: towards the return of the USSR in another form; towards the creation of modern states or Islamic emirates; the breakthrough of China; a link to the West through a sudden network of gas pipelines; war by proxy with Iran; the return of Turkey; pan-Turanism; pan-Iranianism; pan-Eurasianism; Pan-Islamism. Everything seemed possible—and it was necessary to be there.

As for researchers of course, there were not many people working on Central Asia and the Caucasus: some historians, some linguists, and, on the question of Islam, the students of Alexandre Bennigsen. But Russians, Turks and Iranians sought to extend their academic territory by expanding their own cultural area, redoubling and rationalising debates on identity and geo-strategy. It was the hour of glory for geo-strategy, a new field introduced to university studies by geographers in the 1970s. It was then that a whole new generation of researchers emerged, almost spontaneously.

Many, like Bayram Balci, found themselves there somewhat by chance—for him it was cultural cooperation in Kazakhstan. But he was leaving with a definite advantage: he already spoke Arabic and Turkish and made the effort to learn Uzbek. This mastery of languages enabled him to take on a new subject: the reconstruction of the religious space

PREFACE

in Central Asia. As Alexandre Bennigsen had foreseen, the Soviet system had not eliminated Islam, even though, aside from a handful of historic buildings, it had almost completely suppressed its visibility.

Salafism, also called Wahhabism, had penetrated Central Asia before the fall of the USSR. But the general emptiness attracted many activist networks, from the Tablighis to the Gülenists and the entire range of Salafists. Coming from Turkey, the Arab countries and the Indian subcontinent, they converted and recruited locals and built schools and mosques, before experiencing state repression.

At the same time, young activists from Central Asia and the Caucasus set out for jihad in Afghanistan and Pakistan. Uzbeks, Chechens and Dagestanis are overrepresented on the international jihadi front. The reaction of the states of Central Asia was to close the borders, to expel all kinds of religious missions, to take up the old Soviet recipes for the control of religion through a functionary clergy and, of course, the traditional values of the family and respect for historical customs.

Secular conservatives and the promoters of state religion have aimed to break up new transnational religious networks. This policy has had some successes, even if they have not been able to reconnect societies with their cultural traditions—that includes Persian and Chaghatay—and it does not take account of the modern linguistic division established by the Soviets and followed up by the new states. Now, the debate is between Cyrillic and Latin, while the Arabic-Persian alphabet is forgotten, even in those places where it could have been rehabilitated (e.g. Tajikistan). But that did not put an end to the circulation of people and ideas. Hundreds of thousands, even millions of Caucasian and Central Asian Muslims have immigrated to Russia to find work. At least one Russian-speaking battalion is fighting against ISIS in Syria, although few of its members are native speakers. The Soviet phantom also haunts the dissidents of the empire, who are united by the old colonial language. The descendants of immigrants who took refuge in the Ottoman Empire to flee the Russian advance are rediscovered Circassians or Bukhariots. Unfortunately, the common religious grammar of these new global citizens is Salafism, which mocks all cultures, especially ones that also claim to be Muslim. This is undoubtedly the tragedy of the erstwhile Central Asian culture: now it belongs only to historians and archaeologists.

INTRODUCTION

THE END OF THE USSR AND A NEW PERCEPTION OF RELIGION

Some twenty-five years after the end of the USSR, the time has come to take stock of the changes in the countries and societies that emerged from that multi-ethnic, multi-confessional state. Here we shall be examining the development of Islam in two parts of the region: Central Asia and the Caucasus. At certain points in its history, the Soviet Union projected itself as a Muslim power, and contemporary Russia boasts several million practising Muslims whom it places at the centre of its policy of rapprochement with the Muslim world. The so-called 'Muslim' countries that emerged from the Soviet Union—i.e. the republics of Azerbaijan, Kazakhstan, Kyrgyzstan, Uzbekistan, Tajikistan and Turkmenistan, which possess a predominantly Muslim population and heritage—are also affirming a new relationship with Islam. And, whether they like it or not, as sovereign subjects on the international scene they are interacting in a new way with various countries from which they import or experience religious influences. Thus, the initial premise of the present work is that from 1991 onwards the Caucasus and Central Asia joined in the globalization of religion. Consequently, in order to understand changes in Islam there, we need to examine the way in which its states have dealt with various foreign influences and the conduct of public policy on religion in the light of such influences. The latter derive from countries which, prior to Russian conquest and Soviet domination, were in contact with Central Asia and the Caucasus.

Turkey, Iran, the Arabian Peninsula and the Indian subcontinent are the main sources of Muslim currents influencing the revival of Islam in the ex-Soviet sphere. The aim of this work is to assess these interactions and influences.

Attitudes to the Muslim Past and the Administration of Religion

The role of religion in society, and the nature of its links with the state prior to independence, are starting points for study and analysis if we wish to arrive at a clearer understanding of the evolution of the post-Soviet societies. I shall, therefore, first seek to disentangle how and why, from 1991 onwards, all the new republics claimed to belong to Islamic civilization, while showing themselves very determined to maintain the secularism inherited from the Soviet experience. Of particular interest will be observing how this claim to be part of Islamic civilization was articulated and the extent to which such identification, inconceivable until 1991, is selective, corresponding to specific political motives and objectives. Thus, the official decision to promote the image and teachings of some particular scholar or historical religious figure, and to root this religious heritage in local geography, extolling a particular city of pilgrimage, form part of a specific policy geared to constructing a certain type of state and society. In this way of seeing things, religion must serve state or society. But it seems just as important to root local traditional Islam in a more general history. The new elites' obsession with endeavouring to demonstrate that their ancestors contributed to the Islamic civilization, and hence the global civilization, to which they belong attests to an ambition to leave behind the international isolation they suffered for almost a century, and which still hampers their development.

In fact, all these Muslim countries saw not only their history, but also their culture and sense of identity, profoundly marked by Russian domination. The nationalist currents that fought Russian colonial domination were themselves marked, even fashioned, by a Russian and European mentality and political culture in the broad sense. The present work, devoted to contemporary religious issues, will not go into the details of Russian colonization and the way it made the modernization and emancipation of revolutionary and anti-colonial intellectual

INTRODUCTION

currents possible. However, they must be recalled as a reminder that the Tsars' policy towards Islam was not as repressive as one might imagine. Thus, we shall see that Russian domination even facilitated the development of modernizing tendencies in Islam, even a Muslim order, by preserving Islamic courts of justice in particular. On the other hand, to clarify the contemporary development of Central Asian and Caucasian Islam, I shall explain why and how the Soviet regime devoted so much effort to controlling and restricting interaction between Muslims in the empire and those abroad.[1] This brief focus on the Russian episode in Central Asian and Caucasian Islam aims to bring out the continuity in the authorities' relationship to religious matters between the colonial, Soviet order and the independent order since the early 1990s.

Even more so than the Russian phase, the Soviet era had a significant influence on the societies of Central Asia and the Caucasus. It was with the onset of Soviet rule that borders, ethnic identities and national constructs were defined and fixed, in a web of administrative statutes and entities more or less directly controlled by the centre. Moscow's claws certainly kept a tight grip on religion, but that grip twisted, undermined and shaped it, rather than destroying it completely. Thus, Islam acquired a number of its current characteristics during the Soviet period. It did not choose them, because they were injunctions imposed by Soviet policy. Relations between Soviet power and Islam have been abundantly studied in the literature, particularly by Shoshana Keller[2] and Yaacov Ro'i.[3] However, it is worth underscoring the relative character of Soviet religious repression or, rather, indicating that, amid repression and anti-religious propaganda, Islam continued to develop. Its survival was certainly not without its distorting constraints, but it survived in its own way, without the support of classical Islamic institutions, in the Soviet system, especially the kolkhozes.[4] As a result, during the Soviet period a particular type of Islam took shape, which was a matter more of identity than dogma, more private and individual than communitarian, generating a form of public secularism that would be adopted by the post-Soviet regimes after 1991.[5] But I also need to broach a point that is often neglected: namely, the endogenous Soviet character of militant, oppositional Islam, which is often characterized as political and/or fundamentalist by some analysts. A recurrent allegation today throughout the post-Soviet sphere maintains that 'bad Islam', radical and obscurantist, has exclusively foreign roots and is incompatible with 'our traditional Islam', by definition tolerant and humanist. In the event, the local and Soviet roots of militant, oppositional Islam originated in the system itself.[6] What are they? And how far did the Soviet policy of denigrating popular religious sites—the mausoleums of saints, in particular—not only boost popular Islam, but also encourage a certain puritanism in official Islam, which was adopted and kept up by a number of fundamentalist tendencies after the end of the Soviet Union?

When it comes to religious affairs, the break represented by the disappearance of the Soviet Union involves not only the perception and selective re-appropriation of the Islamic heritage, but also the way that Islamic affairs are controlled and administered by the state. In effect, the latter is in charge of organizing worship in mosques, religious education, and the construction or restoration of mosques and madrasas. Thus, it has entered into a new phase where it is no longer opposed to Islam, but seeks to encourage it, on condition that Islam obeys the authorities and satisfies the state's particular interests. In this new context, how does the existing regime's desire to continue the secular tradition forged during the Soviet period find expression? What form of secularism do they now seek to implement? The degree of state intervention in the religious sphere conveys the impression that it is a highly militant, interventionist secularism which, rather than a separation of powers, seeks to legitimate a central government monopoly on religion. How is this task performed? And what is the impact of the apparatus of control on society and the various religious tendencies? Do the Spiritual Directorates inherited from the Soviet era and the newly created Committees on Religious Affairs act in concert, or competition, with one another?

Religious education in the states' new policy towards Islam will be the focus of particular attention. In fact, the new elites are trained in the schools and madrasas. The role allocated to Islamic teaching, as stipulated by the regime and official institutions, says a lot about the new ideology and nature of these young states.[7] However, in the sphere of education, as elsewhere, not all central governments have adopted the same attitude. They are not all obsessed with controlling

INTRODUCTION

and dominating populations and consciences. Thus, although liberated at the same time and bearers of a shared Soviet experience, these states have gradually freed themselves from the Soviet approach to religion and, each in its own way, reinvented their relationship to religion. Coupled with growing nationalism and ethnocentrism, the manacles of traditional Central Asian and Caucasian Islam have burst into a myriad of different forms, peculiar to each country. In each of these contexts, the state's position on religion varies and largely depends on the intensity of Islamist opposition, whether it takes the form of silent dissidence from official Islam or a more assertive, militant form—even a jihadist one in some instances. Radical Islam, or what is deemed such, will not be a central concern of the present work, for it is already the subject of numerous wide-ranging studies. But reference will be made to it as and when it is relevant to aspects of my analysis—notably, as regards the links between state religious policy and the intensity of Islamic opposition.

Having detailed the Islamic heritage and the state's everyday administration of Islam, I shall broach the novel contributions of foreign currents, ideas and influences to Central Asian and Caucasian Islam—and this in the already established order of the major poles of attraction represented by Turkey, Iran, Saudi Arabia and the Indian subcontinent.

Secular Turkey as a Major Islamic Actor in the Post-Soviet Sphere

Paradoxically, the first and doubtless most influential country to have had an impact on post-Soviet Islam is Kemalist, secular Turkey. This republic, loyal to the secular principles of its founder Atatürk until the current deviation from them of Recep Tayyip Erdoğan's AKP regime, was perceived as a model of liberal, secular development to be emulated by the Muslim societies that had escaped the Soviet fold. But history has decided differently and the present work will seek to identify the pragmatic reasons behind Ankara's decision to develop a veritable Islamic policy towards these countries. Since 1991, private Turkish Islamic currents have engaged and participated in the re-Islamization of Central Asia and the Caucasus. But the Turkish state has itself established mechanisms of cooperation in the religious sphere. To what end and with what results? Such are the questions I shall be addressing.

Although developing outside the framework of the state, these private Turkish movements inevitably interact with Turkey's official policy in Central Asia and, obviously, with the Central Asian governments themselves, which have a monopoly on religious affairs and official registration of foreign organizations wishing to pursue their activities in the country. So how does the encounter between Turkish Islam and Azeri, Uzbek, Kazakh, Kyrgyz, Turkmen and Tajik Islam take place on the ground?

In the second chapter, particular attention will be paid to the *cemaat* (the community) or *hizmet* (service) founded by Fethullah Gülen. Within and without Turkey's national borders, this socio-religious movement has gradually and significantly invested in the economy, the media, and especially the education sector. Initially allied with Erdoğan, today Gülen is his worst enemy. What are the consequences of this rift for the movement's educational and missionary activities? How have the Central Asian states reacted to the unanticipated power struggle between Erdoğan and Gülen? How do they react to the movement's patent politicization, when they have themselves always been suspicious of its ambitions? Presented and analysed in its various dimensions, the Islamic influence of the secular Turkish republic will help us arrive at a better understanding of the much weaker impact of another regional power: the Islamic Republic of Iran.

The Role of the Islamic Republic of Iran in Reconstructing Islam in Central Asia and the Caucasus

In the months preceding the collapse of the USSR, Turkey was not the only country to discover an immense region of great strategic and political potential opening up on its borders, to which it was linked by history. Another state, Iran, took a close interest in its new neighbours to the north. With as much legitimacy as Turkey, if not more, the Islamic Republic asserted a shared heritage with the countries of the Caucasus and Central Asia. The deconstruction of Iranian power in the post-Soviet sphere requires us to analyse the numerous obstacles it confronted. Iran's religious policy, but especially the way the Islamic Republic's religious peculiarities are perceived, will be at the forefront of a chapter wholly devoted to Iran in the post-Soviet sphere. This

INTRODUCTION

influence, whose *modus operandi*—its channels and its public or private modality—we shall observe, is very unequally shared between Central Asia and the Caucasus. What is Iran's role among the Shia communities of the post-Soviet sphere? And does its influence measure up to that of its great regional rival, Saudi Arabia?

The Influence of the Arabian Peninsula in Revitalizing Islam in Central Asia and the Caucasus: Between Myth and Reality

Cradle of Islam, home to the holy cities of Medina and Mecca, and leader of Sunni Islam, Saudi Arabia plays a prominent part in debates on religious issues in Central Asia and the Caucasus. In the early 1990s, Western diplomatic corps feared a lightning advance by all-conquering Wahhabism into the ancient lands abandoned by Soviet ideology. A nuanced retrospective analysis of Arab influence in general, and Saudi influence in particular, will disentangle legend from reality as regards Wahhabism's expansion into Central Asia. This will involve not denying the fact of the circulation of this fundamentalist Islam between the holy cities and the cities of Central Asia, but explaining it and identifying its routes. Three in number, they are complementary.

The first is Saudi diplomacy and *Rabita*, the Muslim World League. However, as we shall see, its record in exercising influence in the region is rather mixed.

In practice, the second route, and much more effective instrument, of Saudi Wahhabi influence is the *hajj* and the *umrah*, the major and lesser pilgrimages to Mecca and Medina. Well-nigh non-existent during the Soviet era, pilgrimages have enjoyed a phenomenal revival of interest in the Caucasus and Central Asia. I shall come back to the organization of the *hajj* from the Tsars' time to the present, as well as the concerns and fears it inspires in official circles, while presenting and assessing the issues and opportunities it creates.

Finally, the third significant vector of the circulation of religious ideas between Saudi Arabia and Central Asia is the descendants of Central Asian immigrants in the kingdom. This historical episode, unacknowledged and neglected by scholars, has created a new bridge between Arabia and the ancestral homeland. In fact, two communities—one Uzbek, the other Uighur—have been settled in Saudi Arabia for decades. Forming two distinct communities, well-established in the holy cities but also in Jeddah, Riyadh and Ta'if, these Uzbeks and Uighurs had few links with their country of origin and were in the process of being completely assimilated into Saudi society. But in 1991, in a way the Uzbek community of Saudi Arabia could not have expected and could scarcely have hoped for, their country of origin—Uzbekistan, which they still call Turkestan—finally emerged from the yoke of communism to become independent. This major historical event was an occasion for making the return journey, finding relatives, recreating ties with the country of origin. What role did religion play in this? To what extent did the restoration of links between the Uzbek diaspora and the country of origin nurture a form of religious revival in Central Asia? Has not this contribution been exaggerated by post-Soviet regimes obsessed with the threat of Wahhabism? How did the combination of the diasporic connection and pilgrimage to Mecca, the encounter between migrants and pilgrims, make possible a kind of export of Saudi Islam to Central Asia? Such are the key questions in this chapter, which will be devoted to Islamic relations between the Arabian Peninsula and Central Asia.

Reconnecting Central Asian and South Asian Islam?

A final chapter will be devoted to South Asia, another large Islamic region closely linked historically to Central Asia, which the vicissitudes of history—Russian and Soviet domination on one side, British colonization on the other—have separated. I shall endeavour to show how the opening up of Central Asia and the development of the Indian sub-continent facilitated the expansion of air and rail links, but also forms of interaction, as in the past. These relations also made it possible to recreate religious links between the two zones, allowing Central Asian Islam to benefit from sources of renewal from the south—India, Pakistan and Bangladesh. This involved the restoration of former relations, because the Mughal legacy was a powerful cement between Central Asia and South Asia, encouraging exchanges of ideas and, *a fortiori*, cultural and religious exchanges. So, now that the obstacles have been cleared away, how have relations between India and Central Asia shaped up since the end of the Soviet era? The renewal of religious

INTRODUCTION

links between the two regions essentially comes down to the work of the most dynamic and transnational of all pietistic and proselytizing organizations, the Tablighi Jamaat.

We shall therefore be concerned with its establishment in various Central Asian cities. How is it effected, by what means and in line with what strategy? How do its missionaries adapt to the diversity of religious policy in the countries of Central Asia and the varying reception accorded them? What obstacles and what opportunities do they encounter in pursuing their proselytism?

The sole Central Asian country where the Tablighi movement is legally recognized and accepted is Kyrgyzstan. How is the understanding between the Kyrgyz government and Tablighi Jamaat to be explained? Why is Tablighi's missionary Islam so well-adapted to the rather superficial Islam of the Kyrgyz? Is it the nomadic heritage that naturally embraces the philosophy of the Tablighi movement? Above all, I shall pose the crucial issue of the degree of penetration of Tabligh ideas among the Kyrgyz and the nature and scale of the links with South Asia. Tablighi Jamaat is certainly highly active in Kyrgyzstan, but can it therefore be claimed that it has singlehandedly succeeded in restoring the former ties between Central Asian Islam and South Asian Islam? Is Tablighi Jamaat improving the negative image that Central Asia still has of South Asia?

In conclusion, I shall show that for the countries of Central Asia and the Caucasus, Islam is a force for integration into the international community. Not only does it represent a gateway to the globalization of religion, but it also provides resources for the struggle against radical Islam. I shall also show how, in and through the struggle against jihadism in Afghanistan and even Syria, the Muslim countries of the ex-USSR are finding a role on the international stage.

1

INHERITED ISLAM

AN ISLAM MARKED BY RUSSIAN AND SOVIET DOMINATION

Introduction: Belonging to Islamic Civilization

Some historical references and contextualization are required for a clearer understanding of the role of Islam in the societies of Central Asia and the Caucasus since the end of the Soviet era. A crucial point, which must constantly be borne in mind and which Muslims in the post-Soviet sphere stress, is the historical profundity of the link between Islamic civilization and the peoples of the Caucasus and Central Asia. Although, following Russia's entry onto the scene, they found themselves rather on the margins or periphery of the Muslim world, the reputation of Islamic civilization greatly benefited from the work of scholars and intellectual centres originating in, or situated at, the heart of Central Asia.

The present chapter seeks to highlight the antiquity and the strength of the ties between Islam and the peoples of Central Asia and the Caucasus. At the same time, an analysis of the Russian and Soviet phases in their history will make it possible to achieve a better understanding of the specificities of Azeri, Kazakh, Kyrgyz, Uzbek, Tajik and Turkmen Islam. With these foundations laid, it will be easier to appreciate what is at stake in current religious policies in countries emerging from the ex-USSR. Thus, we shall see that Russian and Soviet domination of Islam did not exclusively take the form of strict control and repression—real as these undoubtedly were—but also involved compromises and negotiations, which made it possible for Islam to maintain a link with society, even a certain salience within it.

The Role of Central Asia and the Caucasus in Islamic Civilization

In the Caucasus and Central Asia alike, the penetration of Islam started very early, from the onset of the Arab conquest, and was rapid and multifaceted.

On their arrival in Central Asia at the start of the eighth century, under the command of Qutayba ibn Muslim, the Arab conquerors discovered a region characterized by a remarkable multi-ethnicity and a way of life with contrasting nomadic and sedentary populations. In religious terms, Zoroastrianism and Buddhism were predominant, although there was a visible Nestorian Christian presence and a small Jewish minority, notably in the Bukhara region. However, Transoxiana as a whole was rapidly incorporated into the Umayyad Caliphate that Islamized the quasi-totality of Central Asia, with more success among sedentary populations than nomadic ones. Scarcely a century after its Islamization, today's Central Asia had made itself the apex of this young civilization. Bukhara, Merv and Samarkand became cultural and intellectual centres that were beacons in the Muslim world. Scholars born in what is part of present-day Central Asia contributed to Islam's advance and influence. To cite only the most illustrious, the theologian Muhammad ibn Ismail al-Bukhari (810–70), respected throughout the Muslim world for his work authenticating the Prophet's *hadiths*, was a native of the Samarkand region in present-day Uzbekistan, and his mausoleum still attracts visitors and pilgrims from across the world. Another famous theologian, Abu Isa Muhammad al-Tirmidhi (825–92), was born in Termez in the south of what is today Uzbekistan. Similarly, the scientist and philosopher Abu Nasr al-Farabi (872–950), famous for having developed the sciences and arts of his time, and who was nicknamed 'the second teacher of the intelligence', was born either in Wasij near Farab (present-day Kazakhstan) or in Faryab in Khorasan (Afghanistan). Whichever, he was a native of Central Asia. Finally, we

INHERITED ISLAM

must not forget Abu Ali al-Hasan Ibn Abdullah Ibn-Sina, Avicenna to Westerners. Born in 980 in the village of Afsana near the city of Bukhara, he died in 1037 in Hamada. He was one of the great scholars of the medieval period, at once philosopher, doctor, mathematician and astronomer. Author of the *Qanun al Tibb*, the 'Canon of Medicine', he is probably the foremost representative of Islam's contribution to world civilization. Because they contributed to Islamic and world civilization, and to the prestige of Central Asia, these figures were made national heroes after the end of the Soviet era. They are used by local political leaders to project their country's image internationally.

This brilliant Islamic civilization, whose main centres in Bukhara and Samarkand were encompassed by the Persian cultural sphere, was destroyed by the Mongol conquest between 1220 and 1223. Yet, in the space of a few decades, the Mongol conquerors were themselves converted to Islam. And this marriage between Turkic–Mongol culture and Muslim religion gave rise to a new civilization. Under the reign of Amir Timur (Tamerlane, 1336–1405) and his descendants, the Timurids, it dominated most of present-day Central Asia until the start of the sixteenth century,[1] making Islam its official religion and, to a large extent, its compass in exercising political power. The astronomer and mathematician prince Ulugh Beg (1409–49) merits mention for creating and directing the team of the *Ziz-i Sultani*, an astronomical catalogue.[2] From the same era hails the illustrious man of letters Mir Ali-Shir Navai (1441–1501), whose writings would be regarded during the Soviet period, but especially after 1991, as the founding texts of Uzbek national literature.[3]

From the late fifteenth century, Timurid civilization began to retreat into isolation and then to decline for a host of reasons. From the early sixteenth century, the roads linking Central Asia to the Arab world were the theatre of wars waged by local sovereigns, divided by political and religious controversies. Thus, the development of Shiism in the Iran of Shah Ismail (1485–1524) fuelled the wars of religion. The Shaybanids,[4] precursors of the Uzbeks and champions of Sunnism, waged war with Iran's Safavids, who were intent on spreading Shiism. This religious war, to be found in virtually identical form in today's Middle East, undermined the existing regimes. In north-west Central Asia, Russia began to develop significantly and to harbour ambitions of expansion towards the south.[5] Finally, and more significantly, the discovery of new trade routes between Europe and the rest of the world brought with it serious competition for the transcontinental routes through Central Asia, resulting in the decline of the Silk Roads whose main intersection it had been for centuries.[6] Three states emerged on the ruins of Timurid civilization: the khanate of Kokand, and that of Khiva, but especially the emirate of Bukhara. Comprising the region between the Amu Darya and Syr Darya rivers, it was the most substantial Muslim state in the region from 1785 to 1920, before the gradual but decisive arrival of Russia.

A form of Sunni Islam predominated in the three states. But small Twelver Shia minorities were settled in the environs of Bukhara and Samarkand and a substantial Ismailist Shia minority was to be found in Badakhshan, present-day Tajikistan. Outside Central Asia, these states were often perceived as theocratic.[7] This needs to be qualified. In the event, *raison d'état* prevailed over religious considerations. Here, as in a fair number of Eastern and Western kingdoms and principalities at the time, there existed 'mirrors for princes'—texts whose purpose was to help those holding power to administer their country's affairs. They were not inspired exclusively by Islam, since they also drew on pre-Islamic practices and rules, particularly Mesopotamian cultures in Byzantium and ancient Iran.[8] In fact, as Adeeb Khalid has eloquently argued, the practice of 'mirrors for princes' had begun before the birth of the emirates and khanates. Already in the Shaybanid state that preceded Bukhara, Ubaidullah Khan had commissioned a scholar called Fazlullah Ruzbihan to write a treatise on good governance. *Suluk-ul muluk* ('The Conduct of Kings') influenced the political authorities of the time and stressed the fundamental point that political authority is a religious obligation.[9] In other words, as had already been argued by Ibn Taymiyya in the tenth century, treatises on good governance stressed that a certain authoritarianism was preferable to chaos and anarchy. The implication was that power may be attained by force and exercised perfectly legitimately as long as Sharia is respected. In accordance with these ideas, and extending Ruzbihan's precepts, the practice of alliance between political power and the *ulama*, the religious caste, developed. Madrasas and hospices were established in the three emirates, but in general political authority dominated the religious caste, even if, in theory, it was obliged to justify its exercise of power in accordance with Islamic precepts. This made Bukhara—the region's most important state on the eve of the Russian invasion—a state that was not theocratic, but one where the principles of Islam were important in political affairs.

As for the Caucasus, its entry into Islam's sphere of influence was equally precocious, dating back to the early stages of the Arab conquest. Islam was initially imposed militarily by the Arab generals Salman ibn Rabiah al-Bahili and Habib ibn Muslim. In 645, the city of Barda was captured and Arab armies soon reached Derbent, in present-day Russian Dagestan. Christianity and Zoroastrianism were the most common religions at the time and for a long time they put up resistance, before retreating in the face of the establishment of Islam, which was gradual and, in some places, superficial. Long a bastion of Sunnism, the region experienced the Mongol conquest after Central Asia. Following the Mongol wave, the bulk of the Caucasian region found itself under Seljuk domination, but especially various Iranian dynasties, including the Safavids. Champions of Shiism, the latter fought numerous battles against the Ottoman Empire, which strove to spread Sunnism everywhere. The Caucasus was one of the main arenas of competition between Shia and Sunnis—a rivalry that we shall encounter again, fortunately in more pacific forms, after 1991. Bogged down in their confessional wars, the two empires ceded the Caucasus to a third power—Russia—which made itself master of the region from the 1750s onwards, but whose total control of the Caucasus dates from 1828, when the Treaty of Turkmenchay fixed its border on the Aras River.[10]

Russian Domination in the Caucasus and Central Asia and its Impact on Islam

A continental power since at least the sixteenth century, Russia embarked on a policy of colonial-style expansion, initially into the Caucasus and then what is now Central Asia. In the Caucasus, its expansionist designs began under the reign of Ivan the Terrible and took the form of spreading Christianity among north Caucasian populations where paganism was still commonplace. From 1600, Tsarist Russia and the Ottoman Empire fought many battles for religious influence in the region, each of them having proclaimed itself protector of its co-religionists in the adversary's empire. The weakening of the Ottoman Empire in the Caucasian region from the nineteenth century meant that Russia's military advance south met with armed resistance from local Muslim brotherhood dignitaries. The Naqshbandi and the Qadiriyya, two major brotherhoods already well-established in the North Caucasus at the time of the Tsarist conquest, led resistance to the Russian advance. The illustrious Imam Shamil's exceptional resistance at the head of a handful of Chechen and Dagestani mountain dwellers has entered into legend; his bravery was saluted by his enemies. In the South Caucasus—present-day Georgia, Azerbaijan and Armenia—it was Iranian power that Russia had to confront. But there too the fragmentation of the South Caucasus into a multitude of khanates, and the weakness of both the Ottoman and Safavid empires, facilitated Russian conquest. In 1828, Russian colonial domination over the whole Caucasus was ratified by signature of the Turkmenchay Treaty.

In Central Asia, conquest followed the same pattern as in the Caucasus. It was slow but inexorable and exploited local rivalries between the political or tribal powers of the coveted region. When the city of Tashkent was captured in 1685, the Russians already had several decades of presence in the region behind them, especially in the nomadic zones of the Kazakh steppe. The capture of Tashkent assumed considerable symbolic significance, because it was the first substantial city in the sedentary zone to fall into Russian hands. As soon as it established its supremacy in Central Asia, Tsarist Russia created a colonial province—Turkestan—composed of nomadic regions and territories taken from the region's three states—Kokand, Bukhara and Khiva. But complete subjugation of the emirates would take longer, with Russia preferring, for tactical and economic reasons, to impose a protectorate initially. Bukhara in particular retained all the attributes of sovereignty, apart from its own foreign policy.

According to Andreas Kappeler, Tsarist Russia demonstrated considerable flexibility towards Central Asian Islam.[11] Basing itself on a tradition inherited from Tsarina Catherine II (1782–96), whose respect, admiration even, for Islam is well-known, the colonial power displayed a certain benevolence towards the Muslim religion, at least during the initial decades of its domination. However, the policy on the spot of

Turkestan's first governor general—General Von Kaufmann (1867–81)—was somewhat different. Aiming at the gradual, long-term integration of the region into the Russian Empire, Von Kaufmann, like the Tsarist civil service, thought it necessary to avoid any direct clash with Islam, which would only serve to crystallize tensions and strengthen it. But in contrast to the respectful benevolence displayed by the Tsars, the general preferred to ignore Islam, in the belief that Russian modernization would condemn it to die out of its own accord.[12]

The attitude of local civilians and intellectuals to Russian conquest varied between resistance and cooperation. An initial phase of resistance occurred in Bukhara in 1866, when local religious authorities inspired a popular revolt, limited in scope, against the Russian occupier. A more serious rebellion against a Russian garrison shook the city of Andijan in May 1898. Led by an influential figure in the Naqshbandi brotherhood, Muhammad Ali Madali, also known as Dukchi Ishan (1856–98), it resulted in the deaths of twenty-two soldiers from the Russian garrison. The rebellion and its instigators were rapidly suppressed.[13]

But resistance to the Russian occupier was in fact of low intensity and, overall, the Central Asian elites, including religious elites, preferred to adopt a cooperative attitude.[14] As Adeeb Khalid points out, this stance was inspired by the precepts elaborated by Fazlullah Ruzbihan in his treatise on good governance, *Suluk-ul muluk*. To protect the community against the new, non-Muslim occupier, the *ulama* legitimated Russian domination to a degree, so long as it afforded Islam complete freedom of action to deal with religious and community affairs. This compromise between Russian settlers and *ulama* in fact made possible a new flourishing of Islam, to the extent that new madrasas were opened and the pilgrimage to Mecca was facilitated by the colonial power. In the Caucasus, the local elites adopted the same attitude, divided as they were between a spirit of resistance and a desire to cooperate so as not to jeopardize the influence they traditionally exercised over the communities of believers. In the different khanates that pre-dated the formation of Azerbaijan, the attitude towards the colonizer was more flexible than in the North Caucasus, where the anti-Russian rebellion lasted much longer, before being put down without having ever been defeated outright by Russian forces. This delicate balance between cooperation and resistance persisted with the emergence of a new indigenous reformist intellectual movement, called Jadidism, which likewise maintained relations with the Russian colonizer that were (to say the least) ambiguous.

Russian domination in Central Asia and the Caucasus was also reinforced by means of modern Russian schools, established by the colonial authorities, where indigenous Kazakh, Tatar, Azerbaijani, Uzbek and other elites were educated. Initially in Russia itself, among the Tatars of the Crimea and Kazan, and then gradually among the elites of other Turcophone and Iranophone peoples, the realization dawned that the empire's Muslims lagged behind the rest of the world. In reality, this crisis of identity and intellectual crisis was not confined to the Muslims of the Russian Empire. In Cairo, Istanbul and Teheran, as in Muslim India, people realized that all was not well with the Muslim world and that, to escape its state of lethargy and subjugation, it must embark on a series of reforms. Throughout the Muslim world, the same nagging questions were posed. How had things come to such a pass? What had happened? Although already very isolated, Islam in the Russian Empire nevertheless felt the reverberation of Turkish, Arab, Iranian and Indian debates. Among the Muslim intellectuals of the Russian Empire who were in the vanguard of the reform programme, let us signal Ismail Gasprinski, a Tatar from Crimea, where he was born in 1851. A journalist and writer, he developed the idea of the need to modernize teaching and education in accordance with a new method—*jadid* (an Arab word meaning new)—as opposed to the old methods deemed responsible for the decline of the Russian Empire's Turkic Muslim populations.[15] His visits to Istanbul and various European cities—particularly Vienna and Paris, which he visited in 1871—influenced and helped flesh out his reformist ideas. On his return, he founded the journal *Terjuman* ('The Interpreter'), which would make him part of Muslim intellectual history. Launched in 1883, it rapidly became the motor force of a powerful movement to modernize Turkic–Muslim societies throughout the Russian Empire. In the Crimean capital of Bakhchisaray, but also in Kazan, Baku, Tashkent and Bukhara, numerous intellectuals were influenced by his ideas and sought ways to rescue society from its spiritual, cultural and identitarian crisis. In the Caucasus, in Azerbaijan, many intellectuals were already concerned with the imperatives of modernization. Abbasgulu Bakikhanov (1794–

1846), an educationalist and founder of schools, and Mirza Fatali Akhundov (1812–78), philosopher and theatre director, had already become aware of the need to reform their society and worked to that end in their respective spheres.[16] But it was in Central Asia that the Jadid movement developed most, won over the largest number of followers, and left its greatest mark. Among its representatives, let us note Sadriddin Ayni, but above all Munnavar Qori and Abdulrauf Fitrat. Conscious of a considerable technological, industrial and societal lag behind Europe, they advocated not a rupture with Islam, but on the contrary a return to its original sources, the founding texts of the Koran and the *hadiths*. Thus, they advocated excluding subsequent glossaries and commentaries, which (in their view) had led to a dilution and corruption of Muslim values. The Jadids put education at the centre of the required community and societal reform. It had to be a standard, functional form of education, not one based on the sacred. In other words, education must seek to interpret the modern world, its sciences and intellectual output, in order to decipher the future and enable as many people as possible to adapt to the new issues it raised, and not remain content with backward-looking, fixed and paralyzing interpretations. This intellectual tendency involved a critique of the traditional madrasa, regarded as a site of indolence and stasis. In its stead the foundation of modern schools was encouraged, where teaching would be conducted in accordance with the new method, *usuli djadid*. In their critical impetus, the Jadids did not spare the classical and traditionalist *ulama*, also called Qadimists, who were held responsible for the decline and retardation of Islamic societies.

Abdulrauf Fitrat is by far the Jadid intellectual most representative of a new intellectual class in revolt against the old elites embodied by the *ulama*. Born in Bukhara in 1886, from 1909 to 1914 he was a student in Istanbul, which was in a state of intense intellectual ferment at the time. There he was initially greatly influenced by the social modernizing movement, the Young Ottomans. On his return to Central Asia, Fitrat joined the society of Young Bukharians and was to become one of its most famous leaders. Like most of his peers, he rebelled against what he considered a sclerotic image of Islam—that of the *ulama*. However, a basic clarification is required here. The controversy between modernist reformers and traditionalist *ulama*—i.e. between

Jadid intellectuals and their Qadimist rivals—was not a rift and polarization between secularists (Jadids) and Islamists (Qadimists). Rather, the divergence revolved around how to interpret Islam, which remained the common basis of both currents for conceiving society and regulating it. Furthermore, in this intellectual configuration, which increasingly polarized the Muslims of Central Asia and the Caucasus, we note that Russian merchants and colonizers were more aligned with the traditional elites, with whom they shared the same conservative ideology and even the same interest in a certain status quo.

In short, Russian colonial domination in the Caucasus and Central Asia had a limited direct impact on Islam. The tsars did not seek to spread Christianity in the conquered zones and, in general, there was little interference in the internal affairs of the communities inhabiting the conquered territories. The key thing for the empire was to control the borders of the khanates or emirates, to harness resources, and to impose Russian geostrategic interests. Nevertheless, the psychological impact of colonial domination was considerable and prompted an existential crisis among the empire's Muslims. This crisis, which combined the need for internal reform, a search for identity, and self-assertion as a nation, diminished considerably with the Soviet Union and its policy of forming or strengthening Uzbek, Kazakh, Turkmen, Kyrgyz, Tajik and Azerbaijani national identities. In fact, in manipulating cultural identities, Soviet power proved much more interventionist in administering religious affairs in the communities under its political and ideological dominion. In this, it was soon replaced by a local elite, sympathetic to the ideals of the Bolshevik Revolution, which endorsed the imposition of a new way of administering religion.

Soviet Power and Islam

The convulsions preceding the Bolshevik Revolution in Russia were not without an impact on the Caucasian and Central Asian fringes of the Russian Empire, where the new regime took several years to achieve complete ascendancy. In Central Asia, the steppe zone and the governorate of Turkestan came under Bolshevik control more quickly. By contrast, in the Emirate of Bukhara, where between 1920 and 1924 a sort of Bukharan Soviet Republic was established in the wake of the new Bolshevik regime, the local government was virtually independent. In the Caucasus, the Bolshevik authorities, grappling with their own problems, were forced to compromise with the demands of local elites on the empire's edges. Thus they permitted the emergence of independent national democratic republics in Armenia, Georgia and Azerbaijan. Their ephemeral existence served only to undermine the Tsarist regime and afford the Bolsheviks a firmer grip on power in Moscow. Once firmly established, and notwithstanding their promises to liberate peoples under the Tsarist yoke, the Bolsheviks simply replaced one form of domination with another. In Azerbaijan, the ephemeral democratic republic disappeared in 1920.[17] In 1925, the whole of Central Asia was subjected to the new masters in the Kremlin, who had just founded the Union of Soviet Socialist Republics. A new territorial and administrative organization had been born. The new borders, fixed between 1924 and 1936, inviolably defined the Soviet Socialist Republics until the end of the USSR in 1991.

Throughout the Muslim east of the Russian Empire, the arrival of the Bolsheviks in power aroused a great many hopes, especially among Jadid reformist elites in Central Asia and their counterparts in Azerbaijan. A fair number of these intellectuals adhered to the ideals of the Bolshevik Revolution, sources of hope for the Muslim populations of the former Russian Empire, to whom they held out the promise of modernization and progress. The goodwill between Jadids and Bolsheviks was based on a sense of convergent interests. Formerly ardent defenders of Western civilization, most Jadid thinkers were disappointed by the attitude of the countries that embodied this civilization—in particular Britain, whose colonizing ambitions in the region were greatly resented. Disappointment with the West facilitated the *entente* between the Bolsheviks and the local modernist elites. Representative of the intellectuals increasingly won over by the Bolsheviks, and embittered by the colonial conduct of the European powers, Abdulrauf Fitrat welcomed the new government's seemingly generous ideas.[18] Having lived in Istanbul and witnessed Western designs on the Ottoman Empire, Fitrat advocated genuine collaboration with the Bolshevik government. In contrast to the Jadids' generally pro-Bolshevik attitude, Qadimist traditional elites proved more distrustful, because they soon divined the Bolsheviks' anti-religious ideas.

ISLAM IN CENTRAL ASIA AND THE CAUCASUS

The Bolshevik objective was to shed the image of Russian colonial power and send a strong message to the Caucasian and Central Asian populations still under the yoke of the old European colonial regimes, enemy of the Bolsheviks and Jadids alike. The latter were convinced that the Kremlin's new masters were going to help them fulfil their national aspirations. Such was the entente that we can speak of a certain golden age in the cultural and artistic sphere, especially for Uzbeks and Azerbaijanis, whose literature, drama and music experienced remarkable development in the first years of Bolshevik power.

On the issue of religion, the early years of the Soviet regime in Central Asia and the Caucasus were relatively untroubled. So as not to offend the sensibilities of Muslim populations and antagonize them, Lenin issued strict instructions about the treatment of believers and respect for Islam. The idea was to project the Bolsheviks, in contrast to the Tsarist regime, as a government respectful of ethnic, religious and cultural specificities. Thus, the new government's first measures were even favourable to Islam. Until 1925, religious freedom was scrupulously respected. Various Islamic institutions continued to operate and new entities were even created. More surprisingly still, Muslim *sharia* courts continued to legislate throughout Central Asia,[19] and in Azerbaijan functioned alongside the Soviet legal system.

However, the initial accord between the Bolsheviks and the Jadids could not last long. For over and above their immediate vital interests, their worldviews were different and created an unbridgeable ideological gulf. In reality, the Bolsheviks' universalistic vision left little room for the toleration of peculiarities displayed by the previous regime. Thus, the alliance between Bolsheviks and Jadids was circumstantial and tactical. Pending full control of the situation, the Soviet regime affected to be on the same wavelength as the modernist elites in the countries inherited from the Tsarist *ancien régime*. But once firmly ensconced in Moscow, at the helm of the whole USSR, a harsh policy of control and then repression of religion was implemented, directed against all religions. In the case of Islam in Central Asia and the Caucasus, the antireligious campaign took several forms. Firstly, a comprehensive propaganda campaign was conducted against religion. Through education and publishing, but also in the form of lectures and seminars, Islam was denounced on the grounds that it encouraged obscurantism and indolence.[20] Campaigns positively promoting atheism accompanied the anti-religious campaigns, but with limited success. In Uzbekistan, for example, an anti-religious magazine, *Hudoysizlar* ('The Godless'),[21] was created and a similar publication appeared in Azerbaijan.[22] This crude anti-religious campaign condemned religion as a poison distracting the people from revolution, the sole source of happiness and progress. It proceeded more smoothly because it enjoyed the active, militant support of a new class of elites, trained Soviet-style, which had scarcely any sympathy for the Jadid elites, regarded as transitional between the Russian and Soviet periods. Anti-religious campaigns were accelerated in the 1930s. Many mosques, madrasas and other religious establishments were forced to close their doors. Reduced to a derisory number, the surviving institutions were easily and totally controllable.[23] At the same time, the policy of confiscating goods said to be endowments and, more tragically, the physical elimination of a number of Jadid intellectuals proceeded relentlessly.[24]

The peculiarity of this anti-religious policy was that it challenged Islam not as an individual practice, but as a moral and ethical corpus which could no longer be given publicly expression. Thus—and we must bear this in mind if we are to understand the post-Soviet Islam that emerged with independence—Islamic values disappeared from the public sphere and withdrew into the private sphere, where they more or less survived. But they have never recovered their erstwhile pre-eminence on the public stage.

The invasion of the USSR by Nazi Germany opened a new phase in Soviet religious policy. The regime needed a certain concord with society, upon whose moral and physical support it called to confront Nazi aggression. The scale of the war and the principle of conscription meant that virtually all Soviet families were affected by this global conflict. Much of industry in the war zone was relocated behind the front, including in Central Asia. The 'Great Patriotic War' became a cement of Soviet identity. For a large number of reservist soldiers, workers and arms industry workers from isolated regions of the Union, it was now that consciousness of Soviet citizenship was acquired, on the battlefield in the face of a common enemy. Thus, to mobilize every population, ethnic group and religion more effectively, the Soviet government granted concessions to the Churches and to Islam. More concretely, religious persecution stopped; some places of worship reopened. In return, the spiritual authorities helped mobilize the masses for the war effort. The most significant change in the administration of Islam in Central Asia and the Caucasus occurred at this point. The Spiritual Administration of the Muslims of Central Asia and Kazakhstan—SADUM in its Russian acronym—was created in Tashkent. In Baku, a similar institution—the Spiritual Administration of the Muslims of the Northern Caucasus—was created. Their mission was to support the Muslim 'clergy' in more effectively organizing the war effort against the Nazi occupier. Scarcely had they been created, when SADUM and the Spiritual Administration of the Northern Caucasus implemented a new Islamic education policy to train religious cadres. The number of establishments remained limited and under control, but even so a degree of openness was apparent, with students being sent to certain Muslim countries to receive higher education in religion and with the creation of a department of religious publications to promote the image of Soviet Islam in several languages—Russian, Uzbek, Arabic, English and French. The purpose of these official structures was not only to make peace with society, but also to associate the traditional religious hierarchy with the propaganda effort directed at Muslim countries in Africa and the Middle East, which were still subject to the colonial order of European countries hostile to the USSR. This relative benevolence towards Islam persisted under Stalin, who (it is agreed) endeavoured in his final years to soften his views on religion. Anti-religious campaigns would emerge under Khrushchev and Brezhnev. However, by the close of the Stalin era Soviet policy had fixed the two main features that Islam must possess in order to accord with the regime's ideological imperatives and interests and be tolerated within the Union. Firstly, throughout the Soviet space, Islam was restricted to its most localized and folkloric forms, reducing it to a form of tradition and custom. Denied public expression, Islam was relegated to the private sphere and the family became the primordial site of conservation and transmission of its precepts. The second characteristic was the role of identity marker it assumed for the Soviet citizens of the Central Asian and Caucasian republics.

The best works on Islam during the Soviet era stress that government policy was by no means restricted to repression, though that was real and massive, especially in the 1920s and 30s. It was also marked by moments of exceptional, paradoxical toleration and accommodation between Islam and communism. Thus, the Soviet Muslim sphere was characterized by a powerful, concurrent internalization of Soviet values and a natural, constant attachment to a certain form of Muslim convention. This surprising cohabitation and marriage of convenience between socialist mindset and Muslim identity was consolidated after Stalin's death, with the establishment throughout the USSR of 'developed socialism' as defined by the experts—that is, a socialism of massive urbanization, potent industrialization, and a record literacy rate. The unspoken social contract established at the time between the Soviet state, guarantor of a certain level of well-being—in housing, education and health—and society, which in return consented to the key features of socialism, accommodated a religious component in the Muslim zone of Central Asia and the Caucasus. It was, to say the least, interesting. As long as the local elites did not come into direct conflict with the spirit of socialism, as long as there was a minimum of adherence to the Party's directives and fulfilment of production quotas (e.g. cotton in the case of Central Asia), the centre adapted to the persistence of various religious practices which, in principle, were incompatible with socialist ideology. Generally speaking, the balance, sometimes renegotiated, between adherence to the principles of socialism and administration of local affairs afforded the general secretaries of the local communist parties a relative autonomy. Combined with the already established Soviet policy of training local elites and indigenizing governing elites, in effect it transformed local leaders into veritable national leaders. Thus, doubtless despite itself, Soviet policy enhanced the national stature of local communist rulers already equipped with their networks of influence and clientelism. In Central Asia, Sharof Rashidov, head of Soviet Uzbekistan (1961–83), served as an example among local leaders who had acquired a national profile and was recognized as such by independent Uzbekistan.[25] In Azerbaijan, Heydar Aliyev, head of the communist party (1969–82), fashioned an image of himself as a national hero and, when his country became independent, was elevated to the status of father of the nation.

The emergence of communist leaders as figureheads of the nation is symptomatic of 1940s Soviet policy, which fostered the development of national identities. As early as 1936, Turkestan and Transcaucasia were sliced up into national entities that would give birth to the socialist republics forming part of the USSR. At the end of the Second World War, Soviet ideology already evinced a quasi-abandonment of class in favour of ethnicity and nation, whose radicalization in Central Asia was the work of Soviet policy.[26] Contrary to an idea commonplace in Western literature on the USSR, the Soviet system did not kill the nation. In many respects, on the contrary, the Soviet Union, in its desire to differentiate itself from Tsarist Russia, but also in a strategy of divide-and-rule, integrated the national factor and ethnicity into its administrative and territorial organization. The Soviet government deemed it more expedient to strengthen national identity, so as to place it at the service of socialism. In fact, Moscow's aim was to induce new identities and cultures that were national in form and socialist in ideological content. In retrospect, we know that virtually the opposite occurred, since the fabrication of ethnic identities in Central Asia and the Caucasus was more national in substance and socialist in form. This policy of creating new ethnic identities or, rather, reinforcing or reinventing them was entrusted to the Academy of Sciences. The work of its researchers made a major contribution to codifying national norms in cuisine, architecture, music, dress and so forth. Promoted with an identity of their own, the communities adhered unreservedly. It is important to stress that this process unfolded legally, in a time and space free of any conflict with the communist authorities.[27] The researchers tasked with developing these codes were ordinary civil servants working for the Academy of Sciences and paid by the Soviet government. The fabrication of habits and customs occurred without any major conflict, with the possible exception of the delicate issue of defining borders and the allocation of certain cities and cultural and architectural treasures. Thus Bukhara and Samarkand, historical cradles of the formation of Tajik culture, were assigned to Uzbekistan, remaining—especially since independence—sources of friction between Uzbeks and Tajiks.

Soviet nationalities policy was not without an impact on Islam. The preservation of Muslim rites of passage in connection with birth, circumcision, marriage and burial, which were observed by much of the population, including representatives and servants of communist ideology, attests not so much to a challenge to the Soviet order as to a sincere, natural attachment to a cultural identity, whether fabricated or not. The culture of these particularities was thus not banned by the government, but encouraged and codified by communist power. Under Brezhnev, a reconciliation was effected between tradition and Sovietism. People could now be loyal to their traditions, to their Uzbek, Azerbaijani, etc., and Muslim way of life, while feeling modern and Soviet. Furthermore, this spirit of symbiosis ended up encompassing certain non- or pre-Islamic customs and practices, such as Navruz, a Turkic–Persian holiday marking the first day of Spring.[28] Through the Soviet policy of fixing identities, this very ancient, originally pagan holiday, which was specific to Central Asia and had nothing Russian and Slav about it, was recuperated to serve local identities, Uzbek, Kazakh and Muslim.

The preservation of rites of passage unquestionably contributed to the preservation of an Islamic consciousness, in spite of an officially atheistic and anti-clerical dominant ideology. Along with rites of passage, unofficial sites of popular religiosity played a fundamental role in preserving Islam. Thus, to cite only the most important, the mausoleums of holy figures, which are very numerous in Central Asia, from the most famous, such as Bahauddin Naqshbandi in Uzbekistan or Akhmet Yassawi in Kazakhstan, to the least illustrious such as Zengi Ata on the periphery of Tashkent or the site of Bibi Heybet on the periphery of Baku, have been popular religious sites. Tolerated by the Soviet authorities, they made it possible to preserve an individual and collective Muslim consciousness. Along the same lines, cemeteries, by dint of the rites that persisted in them, aided the transmission of Islamic knowledge and practices. In her work on Islam in Tajikistan during the Soviet period, Ariane Zevaco explains how cemeteries were 'silent mosques',[29] because of their role in transmitting rites and knowledge in the absence of other public stages where religion could find expression.

Certainly, the role of official Islamic structures—the Spiritual Administration in Tashkent and that of Baku for the Caucasus—must not be ignored in the preservation of traditional Islam. But it was in and through the rituals conserved in family circles and popular religious sites that Islam was able to survive, in individual and collective consciousness alike. We may note that members of communist local government respected these practices, paradoxical as this might seem given their professed ideological convictions. This attests to the power of Islam as an exclusive identity marker, in the absence of irrefutable proof of an authentically religious practice.

A good example of such coexistence between Soviet mindset and Islam was evident in kolkhozes at the height of the Soviet era, in the Caucasus and Central Asia alike. Islam not only survived in these arenas of collectivism, but was given expression to the point of genuinely interacting with Soviet institutions and their representatives.[30] The strong connection between religious authorities in kolkhozes and Soviet administrative personnel—a phenomenon that Olivier Roy was one of the first to describe[31]—paved the way for the emergence of alternative religious communities in the Soviet Union after Stalin, well before the phenomenon of re-Islamization became more visible in the 1970s and 80s.

It is interesting to track the Soviet government's attitude towards the persistence of customs tinged with Islam. *Prima facie* outdated and retrograde from the Party's progressivist viewpoint, such practices never really escaped surveillance by the authorities and their security organs. A plethora of internal reports lamented their survival, even as they were tolerated so long as they did not drift into a direct threat or challenge to the powers that be. Basically, this Islam, disseminated via customs and traditions, contained no political dimension, at least in the 1950s and 60s. As has been underscored by Adeeb Khalid, in as much as it derived from a Hanafi tradition advocating introspection, it harboured no political ambitions.[32]

The state of peaceful coexistence between a cultural, customary Islam and a Soviet state that was undemanding about adherence to socialist principles persisted during the 1960s and 70s. As to the role of Islam in the public sphere and public debate, it was virtually non-existent. We might even speak of a de-Islamization of public debate. This is too often forgotten, when it is actually a fundamental phenomenon. Having reassured Soviet power about the inoffensive character of Islam, it made it possible for ideas of nation, ethnicity and group solidarity to take root. Yet all these notions incorporated cultural and identitarian elements associated with Islam. Thus, prior to the end of the Soviet era, individuals defined themselves as Muslim and attested

INHERITED ISLAM

to a developed but particular Muslim consciousness, peculiar to the Soviet sphere and experience. It was distinguished from that of their co-religionists in Turkey, the Arab world or Iran, where secularization campaigns, even violent ones, never completely expelled Islam from public debate. Moreover, contrary to many received ideas, the Muslims of Central Asia and the Caucasus never felt the need to conceal their Muslim identity. But they internalized it and adapted it to the Soviet social ethic, which required them to confine it to the private sphere. As regards erudite Islam—that is, the creation of an Islamic literature and the formation of elites—here too, things must be put in perspective. Certainly, no establishment in the Soviet Union could claim the transnational prestige and influence of an Al-Azhar University or the theology faculties of Turkey or Iran. But an erudite Islam prospered to some extent in the USSR, albeit in precarious circumstances. In particular, it benefited from the body of knowledge deposited with the Spiritual Administration of Tashkent, whose *ulama*, educated in the old school, were sophisticated men of letters, with a high level of theological knowledge. These *ulama* have often been caricatured as servants of the Soviet state, whose legitimation they allegedly promoted among the community out of sheer personal opportunism. The truth was much more complex. But before the open clash between Soviet and post-Soviet cadres, let us briefly study the beginnings of the revival of Islam in the region from the 1970s and especially the 1980s.

The Predominantly Internal Resources of the Islamic Revival

The Islamic revival we are concerned with here must be situated in its specific temporal context. It did not consist in the emergence of a powerful intellectual tendency, comparable to the Jadid phenomenon among the Russian Empire's Muslims, but instead in a change of attitude towards religious practice and religious establishments, among governing elites and populations alike.[33] For a start, the religious revival in the USSR at the end of the Soviet era was not confined to Islam. It was even stronger in countries with a Christian culture, such as Armenia or Georgia.[34] Even in Russia, churches enjoyed unprecedented popularity and attendance. Furthermore, the revival of Islam in Central Asia and the Caucasus is difficult to date with precision, in the absence of a milestone that might be regarded as a decisive turning point in the life of Soviet Muslims. Even during what is said to be the period of religious repression, there was—a paradox and ambiguity of Soviet domination—tolerance, or ignorance, on the authorities' part, of Islamic practices that were incompatible with the spirit of socialism. The most frequently invoked example in this respect is the life and monumental *oeuvre* of Domullah Hindustani. Throughout the Soviet period, he trained a large number of followers who participated in the Islamic revival at the end of the Soviet era and the early months and years of independence. Born in the city of Kokand in 1892, Hindustani completed his religious training in India in the 1920s, before returning to Central Asia to play a crucial role in the renewal of Islamic thought. Among his most influential followers, we should note Rahmatullah Qori Alloma and Abduvali Qori Mirzoev who, having benefited from his teaching, criticized him for his unduly conciliatory position on Soviet power and adopted a more intransigent line.[35] In the Caucasus too, in Dagestan as well as Azerbaijan, seeds of religious revival developed in the shadow of the Soviets. But the most eloquent example is the kolkhozes and sovkhozes at the heart of the Soviet system, where there was complicity between officials and religious authorities, which allowed for the creation of new Islamic congregations whose role in the development of a certain political Islam was not insignificant.[36]

Nevertheless, the major change that made the renaissance of Islam possible derived, paradoxically and inadvertently, from the centre and was prompted by a non-Muslim government unsympathetic in principle to any Islamic revival. In fact, if we must identify a key date, a turning point in the liberalization of Islam in the Soviet Union, it would doubtless be Mikhail Gorbachev's arrival in power and his policy of *glasnost* and *perestroika*. Contrary to what people sensed and even argued in the West at the time, it was not from the periphery and Islam that change came to the Muslim part of the Soviet Union, but from the centre. Gorbachev's policy initiated a series of reforms that caused breaches in the system into which stepped partisans of renewal, including religious renewal. In effect, *glasnost* and *perestroika* caused the framework to implode and allowed cultural, identitarian, scientific and historical phenomena to find expression. Renewal also affected the way that each people understood its own past. Environment and ecology became sources of concern, particularly in Kazakhstan with the emergence of the Nevada Sempalatinsk movement around the charismatic poet Olzhas Suleimenov,[37] and in Uzbekistan with awareness of the tragedy of the Aral Sea. Above all, the spirit of freedom inspired by Gorbachev's reforms made it possible to rekindle the debate on national languages, identity and also each people's relationship to its past, its ancestors and hence its future. Among peoples with a sedentary, urban tradition—Uzbeks and Tajiks—reference to the past sought to highlight the greatness of their ancestors and national culture. Among more nomadic peoples—Kazakhs and Kyrgyz—the debate on identity was aimed predominantly at self-reassertion against the Russian element that remained predominant in each republic. National movements emerged throughout the Caucasian and Central Asian zone. In Azerbaijan, the *Halk Cephesi* (Popular Front) developed around the charismatic figure of Ebulfeyz Elçibey. In Kazakhstan, the *Jeltoksan* movement was founded in 1986, when Moscow sought to replace the head of the local communist party—the Kazakh Dinmukhamed Kunaev—with a Slav, Gennady Kolbin.[38] In Uzbekistan, the *Birlik* (Unity) movement, led by Abdurrahman Polatov, emerged in the context of Gorbachev's reforms.[39]

The religious dimension of this revival was mainly characterized by the reopening of old mosques that had been closed or confiscated. New mosques were built, almost as a fashion phenomenon: each *mahalla*, each traditional district, sought to erect a more beautiful mosque than its neighbour. However, economic difficulties and growing mistrust on the part of the authorities slowed the pace of construction after independence. The revival of interest in religion is even more visible as regards places of pilgrimage and establishments connected to Sufism. As we have seen, Central Asia was an important centre of Muslim Sufism. The Naqshbandi brotherhood, the most widespread in the Muslim world, emerged in Central Asia during the Soviet era. Along with other, less prestigious places of pilgrimage, the mausoleums of saints were, and remain, sites where religiosity has been preserved. In Azerbaijan, the revival connected with places of pilgrimage centred on the *imamzade*—the tombs and mausoleums of figures 'venerated' on account of their descent from Ali, key figure in Shiism. Thus, the mausoleum of Bibi Heybat on the outskirts of Baku and, still more, the village of Nardaran, which is home to the mausoleum of Rahim Hanim,[40] daughter of the seventh imam Musa al-Kazim (and therefore sister of the eighth Imam Reza), are among the main sites of popular religion and became objects of fervent enthusiasm with the onset of *perestroika*. The novel attention paid to identity, religion and the past was not restricted to ordinary people, but also affected intellectuals and even senior official cadres. Above all, the quest for identity signified that the people and elites had become aware that they belonged to the world, to Islam and especially to Islam as a civilization and system of fundamental values, and were affirming it. This interest in Islam was also the sign of a 'return' to national values or, rather, a rediscovery of them. However, such passion about identity was definitely not accompanied by more religious observance or by contempt for the Soviet order. On the contrary, in everyday life religious observance remained weak,[41] and the new-found passion for the national tongue and culture was accompanied by pride in belonging to the great Soviet power. When a referendum on the future of the USSR was held throughout the Soviet Union, it was in Central Asia and the Caucasus that the population proved most attached to maintaining it.

At the same time, the revival of Islam in the Soviet Union drew on various external sources. Minor or even marginal, they nevertheless warrant a mention. Some, notably Russian researchers like Alexei Malashenko or Vitaly Naumkin, tend to overestimate the importance of the Islamic Revolution in Iran or the Soviet invasion of Afghanistan in explaining the resurgence of Islam among the peoples of Central Asia and the Caucasus. The correlation is not inapt. In reality, however, these two major events, which unquestionably had a strong international echo, scarcely registered with Central Asian and Caucasian Muslims. The Iranian Islamic Revolution, if only on account of its Shia particularism, passed unnoticed or was badly received in Central Asia. In Azerbaijan, where a good half of the population identified with Iranian Twelver Shiism, only a handful of religious figures appreciated the major political and social upheaval represented by the revolution in the great neighbour to the south. As for the war in Afghanistan, there too many Muslim Soviet soldiers were shocked by the violence of the fighting, but very few of them fed Islamist intellectual tendencies from the Afghan front. The leading light in Central Asian jihadism—Juma Namangani—

was certainly a Soviet parachutist in Afghanistan. But this does not prove the Afghan origins of Islamic revival in Central Asia—and for a simple reason: that revival had already started. As we have seen, it emerged from the 1970s and not in the 1980s, marked by the Afghan War. In reality, if an external phenomenon must be identified as contributing to the revival of Islam in the Soviet Union, it is the official policy of religious cooperation with certain socialist Arab countries, such as Libya and Syria. Although limited in number, some Soviet Muslim aid workers had the opportunity to spend time in religious residence in the Arab world, enabling them to make a small contribution to the revival of Islam, whose resources were almost exclusively endogenous.

Conclusion: Participating in the Globalization of Religion

At the centre of the world and the cradle of several civilizations, some of them Islamic,[42] and long at the intersection of several cultural zones by dint of its location on the Silk Road, Central Asia in the broad sense became ever more marginal after the discovery of the New World and the emergence of new trade routes.[43] Already in decline during the Russian conquest, its subjugation by the Tsars and then the Soviets only served to isolate it further from the rest of the great Islamic community, the *ummah*. Certainly, during the Soviet era, it was scarcely affected (if at all) by a very limited globalization confined to the Soviet sphere, whose horizon was restricted to COMECON and the Warsaw Pact.[44] The end of the Soviet Union put it under the spotlight. Central Asia and the Caucasus emerged from their prolonged torpor endowed with political entities that were now independent, open to the world, and constructed on the basis of national communities whose majority populations were Muslim. There was an urgent need to define their identity, which would have two major ongoing impacts on these countries' Islam. The first is that the new authorities found themselves tasked with giving birth to a novel national and ethnic identity, legitimating and distinctive, wherein Islam was a basic element whether they liked it or not. The second was globalization, in the grip of which these new countries found themselves. This globalization was also religious, and the diversity and intensity of foreign intellectual currents that arrived to test their power of influence on Central Asian territory posed a real challenge to the political and religious authorities. Building new republics largely inherited from the Soviet era, but demarcating themselves from it, while determining the role that Islam might appropriately take without crushing everything in its wake, was not an easy task. Thus, relations between their form of Islam and the enormous variety of religious tendencies injected by globalization were among the new states' priorities. In the following chapters, we shall analyse how these religious policies, which differed from country to country, were implemented and how post-Soviet Islam's participation in the globalization of religion contributed to its diversification, thanks to novel input from Turkey, Iran, the Arab world, and Muslims in the Indian subcontinent, and to continual national reinterpretation.

2

TURKEY AS AN ISLAMIC ACTOR IN CENTRAL ASIA AND THE CAUCASUS

Introduction: 'Reunions' between Turkey and the Turkic World

Turkey is no insignificant neighbour for the new republics of Central Asia and the Caucasus. It has powerful ethnic, historical, cultural and religious ties with them. Originating in their great majority from Siberia and Central Asia, Anatolian Turks mythologize this kinship with the Turkic peoples of Central Asia—Uzbeks, Kazakhs, Kyrgyz, Turkmens and Azerbaijanis. In fact, it should be pointed out, the languages spoken in Central Asia—Uzbek, Kyrgyz, Kazakh, Turkmen and Azeri—belong to the same linguistic family as Anatolian Turkish. The common core is estimated at 80 per cent in the case of Anatolian and Azeri and decreases with distance. But the proximity of the Turkic languages remains a unifying factor. In addition, in some pan-Turkic intellectual circles, the memory of currents that sought to unify the Turkic languages is still alive. In this regard, the thought of the Jadid Ismail Gaspirali has (as we shall see) been the subject of a postmodern rereading since 1991.

However, we should make it clear that not all the countries in the great Turkic family perceive their Turkishness in the same way. Initially, official Turkish policy employed the same word—'Türk'—to refer to any form of kinship between Turkey and the new republics, and this usage persists in some instances. Thus, in its policy of rapprochement with Central Asia, Ankara referred to *Türk dünyasi* (Turkish world) and *Türk edebiyati* (Turkish literature), just as it specified the geographical particularity of the Central Asian languages in the early 1990s—*Özbek türkçesi*, *Kazak türkçesi*, *Azeri türkçesi*, which were thereby put on a par with *Türkiye türkçesi* (the Turkic language of Turkey)—to underscore the kinship of the Turkic languages. This cumbersome, emphatic way of referring to Turkey and the ex-Soviet republics with the same notions and adjectives was gradually abandoned. It actually prompted resistance and rejection in Central Asia, where it cast the undesirable shadow of a 'new big brother' and contradicted the ethno-nationalism nascent in each republic.

Finally, with the end of the USSR, the community of belief between Turkey and Central Asia was rapidly prioritized by Ankara to support the rapprochement. Most Muslims in Central Asia, even the Persian-speaking Tajiks, are Sunnis of the Hanafi rite, as are Turks. Similarly, mystical currents native to Central Asia—particularly the Naqshbandi following its foundation in the twelfth century—soon spread to Anatolia. The only damper on this religious proximity between Turkey and the Turkic-speaking peoples of the ex-USSR is Azerbaijan, where the majority of the population are Twelver Shia. Turkist nationalist currents are nevertheless so strong in the two countries that they make excellent cooperation possible, including in the religious sphere.

The multifaceted kinship between Turkey and the new states that escaped the Soviet orbit in 1991 led Ankara to pursue a multi-pronged policy to develop relations with these newcomers on the international scene. The ambitious objective was to construct a political bloc with them, whose contours were certainly imprecise but which revolved around Turkic solidarity, and thereby indirectly endow Turkey with a new sphere of influence. Understanding Turkey's political context and ambitions at the time of *perestroika* will aid a better appreciation of its Islamic influence, religion being one of the central planks of this secular republic's policy in Central Asia.

Between 1923, the date of its foundation on the ruins of the Ottoman Empire, and the break-up of the USSR in 1991, Turkey's official policy towards the Turkic peoples of its Soviet neighbour was well-nigh non-existent. In fact, the Kemalist republic was initially attached to a 'little Turkish' nationalism, indifferent or even hostile to any 'great Turkish' discourse such as existed among certain Ottoman intellectuals and politicians, like Enver Pasha, at the close of the empire. Conscious of the geopolitical realities and context of his era, Mustafa Kemal Atatürk did not endeavour to develop particular relations with the Turkic peoples of the Soviet Union—a USSR with whom good neighbourly relations were fundamentally useful when it came to pursuing his national project. With the exception of the Azerbaijanis, geographically close to Turkey, the Turkic peoples held virtually no interest for Atatürk. However, contrasting with such official state indifference towards the Turkic and Muslim peoples of the Soviet Union, various migrant associations, intellectual circles and even political parties existed that were sensitive to the cause of the Turkic peoples living outside the borders of Anatolian Turkey—the *diş Türkler* (Turks abroad)—and acted as vehicles of a fundamentally anti-Soviet and anti-Communist nationalist discourse.[1]

In fact, from the end of the nineteenth century, the Russian advance into the Caucasus and Central Asia put numerous Muslim populations in the Russian Empire on the road to exile, because they could not conceive of living under a non-Islamic government. Thus, significant Circassian populations found refuge in the Ottoman Empire and settled in various Ottoman provinces—Anatolia, the Balkans and several of the empire's Arab cities. Today, considerable populations of Caucasian origin are still to be found in Amman in Jordan, in Homs in Syria, and in Palestine—at least until the birth of the state of Israel. The fall of the empire of the Tsars and the advent of the Soviet Union did not put an end to the migration of Muslim groups, Turkic in the main, from the USSR to republican Turkey. Thus, the forced Sovietization of Central Asia, particularly in the 1930s, prompted the exile of inhabitants of Turkestan (particularly Uzbeks) to Turkey, via several other Muslim countries, especially Afghanistan and Saudi Arabia. These migrants and their descendants were in the vanguard of a discourse addressed to their brothers 'under the yoke' of communism, or at least took an interest in them.[2] Throughout the Soviet period, their numerous cultural associations continued to publish papers and magazines in Turkey to promote awareness and even state action on behalf of these peoples. Militantly anti-communist, such circles were very close to the party of the Turkish extreme Right, *Milliyetçi Harkekt Partisi* (National Action Party), and its historical leader Alparslan Türkeş. At the time of the Soviet Union's break-up, they played a crucial role in Turkish policy towards the new independent republics. Their romantic, pan-Turkic discourse rubbed off on the Turkish state and the policy interest it subsequently developed in these countries.[3]

Turkish Dreams of Grandeur in the Turcophone Sphere in the Early 1990s: Between Fantasy and Reality

The fall of the Soviet Union and the independence of its Turco-Islamic republics were major international events, for which Turkey was not really prepared.[4] The pragmatic prime minister of the time, Turgut Özal, had sensed the coming upheaval and, during his final visit to the Soviet Union, included last-minute stops at Baku and Tashkent. Generally speaking, however, the Turkish state was not prepared for the implosion of the USSR and the birth, on its ruins, of so many independent states, new neighbours and Turkic, Turcophone and Muslim cousins. It did not have a comprehensive policy for them in its bottom drawer. Their past and future destiny was largely unknown to public opinion. Nor did it elicit interest from Turkish academic circles, whose studies and focus were directed more to the West at the time. However, in a context of euphoria and pressed by its Western allies, who feared the development of an Iranian or Saudi Islam—as if these societies were condemned to opt for political Islam as a developmental project—Turkey entertained the wildest dreams in its policy of rapprochement, which was hastily implemented. Although it did not yield the anticipated success, this policy, which was coherent but vitiated by overly ambitious objectives, at least had the merit of existing.[5] The present chapter seeks to analyse Turkey's Islamic activity in the Turkic world. I shall situate it in the more general context of the political, cultural, educational and linguistic initiatives pursued by the Turkish leaders of the time to endow Turkey with a new sphere of influence, extending 'from the Adriatic to the Great Wall of China'.

Analysis of Turkey's overall policy towards the Turkic republics of Central Asia conveys the impression that it put the cart before the horse. In effect, Ankara at once sought to lay the foundations of a political union based on Turkishness. This ambition led to the staging of Turcophone summits between Turkish and Central Asian leaders.[6] There could be no union without mutual knowledge, without respect, without a shared desire to link their destinies. Only just freed from the claws of the 'Russian big brother', Central Asia aspired to stand on its own two feet, rather than be chained to a new 'big brother'. Despite common heritages, relations were non-existent and everything had to be constructed. The sense of having a Turkic identity and belonging to a Turcophone world—i.e. the Turkish dialects on either side—did not have the same meaning in Turkey and in the new republics. Novices on the international stage, of which they were ignorant, the leaders of the new republics initially responded favourably to Turkey's invitations to participate in the summits. But they were sufficiently cautious and detached not to commit themselves unreservedly. Divergent interests between Central Asian states, sometimes engaged in regional disputes, and the fear of having to surrender some of the sovereignty they had just recovered to further Turkey's integrationist proposals, led the summits to founder. More so than the Azerbaijanis, the leaders of Central Asia were responsible for this. Openly boycotted by Uzbekistan, which rapidly distanced itself from Turkey, and by Turkmenistan, standing firm on the principles of neutrality stipulated in its constitution, the Turcophone summits soon became informal meetings at irregular intervals, whose closing declarations, vague and imprecise, convinced no one. While they were scheduled to be annual, the meetings were actually staged eleven times between 1991 and 2015.

The economic plank of Turkish policy in Central Asia and the Caucasus was probably the most considered and thought out, but this does not mean that it satisfied all Turkey's ambitions. In 1991, the commonly held view, ardently defended by Turkey and its Western allies (the USA at their head), was that Turkey, a secular, democratic and liberal Muslim republic, furnished an economic model for the republics just liberated from the socialist system.[7] In this spirit, for the first time in its history Turkey conceived an instrument of economic cooperation and development, creating the *Türk İşbirliği ve Koordinasyon Ajansi* (Turkish International Cooperation and Development Agency, TIKA), which bore a strong resemblance to the German GTZ, the Japanese JICA or the French AFD. The idea was a good one, but the resources were insufficient. In fact, for Turkey to make a difference in the sum total of international aid (European and American) granted to the ex-Soviet republics at the time, it would have required much greater financial and economic resources at its disposal. Nevertheless, it would not be right to say that Turkey's economic objectives in the region failed completely. Even if Turkey was not the motor force in financing and modernizing the economies of the new republics, it hit the mark in two respects worth mentioning. Firstly, Turkish firms penetrated Central Asian markets particularly successfully and created a dense, enduring web of small and medium-sized enterprises. In the construction sector, Turkey was a big player, with a number of major projects entrusted to Turkish firms. The new Kazakh capital of Astana was partly built by Turks, and the megalomaniac constructions of the Turkmen Presidents in Ashgabat were due to the French giant Bouygues, but with its Turkish competitors following close behind. Obviously, in the energy sector we must highlight the success of the 'contract of the century': the construction of the Baku Tbilisi Ceyhan (BTC) pipeline. It singlehandedly illustrates the economic victory of Turkey and its Western allies over Russia, which did everything to prevent its completion.[8] Firmly connecting Turkey to Azerbaijan, over time this pipeline also promised to open up Turkmen and Kazakh hydrocarbons. If the project is completed, it will further strengthen cooperation between four of the six Turcophone states—Turkey, Azerbaijan, Turkmenistan and Kazakhstan.

In the area of cultural and educational cooperation, Turkish initiatives were more attuned to the needs of the relevant parties. Thus, with the declarations of independence, a programme of study grants was established to enable thousands of students from the Turkic world to study in Turkey's schools and universities. Similarly, thousands of students from Turkey have been encouraged to pursue careers in the Turkic republics, in all manner of fields.[9] Moreover, the Turkish state undertook the establishment of several secondary schools, but especially two universities, in the new republics: the Manas University in Kyrgyzstan and the Akhmet Yassawi University in Kazakhstan.[10] Although Turks, Kazakhs and Kyrgyz sometimes held different views about the long-term objectives of these universities, they made possible not only student exchange programmes, but also opportunities for thousands of students from Turkey and the countries of the Turcophone sphere to meet and mingle. If only at the level of language, Turkey now has more people who know and speak the Russian and Turkic languages of Central Asia than before. Similarly, the dissemination of Turkey's Turkish has expanded remarkably in these republics.

Alongside these educational initiatives, important measures have been taken for the culture and literature, and also the intellectual figures and authors, of Turkey and the Turkic states to be promoted and known throughout the Turcophone space. Ankara's first priority was to do everything possible to get the new republics to abandon Cyrillic script in favour of the Latin alphabet. As in a fair number of other areas, the upshot of this policy of inducements was limited. Azerbaijan, Turkmenistan and Uzbekistan adopted a Latin alphabet, but each of them made it a point of honour to distinguish themselves from their neighbour by creating letters exclusive to their own language. Thus, the various Latin alphabets differed significantly from one country to the next, contrary to what had been proposed by Turkish linguists bent on harmonization and unification.[11] Furthermore, the three countries made the transition to the Latin alphabet more in order to demarcate themselves from the Russo-Soviet legacy and approximate to the West than to respond favourably to the integrationist promptings of Turkey, which hoped to realize Gaspirali's dream of creating a single language for the whole Turkic world.

In the same spirit, history and literature textbooks were designed in Turkey and offered to the peoples of Central Asia, so that schoolchildren throughout the Turkic world might have shared literary references. They were not always well-received, although some successes should be noted. Whereas during the Soviet period only the Turkish communist writer Nazim Hikmet was known to a Central Asian audience, after 1991 there was a very considerable opening up to Turkish culture. Turkish television channels, soap operas and music were highly appreciated throughout the region,[12] to the extent that the Uzbek regime, distrustful of too much foreign influence whatever its provenance, had to take practical measures to prohibit them in Uzbekistan.[13] Conscious that it was in the sphere of the humanities (literature, sciences, architectural heritage) that it had most chance of strengthening ties with the Turkic world, Turkey created a specialist agency, the *Türk*

ISLAM IN CENTRAL ASIA AND THE CAUCASUS

Kültur ve Sanatlari Ortak Yönetimi (the International Organization of Turkic Culture, TURKSOY), to be responsible for all projects of cooperation with the Turkic world. Equipped with significant resources, TURKSOY is probably the least politicized body in the Turkish policy of cooperation with Central Asia, but the most conducive to strengthening the links between Turkey and its sister republics in the long run.[14]

An initial assessment of Turkish policy in the region, over and above its religious dimension (which we shall now examine), brings out two important points. Turkey's policy objectives in 1991 were too ambitious to be realistic and feasible. In view of the limited results, it would be more accurate to speak of semi-failure or semi-success, depending on whether the glass is regarded as half-empty or half-full. Turkey's policy of integration into a Turkic union failed, and in retrospect we can see why it had no chance of achieving this goal. New on the international stage and fragile in their altogether novel national identity, the Central Asian republics aspired above all to strengthen their new nation-states.[15] Defeated in its integrationist or even pan-Turkic aims, Turkey nonetheless envisaged good bilateral relations with most of these countries. Once again, Uzbekistan was the exception, for the latter never forgave Turkey for having tolerated the subversive activities of the Uzbek opposition on its soil.[16] Brought to their senses, Turkey's leaders gradually abandoned their ambitions in favour of a more realistic policy, adapted to the domestic and regional context and more attuned to their means.

When it came to power in 2002, the AKP (*Adalet ve Kalkinma Partisi*, the Justice and Development Party), which originated in political Islam, making it more sensitive to an Islamic disposition than a Turkic one, re-orientated its foreign policy in the etymological sense of the term. Won to Euroscepticism, the AKP turned towards the Middle East and the Caucasus out of economic and political pragmatism.[17] Central Asia therewith lost the centrality to Turkish foreign policy that it had possessed since the 1990s.[18] As to what was achieved in political, cultural and economic terms, the Islamic plank of Turkish policy in Central Asia is nevertheless distinguished by notable success, thanks in part to an improved combination of public activity, via *Diyanet*, and private activity, involving various Turkish Islamic movements.

TURKEY AS AN ISLAMIC ACTOR

Diyanet—*Turkey's Official Arm for Helping to Reshape Islam in the New Caucasian and Central Asian Zone*

Although constitutionally lay and secular, and despite the fact that since the end of the USSR Turkey has been elevated by the West into a model of secular, democratic, liberal development for the new republics, Turkey has made full use of Islam as a lever of influence in its new geopolitical space.[19]

The Islamic dimension of Turkish foreign policy was based on a specific structure, whose existence dates back to the foundation of modern Turkey, and which has fuelled intense debates about its compatibility with the Turkish republic's secular principles. This instrument is the *Diyanet İşleri Başkanlığı* (Religious Affairs Directorate), more commonly called *Diyanet*. Conceived in 1924 at the time of the Turkish Republic's creation by Mustafa Kemal Atatürk, its function was administration of the country's religious affairs and, in particular, Islamic education, the administration of places of worship, and the organization of pilgrimages to the holy cities.[20] Its existence has been criticized by fervent defenders of the Turkish state and its lay character. According to the latter, in a secular republic like Turkey, the existence of a structure like *Diyanet*, financed by the state, is contrary to the constitution, which stipulates a strict separation between religious and public affairs.[21] Despite these criticisms, *Diyanet* has been cosseted and respected by all Turkish governments, since it served religion while providing an excellent tool with which to control it. Instrumentalized by the authorities, it was able to exercise maximum influence over the population electorally. Over the years, *Diyanet* has become a tool for defending Turkish-style secularism—that is, not a separation *sensu stricto* between public and religious affairs, but an instrument for controlling and orientating religious life for the state. In many respects, *Diyanet* has played a role of harmonizing centrifuge for Turkish Islam, in that it has contributed to the standardization and dissemination of a majority Hanafi Sunni Islam throughout the country.

Between its foundation in the 1920s and the end of the USSR in 1991, *Diyanet*'s activity was confined to administering Turkish Islam within national borders. It remained very weak abroad, because the main role assigned to it by the Turkish government was moulding

Turkish citizens in accordance with criteria fixed by the Kemalist republic—that is, an internalization of the faith and its expression in accordance with norms and at sites predetermined by the state. From the 1970s and 80s, with the phenomenon of Turkish migration to Europe, sizeable expatriate Turkish communities developed in the major European metropolises. Anxious to retain control, to avoid any drift by the expatriate community towards different forms of Islam, but also to prevent it dissolving into the host societies through loss of its cultural and religious roots, *Diyanet* made a range of religious services available to migrant Turks.[22] Thus began the extra-territorial expansion of *Diyanet*, which became an agent of international cooperation in the service of Turkish diplomacy. Concretely, *Diyanet*'s initiatives on behalf of Turks living in Germany, France and other European counties were mainly limited to despatching imams to preach in mosques and places of worship founded by migrant Turks or directly financed by Turkey, as well as organizing funeral services and distributing Islamic literature devised in Turkey but addressed to expatriate Turks.

The end of the Eastern bloc at the start of the 1990s was a key date in the history of *Diyanet*'s external activities. The opening up of Central Asia and the Caucasus, but also of the countries of the East Balkans, where a significant Turkic–Muslim legacy survived from the Ottoman period, enabled *Diyanet* to extend its activities considerably. Establishment abroad was made easier by the fact that the Turkish political context was conducive to the introduction of more Islam into Turkish foreign policy. In fact, since the military *coup d'état* of 1980, the Turkish generals, anxious to block the road to communism in Turkey and find a solution to the country's identity problem, fostered the emergence of an intellectual current characterized as a Turko-Islamic synthesis which, in the event, amounted to injecting a dose of religiosity into the new national ideology.[23] Above all, as the Eastern bloc foundered, Turkish political life was dominated by the Motherland Party (*Anavatan Partisi*, ANAP), whose charismatic leading figure—Özal—was well-known for his religious conservatism and ideal of rapprochement with the Muslim world.[24] More prosaically, at a time when a Turkish policy for the Balkans, the Caucasus, Central Asia and the Russian Federation was being put in place, the Turkish government considered using the Islamic factor to engage in dialogue with the new countries from the old Eastern bloc and draw closer to them, so as to integrate them into the sphere of influence that Turkey was seeking to create 'from the Atlantic to the Great Wall of China'. Similarly, Turkey was intent on restricting the development in Central Asia of any form of Salafist or Wahhabi Islam of the Saudi variety. In this it enjoyed the West's moral support in the early 1990s.

Although *Diyanet*'s services now extend to the whole of Eurasia and even to Africa, given Turkish designs on that continent thanks to the actions of successive AKP governments,[25] we shall focus on its activities and impact in the republics of Central Asia and Azerbaijan. Enjoying a greatly increased budget of almost 4 billion Turkish liras in 2013, *Diyanet*'s first major initiative was to set up a directorate of 'foreign relations' for the creation of an *Avrasya Islam Surasi* (Eurasian Islamic Council). Concretely, this involved a body containing the Muslim leaders of practically all twenty-eight member countries of the Balkans, the Caucasus, Central Asia and autonomous entities with significant Muslim communities in the Russian Federation. Under Ankara's supervision, these summit meetings between Islamic authorities were an opportunity for Turkey to position itself as a regional power and source of inspiration and influence for Islam over a vast area. The summits were also an opportunity to strengthen educational cooperation between member countries, to coordinate the struggle against the radical, undesirable forms of Wahhabism and Salafism. During them, spiritual leaders also liaised to agree a calendar of the main Muslim feast days that remained movable. Most of the summits were held in Turkey, but Sarajevo and Cyprus hosted one each.[26] They enjoyed support from the political authorities in virtually all the countries in the Balkans, Caucasus and Central Asia, with the exception of Uzbekistan, which did not wish to cooperate. It goes without saying that the Eurasian Council afforded Turkey a veritable instrument of political influence.

Diyanet did not limit itself to this initiative. On the ground it performed valuable religious services on a daily basis and assisted in the revival of Islam in the new republics, just as in a way it facilitated the development of a Turkish presence in a zone that represented Turkish diplomacy's new priority in the 1990s.[27]

Even before the establishment of the Eurasian Islamic Council that followed the independence of the ex-Soviet states, Turkey posted a religious affairs attaché to each of its new diplomatic missions. Like the attaché for cultural, military or economic cooperation, this civil servant seconded from *Diyanet* had the task of developing and administering a programme of bilateral cooperation in the religious sphere. He reported to Ankara on the state of Islam in the country and identified requirements and opportunities for cooperation with Turkey, just as he briefed the country's religious elites on how Turkey administers its Islam. Thus, he played a crucial role in transmitting the Turkish model of religious administration to Central Asia and the Caucasus. All the countries of the region accepted this cooperation and the posting of a Turkish religious attaché, but Uzbekistan terminated it in 2002 and Turkmenistan in 2011, for reasons that we shall spell out later. In Azerbaijan and Kazakhstan, the post still exists.

Even before the end of the USSR, from the Caucasus to the easternmost part of Central Asia, more and more voices were raised demanding the reopening of mosques that had been closed and expressing the need for others to be built. To respond to this demand, Turkey financed the restoration of several religious buildings via *Diyanet*. Above all, it tried to construct new mosques in these countries, in the Ottoman style inspired by the Blue Mosque. In addition to a multitude of small mosques constructed in various Azerbaijani, Kyrgyz or Kazakh cities, we may note the construction of various gigantic mosques in the capitals to mark the new urban space. In Baku, *Diyanet* financed the mosque of the monument to the martyrs of the Nagorno-Karabakh war—an iconic site in the new Azerbaijani national ideology. The young republic's protocol requires every official foreign delegation to pass through the Park of Martyrs, whose architecture is dominated by the new Turkish mosque. An even grander mosque has appeared in the city of Nakhchivan. It bears the name of Kazim Karabekir, an Ottoman general who commanded the Eastern Army at the end of the First World War and was the first president of the Turkish National Assembly when the Republic was created.

As we saw in the previous chapter, the new republics, anxious to create strong links between Islam and the new national ideology, prioritized Islamic educational structures in order to train their own cadres and control official discourse and preaching to the faithful. With extensive experience when it came to Islamic education and training religious cadres, notably through its network of *Imam Hatip Okullari*—training schools for imams and preachers[28]—and theological faculties, *Diyanet* possessed persuasive assets for offering its services to the new republics. Thus, in addition to sending hundreds of imams to towns and villages in Eurasia, it received students from these countries to train in the theology faculties of Ankara, Istanbul and other Turkish cities. More ambitiously, theology faculties were established by *Diyanet* in Osh in Kyrgyzstan, in Ashkhabad in Turkmenistan, and Baku in Azerbaijan. Like most of the Islamic establishments founded in these countries, they attracted youth from modest backgrounds or failed students from other, more prestigious university courses. This is another phenomenon demonstrating the unattractiveness of 'Islamic professions' and attesting to the importance of secularism in all countries stamped by the Soviet legacy. The educational programme and content of the disciplines taught in these faculties are inspired by the model of the theology faculty in the University of Marmara in Istanbul. Moreover, a large number of the Turkish teachers appointed to these faculties are graduates of Marmara and are sent to Central Asia to take charge of occasional courses.

Finally, to leave its imprint on the Islam of Central Asia and the Caucasus, *Diyanet* has promoted the production of an abundance of Islamic literature in local languages, so as to diffuse the basics of the Hanafi Sunni Islam that is majoritarian in Turkey and these countries—with the exception of Azerbaijan, where around 70 per cent of the population is of Shia observance. Printed in Turkey, these works have been distributed throughout Central Asia, in the mosques or institutions cooperating with *Diyanet*. The two most widely distributed works are basic textbooks, and *I Learn My Religion* and *The Life of the Prophet*, which (as their titles imply) are far from being major theological treatises, but answer the elementary questions of those secularized Muslims who are returning to religion in a quest for identity.

Two remarks are in order when it comes to assessing the Turkish state's public actions via its Islamic arm, *Diyanet*, in matters of religious cooperation and influence. Firstly, for all the criticisms levelled by analysts and agents of Turkish policy in Central Asia, *Diyanet* carried out its mission successfully. This is attested by the large number of Islamic cadres 'officiating' in mosques and Islamic establishments who were trained in Turkey or *in situ* thanks to *Diyanet*. The creation of state committees for religious affairs and the conversion of Muslim clergy into civil servants show that *Diyanet* has, to a certain extent, served as a model of inspiration for the new states in organizing and regulating Islam. Certainly, after some years of good and loyal service, various *Diyanet* offices—in Ashkhabad and Tashkent notably—have been closed by the local authorities. Aside from the Uzbek case, however, these closures do not indicate *Diyanet*'s failure, but, on the contrary, its success. In line with its initial objectives, the idea was not to settle permanently in these countries, but to cooperate with them while their states were training their own cadres. *Diyanet*'s activities made it possible to support this effort and to train hundreds, even thousands, of Islamic cadres, in sufficient number to meet demand. Moreover, the latter is not excessive, ex-Soviet Muslims remaining very much marked by the secular heritage. However, the Turkish imprint on Caucasian and Central Asian Islam is not attributable solely to *Diyanet*. Several Turkish religious movements have made, and are still making, a major contribution to the success of Turkish Islam in Central Asia and the Caucasus.

The Dynamism of Non-State Actors in the Dissemination of a Turkish Islam

Observation of the relations between Turkey and the Turco-Islamic sphere, from the Soviet period to the present, throws up an initial paradox. During the Soviet period, nationalist and pan-Turkist movements in Turkey were virtually alone in articulating a discourse of inclusion and an interest in Central Asia and the Caucasus, whereas Turkish Islamist movements were focused on themselves, the national community or, in some cases, orientated towards Europe in order to address Turkish migrants. Their focus changed in 1991 when, with the 'liberation of our brothers from the communist yoke', it was religious movements, rather than nationalist circles, that embraced the post-Soviet sphere and sought to establish themselves there in order to acquire a supra-national stature. The ethnic and national identities of the states in the Caucasus and Central Asia, fixed during the Soviet era, were transplanted and reinforced by the nationalist turn taken by the new regimes. They indicate that the pan-Turkist discourse disseminated by Turkish nationalist circles had little chance of finding a positive echo in Central Asia and the Caucasus. In other words, in 1991 Turkish Islamist circles in Turkey had much more wind in their sails than nationalist circles, for the new countries were seeking a distinct Islamic identity, not dissolution into a pan-Turkist integrationist project.

Moreover, committed to a liberal economic policy since the reforms introduced by Turgut Özal from January 1980 onwards, Turkey witnessed the emergence of a dynamic, conservative private sector. As a semi-official ideology launched by the military in 1980, the Turco-Islamic synthesis generated a new caste of Islamic private entrepreneurs, attracted by the new economic opportunities, but also by the missionary and spiritual opportunities offered them abroad. The opening of the Islamic market in Central Asia and the Caucasus, and the dynamism of the Turkish conservative private sector, helped several Turkish brotherhoods or neo-brotherhoods to establish themselves in the Central Asian, Caucasian and Balkan zones. These three regions, marked to different degrees by Turcophone populations or the Ottoman heritage, and characterized by a majority Hanafi Sunni Islam as in Turkey, were receptive to the influence of Anatolian Islam. Adopting and espousing different strategies and causes, like trade or pilgrimages, various Turkish movements were more active and successful than the Turkish state in their engagement and influence in Central Asia and the Caucasus. These Turkish agencies of Islamic cooperation were very often members of brotherhoods, like the Naqshbandi or the Suleymanci, or new actors called neo-brotherhoods for want of a better term—that is, followers of Said Nursi and Fethullah Gülen.

Mystical currents: The Naqshbandi

At the risk of repeating the point, in the religious dynamics between Turkey and the ex-USSR, Turkish Islam's major asset is that it is informed to a considerable extent by various mystical currents that have their roots in Central Asia. As we have seen, the Naqshbandi, still the most important mystical brotherhood in the Muslim world and highly active in Turkey in various branches, was born in Central Asia in Bukhara, in what is today Uzbekistan. During the Soviet period, relations between the Naqshbandi of Turkey and those of Central Asia were difficult, but after 1991 exchanges became easier. In the first instance, this was because the regime in Uzbekistan was particularly attached to genuinely promoting the Naqshbandi Sufi heritage, including in the context of cooperation with Turkey. Thus, during his visit to Uzbekistan in 1992, the then Turkish head of state, Turgut Özal, visited the mausoleum and museum dedicated to the great mystic Bahauddin Naqshband. He also made an official contribution to the restoration of the complex with a donation. Good Turkish–Uzbek relations over a common mystical heritage enabled Turkey's Naqshbandi to establish themselves more easily in Central Asia.

A Naqshbandi authority from Turkey merits particular attention when it comes to cooperation between Turkey's Naqshbandi and their brothers in the ex-USSR. This is Osman Nuri Topbaş, born in 1942, who was leader of a community gravitating around the *Aziz Mahmud Hudayi Vafki* foundation. His community organized various religious and educational services, but also humanitarian ones, for charitable associations supported by the brotherhood regularly sent aid to Central Asia. Paradoxically, however, it was not in Uzbekistan—birthplace of Naqshbandi—that Osman Nuri Topbaş and his followers ended up becoming firmly rooted. In fact, after an initial phase of openness, the Uzbek regime decided to close its doors to Islamic cooperation, including with the Sufi authorities of Turkey and elsewhere. Osman Nuri Topbaş's most obvious impact is his activity in Azerbaijan, where his followers set up a major educational centre for youth. With minor educational structures in several of the country's cities, the aid foundation for Azerbaijani youth also had a cooperation agreement with Azerbaijan's Spiritual Directorate, which entrusted it with managing two branches of the Islamic University of Baku in the provinces, in Zakatala and Sheki. Along with educational services, this Naqshbandi leader also succeeded in disseminating his works, translated into local languages, including Russian. His literature deals with doctrinal and philosophical questions, stressing the importance of faith and practice, and rarely alluding to political issues.

Likewise deriving from the Naqshbandi, Süleyman Hilmi Tunahan's community is another Turkish Islamic organization that has attracted attention for its Islamic educational missions throughout the ex-USSR. The leader of the community, a native of Bulgaria in the

TURKEY AS AN ISLAMIC ACTOR

Ottoman era, was influential in Turkey, where he often came into conflict with *Diyanet*, whose monopoly on Islamic affairs—notably courses on the Koran—he denounced as illegitimate. The community's watchword throughout its existence has been that every Muslim must be capable of reading the Koran in the language in which it was revealed: Arabic. For Süleyman Tunahan's followers, often referred to by the pejorative term Suleymanci, anyone who cannot read the Koran in Arabic cannot be regarded as a Muslim. Consequently, the community specializes in opening and running Koranic schools in Turkey.

In Central Asia and the Caucasus, dozens of small madrasas have been created by Süleyman Tunahan's community, which does not really engage in other activities aside from a few publishing projects. In Kyrgyzstan, in the cities of Osh and Jalalabad, but also Bishkek and Narin, the community has opened small madrasas, registered and recognized by the country's Spiritual Directorate. In Kazakhstan too it has small madrasas. Turkmenistan and Uzbekistan being more closed to this kind of cooperation, they have not allowed Tunahan's followers to pursue their activities there. The community's presence is more significant in Azerbaijan, but also, and especially, at the heart of Georgia, in Adjara, where the largely Muslim population welcomes cooperation with its Turkish co-religionists and immediate neighbours.

In both instances, in the communities of Osman Nuri Topbaş and Süleyman Tunahan alike, trade and study are important media for disseminating their discourse. Trade between Turkey and these countries, but also the development of educational exchanges—the opening of Central Asian universities to Turkish students and the welcoming of Central Asian students in Turkey thanks to recognition of equivalent qualifications—have facilitated greater circulation of ideas, including those of religious movements, and Topbaş' and Tunahan's movements have benefited. In both cases, the aim of performing an Islamic educational service has always been clearly expressed and often negotiated and overseen by official cooperation agreements with the host countries. Such has not been the case with two other religious movements, which are closely linked: Said Nursi's and Fethullah Gülen's. However, they are the most important and most effective in exporting a Turkish Islamic discourse from Anatolia to Central Asia and the Caucasus.

ISLAM IN CENTRAL ASIA AND THE CAUCASUS

Said Nursi's followers in Central Asia and the Caucasus

Intellectually close, since the former strongly influenced the latter, Said Nursi and Fethullah Gülen are among the religious figures who have made the biggest contribution to the diffusion of a Turkish Islam in the ex-USSR. The initial philosophical proximity between the two movements often results in confusion in Central Asia, where, however, their representatives by no means get established in the same way or possess the same aims. Clearer in their ambitions, Said Nursi's followers—let us call them classical so as not to confuse them with Gülen's—are easier to get an analytical grip on.

Said Nursi was born in 1876 in eastern Turkey, in the village of Nurs near Erzurum. Marked by a mystical Islam, he first became an influential religious authority in his native province, and then grew in notoriety thanks to his engagement on the eastern front against Russia during the First World War. At the time of the foundation of the Turkish Republic on the ruins of the Ottoman Empire, he militated in favour of a new political regime based on Islam. Profoundly disagreeing with Mustafa Kemal Atatürk and his lay, secular vision, he renounced political involvement and founded a mystical movement, which was apolitical and pietistic.[29] In this he is comparable to other Muslim thinkers of his time—Muhammad Ilyas and Maududi in India, for example—who, conscious of the crisis that the Muslim world was experiencing, sought to solve it by advocating greater attachment to a modernized Islam. In Said Nursi's thought, the key idea is to prove that Islam, science and modernity are compatible, on condition that the religious sciences enter modern schools and madrasas are opened to the profane sciences. Poised between a clandestine and semi-legal existence, his movement became popular throughout the country. Under his impetus, here and there groups formed to read his fundamental work, the *Risale-i Nur* ('The Epistle of Light'), an exegesis of the Koran. Its content is not political, but exclusively spiritual, and its sole ambition is to explain the Koran and the other basic texts of Islam, the *hadiths* in particular. Said Nursi died in 1960, leaving behind him a movement active throughout the country, but which could not resist the secessionist tendencies of various groups, each of them led by one of his followers and dedicated to a particular task: dissemination of his master work, promotion of his ideas in academic circles, or education. His most notable followers are Mehmet Kutlular, who still edits the daily *Yeni Asya* ('New Asia'); Mehmet Kirkinci, who died in February 2016; and Mustafa Sungur, who died in December 2012. Fethullah Gülen is another of Said Nursi's followers, the most influential at present, who has become so independent of Nursi's classical teachings that we shall deal with him separately. Meanwhile, let us review the activity of the other branches identifying with Said Nursi's teachings in Central Asia.

Dubbed *Nurcu* on account of their affiliation to Said Nursi's philosophy, from 1990, various unstructured groups set out from Turkey for the post-socialist Muslim sphere, but especially for the Turcophone republics, to distribute the *nurcu* movement's key work, the *Risale-i Nur*—an exegesis of the Koran composed in Turkish, but translated into nearly all the languages of Central Asia. Reading groups devoted to Said Nursi's work are inconspicuous, however. In fact, they do not operate within the framework of educational establishments, but in private apartments. These networks do not regard themselves as a specific movement. They do not demand official recognition as a religious community in the countries where they operate. In all the republics of Central Asia save Uzbekistan, where a *nurcu* presence is banned, the *Nurcus* diffuse their master's ideas in the context of their commercial or student activities; a fair number of Turkish expatriates in Central Asia are managers of small and medium-sized enterprises, or young students enrolled in Central Asian universities via academic exchanges between Turkey and Turcophone countries. For these *nurcu* circles, whose size and influence are often exaggerated by the political authorities, the aim of disseminating the master's ideas is perfectly clear; this is where the group founded by Fethullah Gülen—the most influential in Central Asia—dissents.

Fethullah Gülen's Community in Central Asia: Modern, Secular Education and Islamic Spirituality

Born into a conservative family in eastern Turkey in 1938, and currently living in voluntary exile in the USA, Fethullah Gülen adopted Said Nursi's discourse while assigning especial importance to its educational dimension. Initially rooted in exclusively mystical religious thinking, which was progressively politicized by implantation in the media, petty commerce and education, Fethullah Gülen's thought aims to form a new, 'golden' generation (*Altin Nesil*), which is modern, in tune with its times, and faithful to its Turco-Islamic traditions.[30] The construction of the movement was slow but resolute. In the 1960s, Fethullah Gülen trained his first followers in the Izmir region, where he was employed as an official imam, paid by *Diyanet*, in the service of the republic. The following decade saw the movement's ideas spread to Turkey's other regions. When Turkey switched to the market economy from January 1980, the movement, boasting hundreds of thousands of sympathizers who financed its activities, reinforced itself by combining economic success and Islamic faith.[31] From 1989 onwards, Turkey's opening to the Balkans, the Caucasus and Central Asia made it possible for Gülen's followers, dubbed Fethullahci, to participate in economic and religious globalization alike. In both Turkey and the countries where it has put down roots, the movement prioritizes four spheres of action in which it is particularly influential.

With the transition to the market economy, Gülen's movement prioritized education and created thousands of private establishments. The media formed the movement's other base. The daily paper *Zaman*[32] (and its Anglophone version *Todayzaman*) was one of the best Turkish dailies, both because of the professionalism of its journalists and because of the quality of its news and analyses.[33] Several TV channels, like STV, were organs for broadcasting Gülen's ideas. A third favoured domain was the intellectual milieu, through the creation of forums dedicated to inter-faith dialogue, initially in Turkey and then gradually abroad. The movement comprised hundreds of cultural centres or associations that encouraged inter-cultural and inter-faith meetings.[34] Finally, these priority areas could not do without the movement's presence in key sectors of the economy and commerce. Hundreds of large companies, but above all thousands of medium and small enterprises, were managed by businessmen who identified with Fethullah Gülen's ideas.

The movement initially defined itself as a community—*cemaat*—before preferring the term *hareket*, 'movement'. For some years, following diversification of its spheres of activity, it defined itself as *hizmet*—a 'house of service' motivated solely by the promotion of ideals of dialogue and social peace globally. To back up this claim, it foregrounds the regular inter-faith meetings it organizes wherever it has a presence and the support enjoyed by the movement's initiatives in non-Muslim circles: Christian, Jewish and other. Fethullah Gülen is, in fact, one of the few Muslim thinkers who has been supported and publicly lauded by Jewish and Christian religious leaders in Turkey and most of the countries where his movement has had a presence.

For the movement's rival Islamic organizations, particularly the most fundamentalist among them, like the Kaplanci, which was active in the Turkish diaspora in Europe, Fethullah Gülen's initiatives are to be condemned. For in their apolitical character, moderation and collaboration with the 'enemies of Islam', they allegedly void Islam of its fighting spirit and perpetuate the Muslim world's submission to the West.

As for Turkey's secular and Kemalist circles (army, Republican People's Party, the main opposition party founded by Atatürk and champion of secularism), they are convinced that the Fethullaci, under cover of moderate Islam, social peace and dialogue between civilizations, are in fact seeking to promote a secret agenda of intellectual Islamization so as to foster the advent, in the medium or long term, of an Islamic state.

In my opinion, each of these claims contains an element of truth. The Gülenist movement unquestionably exudes a generous, humanist spirit which is not, however, incompatible with the progressive politicization for which it has been criticized by secular circles. Gülen's movement resembles a Turco-Islamic version of the Jesuit phenomenon. It probably derived inspiration from the missionary schools created by Westerners in the Ottoman Empire, which trained the post-Ottoman, republican elites.[35] More recent research on the movement compares it with the Christian organization World Vision,[36] on account, in particular, of its prioritization of dissemination of its discourse and a method of proselytizing that foregrounds exemplary conduct and attitudes in society at the expense of classical proselytism.[37] In reality, Gülen's original idea was to transpose a Jesuit-inspired Western model of training to educate Turco-Islamic elites capable in their turn of training the elites of other countries: in Central Asia and the Caucasus to begin with, then in the rest of the world and, in more recent years, Africa in particular. Like the Jesuits before them, the Fethullahci put 'total' education at the centre of their concerns and, like them, cultivate elitism and entryism, which barely conceal their taste for influence and power.[38] Central Asia was the movement's experimental field, prior to its becoming a transnational movement operating on all continents.

The settlement and activities of Fethullah Gülen's followers in Central Asia

Unquestionably, the educational services rendered by Gülen's community (*cemaat*) to the post-Soviet societies are what furthered and legitimated its activity most in those countries. From Azerbaijan to Kazakhstan, Gülen's followers—minor entrepreneurs, teachers and students influenced by his Islamic thinking tinged with Turkish patriotism—set up secondary schools and universities that satisfied a real need on the part of local populations. Weakened by exit from the Soviet Union, and in a period of rediscovery of ethnic and religious identity, the societies and regimes of Central Asia responded very favourably to the community's requests to open schools in their countries. Let us nevertheless note that Fethullah Gülen's schools did not explicitly present themselves as such in Central Asia—that is, as openly representing the teaching of a Turkish imam idolized by some in Turkey and reviled by others. Installation was more discreet and did not directly refer to any religious discourse.

The first contacts were made by entrepreneurs who arrived in Central Asia as representatives of business associations. They developed economic cooperation between their native region in Turkey and various Central Asian cities, before proposing to local partners that they create schools on the model of private establishments in Turkey. As we have seen, the context was highly conducive to such cooperation, economic, cultural and educational. In fact, although in the early 1990s the Turkish state, the Kemalist elites and the army distrusted the movement, the key figure in Turkish political life at the time, Turgut Özal, strongly supported Fethullah Gülen's activities for pragmatic and political reasons, but also out of religious conviction. Moreover, though they deny it today, the Central Asian governments were very well-disposed towards Turkish influence, only later developing reservations about the ambitions of a Turkey that seemed to them to be behaving like a 'new big brother' in place of the 'Russian big brother'. Turkey and its multifaceted influence were a source of inspiration for development divested of the Soviet legacy. Thus, in the early years of independence, the *cemaat*'s educational services, which on the ground did not openly advertise its spiritual links with Fethullah Gülen, were greatly appreciated. Within a few years, several educational services developed a solid network throughout Central Asia. Kazakhstan rapidly developed a Gülenist network containing thirty secondary schools, a university and dozens—even hundreds—of medium and small enterprises run by Turks affiliated or linked to Gülen's movement.[39] To start off with, Uzbekistan looked favourably on the development of twenty schools—of all kinds—by the *cemaat*, before closing them down in 2000. Their closure is explained more by deteriorating relations between Turkey and Uzbekistan than by the actual nature of the *cemaat*'s activities. In Kyrgyzstan, a dozen secondary schools and a university are still run by followers of Gülen, and a new school was set up in the city of Kara Balta in 2013, despite the crisis involving the movement and Erdoğan's government in Turkey.[40] In Tajikistan, and even more so in Azerbaijan, Gülen's movement had a strong educational presence and it is still growing despite some apprehension on the part of the local authorities.[41] In many countries, such developments were eventually compromised by the war at the summit of the Turkish state between Fethullah Gülen and the president, Recep Tayyip Erdoğan.

The success of *cemaat*'s schools accounts for the movement's popularity in Central Asia, and thanks to them the community has held up well in all these states, with the notable permanent exception of Uzbekistan. The attacks of 11 September 2001, which contributed to the Central Asian regimes becoming less relaxed about religious matters, significantly curbed the active potential of the Islamist movements, even the most moderate among them, in Central Asia. But they barely made a dent in the positive image of Fethullah Gülen's schools. There are at least two reasons for this. Firstly, Gülen's followers have never presented themselves as a religious community in Central Asia. Moreover, especially at the outset, the schools were called 'Turkish schools' and rarely identified with Fethullah Gülen, except perhaps in the last few years, now that the community is globally well-known. On the morrow of the 11 September attacks, the Fethullahci began to advertise their affiliation to Fethullah Gülen more openly, while taking care to present him as more of an intellectual than a religious authority. Invisible until 2001, Gülen's books began to appear more frequently on the desks of secondary-school heads, to highlight and promote his works on peace, inter-faith dialogue, tolerance and the moderate character of his religious beliefs. In the wake of the attacks, Fethullah Gülen wrote a significant number of books and articles denouncing any act of violence perpetrated in the name of Islam.[42] His moderate discourse, open to inter-faith dialogue, intensified after 11 September and naturally was disseminated in all the institutions inspired by his movement. Taking a significant step towards greater transparency in their activities, the schools were strengthened after 2001, despite an unfavourable context of anti-religious suspicion and distrust. However, Uzbekistan, which had displayed its hostility to the schools by banning them well before 11 September, out of a general rejection of Turkish policy in Central Asia, has always been a separate case.[43]

The development of Gülen's Islamic discourse in Central Asia

This is a difficult issue, because from the start of its settlement in Central Asia the *cemaat* (or *hizmet* in current terminology) has never avowed any proselytizing objective vis-à-vis the societies of Central Asia, traditionally Muslim but secularized for more than three generations by Soviet repression and atheism. Reinforcement of the faith and its reconciliation with science and modernity—fundamental objectives in Said Nursi—remain the ultimate goals of his disciple Fethullah Gülen. However, his intentions have never been openly avowed in Central Asia. At the outset, between 1990 and 1995, the movement's leaders in Central Asia sought to disseminate an Islamic discourse and provide religious instruction outside the schools to train followers.[44] This initial phase in the general strategy of establishing the *cemaat* was short-lived, for the Gülenists soon realized that it would fuel the local authorities' distrust and hamper, even imperil, their educational activities. Above all, the movement's cadres soon came to understand that the local population appreciated the schools for their educational provision, discipline and rigour, but remained averse, even hostile, to any explicitly religious activity.

Having registered this distrust of any form of Islamic activity, a new strategy was implemented, which Fethullah Gülen calls *temsil*. It no longer involves spreading Islam via *da'wa* ('invitation' to the non-Muslim to listen to the message of Islam), or *tabligh* ('transmission' of the message, generally literally), which are the classical methods of preaching and disseminating Islam, but by *temsil*, i.e. exemplariness (*missal* signifying 'example' in Arabic and Turkish). This method involves the bearer of the message living his religion nobly, by being morally impeccable, well-educated and virtuous. Attraction by example is intended to attract the faithful, who are spontaneously tempted to adopt the religious vision of the *cemaat*, without the latter imposing it.[45] In this sense, *temsil* operates as a kind of soft power, a method of persuasion that imposes itself naturally. We even observe *temsil* preceding soft power and inspiring other forms of it. The *cemaat* has seen its influence strengthened in Central Asia and then other continents thanks to this method of preaching, which has no equivalent in the Muslim world.

Curiously, the tried-and-tested strategy of subtle proselytizing 'by example' has now been abandoned; at least, it is no longer central to the Gülenists' strategy for strengthening their position in Central Asia. In fact there, like everywhere else, the *cemaat* is developing into a form of community that no longer refers to religion, but to service—*hizmet*. It thus advertises its desire to serve humanity by helping it to perfect itself via initiatives in inter-faith dialogue and international peace, but also more concrete services—particularly education—which are sometimes charged for, sometimes free, throughout the world. Thus, at the time of writing, while Gülen's followers in Central Asia follow a conservative Muslim way of life, their engagement is not such, strictly speaking. Unlike other religious movements in the region, they do not create madrasas, mosques or Koranic schools, and do not even advertise themselves as an Islamic community. There is nothing in common between Fethullah Gülen's educational activities and the purely Islamic activities of Suleyman Tunahan's group or Osman Nuri Topbaş' Naqshbandi. Just as those two groups concentrate on constructing mosques and madrasas and distributing Islamic literature in bulk, so Gülen's followers do not convey the impression of being an Islamic organization. The movement's members prefer to practise their faith discreetly and it is reserved exclusively for the private sphere. In some respects, Gülen's community has features in common with Western NGOs whose religious discourse is increasingly effaced behind more humanist and universalistic considerations. In this respect, the *modus operandi* of New World Vision, for example, is strangely similar to that of Gülen's movement. The resemblance between the latter and certain Christian organizations is striking. I noted it on several occasions, particularly in ways of communicating in the media. It should not be so surprising given a certain global standardization of methods of proselytism, which in Fethullah Gülen's case is readily intelligible. Based in the USA since 1999, his interlocutors and strongest advocates are Christian religious organizations, from which he doubtless indirectly draws inspiration to strengthen his community globally.

Despite its discretion, in some Central Asian countries fear of Islam posed a serious threat to the *cemaat* from 2002, less on account of the 11 September attacks than the arrival of Islamo-conservatives in power in Turkey, with the victory of Recep Tayyip Erdoğan and his Justice and Development Party (*Adalet ve Kalkinma Partisi*, AKP). The first concerns emerged in the Russian Federation, in the Caucasian region, in Tatarstan and Bashkortostan (Bashkiria). In the Russian state, particularly the intelligence services, distrust of the Turkish schools gradually crystallized. They were soon banned and closed, on the grounds that they served as a channel for disseminating Islamism and pan-Turkism. In Central Asia, courtesy of the Soviet past and tradition, events in Moscow resonated in the periphery. Thus, retaliatory measures in Moscow inspired some Central Asian countries to increase their surveillance of the movement's activities. In Uzbekistan, the issue did not arise because the schools had already been closed. By contrast, in Turkmenistan, where relations with Turkey were excellent and where an intimate of Fethullah Gülen—Ahmet Calik—was an adviser to President Turkmenbashi for several years, the decision was taken in 2011 to close certain establishments, with the notable exception of the International Turkmen-Turkish University and the Lycée Turgut Özal situated in the capital. In Azerbaijan, where Turkey's image had likewise been excellent for nearly twenty years, from 2000 to 2005 the government considered reinforcing control of the *cemaat* and its schools.[46] Why are the authorities succumbing to anxiety today, when they used to appreciate the educational services without worrying unduly about their possible future political impact?

The reason for the sudden mistrust is probably to be found in the AKP's arrival in power in Turkey. The Central Asian elites are still for the most part the old, profoundly secularized Soviet elites, and they interpreted the success of the AKP's moderate Islamists as a sign that educational activities like Gülen's would eventually lead to a conservative political government—a prospect they reject. Taxing the AKP with Islamism is excessive, but its conservatism, which is deemed 'too Muslim' by the Central Asians, is sufficient to arouse suspicion and criticism of the *cemaat*. Moreover, the progressive politicization of the movement in Turkey, and the impact of the Ergenekon affair,[47] were seen in Central Asia as tangible proof that the *cemaat* was neither the innocent mystical order it would have people believe it to be, nor the pious organization involved in education and without political ambition it pretended to be.

However, while the *cemaat* aroused mistrust, it remained a marked presence in all the countries of the zone (apart from Uzbekistan) and continued to exercise a certain influence there, with all the subtlety of the soft power of which it is a master. Its establishments in Kazakhstan, Kyrgyzstan, Tajikistan and Azerbaijan operated without too many fetters and until the rupture of December 2013—the divorce between the state and Gülen's movement in Turkey—openly enjoyed the support of Turkish diplomacy, which included its activities in its regional policy.

Three remarks are in order concerning the Gülen contribution to Turkey's prestige and influence in the region. More than the Turkish state and a few cultural centres, it is Gülen's schools that have facilitated dissemination of the Turkish language throughout Central Asia. In the economic sphere, entrepreneurs close to the movement have created strong ties between Turkey and the countries of Central Asia. Moreover, Gülen's movement, which has become transnational, enables students and businessmen from Central Asia to travel throughout the world, to participate in international educational meetings and competitions or in business forums. The *cemaat*'s prestige and reputation in Central Asia are, in fact, of more benefit to Turkey than to the *cemaat* itself. This is indicated by the fact (already noted above) that the schools were more commonly referred to by communities, authorities and media as 'Turkish schools' than Fethullahci schools, directly affiliated to Fethullah Gülen's movement.

The schools' uncertain future

Since December 2013, when a major conflict erupted in Turkey between Fethullah Gülen's movement and the prime minister, and since the failed coup d'état of July 2016, a new, more uncertain era has begun for the *cemaat* in all the countries where it is established. For a long time natural allies by virtue of the complementary character of their visions of Islam—politically moderate in the AKP and socially liberal in the Gülenists—the two groups literally divorced in December 2013. The causes of the rift are still unclear, but it seems that the initial rationale for the union between two major forces in Turkey gradually disappeared. Natural allies against Kemalism and its main pillar—the Turkish army—Gülen and Erdoğan had united their forces in Turkey and succeeded in politically neutralizing their common enemy, the Kemalist establishment. Once this enemy had faded, the two most powerful forces in Turkey became rivals for power.[48] A taste for power, entryism and infiltration of state structures—second nature to the movement, although it has always denied it—ended up riling the Turkish prime minister who, in the interim, had become more authoritarian and disinclined to share power.

The break was violent and continues to affect Turkish political and social life. In December 2013, civil servants allegedly subservient to their master, Fethullah Gülen, and infiltrated into the Turkish legal and political systems exposed massive corruption involving ministers, close collaborators and even the son of Prime Minister Erdoğan. For the latter, these affairs of 'alleged' corruption merely revealed the politicization of the movement, which he characterized as a 'parallel structure'. The mutual accusations are justified in the main: there is unquestionably an authoritarian drift on the part of Erdoğan, who wishes to reign like a new sultan and is sinking into corruption; similarly, Gülen's movement has gone too far, becoming 'cocksure and domineering'.

In July 2016, the rupture between the AKP government in Turkey and the Gülen movement reached a new momentum and became total and irremediable. Indeed, the attempted *coup* that considerably destabilized the country was attributed by the government to the Gülenists who, thanks to their long infiltration of the state apparatus, have sought to topple Erdoğan's government. Be their participation to the *coup* incontestable or not, yet seemingly involved as a major force among others, the Gülenists' contribution has accelerated the purges against the movement in Turkey, where it has been *de facto* uprooted.[49] The all-out war declared on the movement was not limited to Turkey, but extended to all countries where there are Gülen schools. In Central Asia and the Caucasus, more than anywhere else, Turkish diplomacy has increased pressure on the movement, asking local countries to close the schools.[50] Some governments, like Tajikistan, have agreed to close them down, while some others, like Kyrgyzstan and Tajikistan, have changed their status. In all these countries the image of the movement has been tarnished, and its role in the future will probably diminish.

The consequences of the rift in Turkey have already made themselves felt abroad, where the excellent understanding between the AKP and Gülen's movement traditionally supplied Turkey with its most effective instance of 'soft power'. Determined to undermine them wherever they are influential, Erdoğan has extended the war declared on the Gülenists abroad. Just after the local elections which his party won comfortably, the prime minister travelled in April 2014 to Azerbaijan, where the Gülenist movement was most firmly rooted after Turkey. During his visit, the movement's schools were at the forefront of the discussions, and a few months later they were closed by the Baku authorities. The question everyone is asking is whether the same fate awaits Gülen's schools in the republics of Central Asia—Kazakhstan, Kyrgyzstan and Tajikistan—where there was still a large number of them in January 2017. The republics have not (yet) changed their attitude towards these establishments, whose services they still appreciate. However, the image of Gülen's movement has been considerably tarnished, and the leaders of these countries are concerned to discover that it has infiltrated their state apparatuses, as in Turkey, to bolster its power and influence. On the face of it, the movement lacks the resources and local networks to repeat what it has done in Turkey in these countries. Nevertheless, doubt persists and has taken hold among Central Asia's ruling elites, who no longer regard it in the same way.

The schools' influence on Islam in Central Asia

The basic issue that arises as regards Gülen's movement in Central Asia is its impact on local societies and Central Asian Islam. Do the schools have an influence, and if so what influence, on local societies and, more especially, youth and elites? Measuring this is difficult, because we lack the wherewithal to establish the sociological profile of a representative sample of pupils from these establishments and assess their position in the social hierarchy, their relationship to religion, and the impact of Gülenist teaching on society. Such research is underway, and we can venture elements of a response.

Firstly, a very large majority of pupils from these schools go to the best universities in their countries and/or abroad, and not only in Turkey. On completion of their higher education, they often secure prestigious jobs in various areas—public administration, academic contexts and the private sector. They are to be found to varying degrees in the civil service and their countries' diplomatic service abroad. Secondly, we observe that these young elites are not necessarily religious, in the sense that religion does not form part of their basic everyday concerns and does not influence their professional life. They are certainly conservative in most instances, but not exclusively so, and do not have the same profile as pupils from religious schools. In this, the resemblance to the Jesuit phenomenon in the West is striking. In both cases, the socialization of pupils in an educational structure run by a religious order does not make them particularly observant religiously. In each instance, however, the phenomenon is totalizing—that is, the community absorbs the individual without destroying his or her individuality.

Conclusion: Turkey has Exported Islam rather than Secularism to the Post-Soviet Sphere

Since Turkish influences are not the only ones to play a role in reconstructing Islam in Central Asia, the question arises as to how they are perceived by other Islamic actors, public and private, all of whom are engaged in religious competition. First and foremost, how do the official religious authorities in each country regard Turkish influence? The states in Central Asia greatly prefer inter-state cooperation to private initiatives, of which they are permanently distrustful for fear of not being able to control them completely. Thus, the Spiritual Directorates generally have a very positive image of *Diyanet*, because they appreciate the services it has rendered, especially in education and in training new religious elites.

As for Turkish influences other than *Diyanet*, the Central Asian authorities accept them reluctantly, very often after having consulted the *Diyanet* representative to learn more about their true character. For example, Suleyman Tunahan's followers in Kyrgyzstan, as in Kazakhstan, have been authorized to operate only if *Diyanet* expresses a positive view, and on the absolute condition that they respect the Spiritual Directorate's supervision and orientation on the ground.

The issue of the states' perception of Fethullah Gülen's movement is more complex. In fact, as we have seen, its activity and comportment have evolved over time, leading to the abandonment of overt proselytism. It has never presented itself either as a religious institution or as an institution *per se*. At most, educational associations identifying with and drawing on Fethullah Gülen's ideas, without always explicitly avowing them, have founded various educational establishments, without apparent religious designs. However, even when discreet and relegated to the background, the religious inspiration behind these establishments is no longer a secret for the authorities of Central Asia. Thus, the movement is no longer judged solely on the basis of its contribution to education, but also in the light of its possible religious impact on youth attending its schools. To guard against potentially harmful influences and prioritize the educational contribution, the authorities vigilantly monitor the schools' operation and the behaviour of Turkish teachers. As a result of the crisis at the summit of the state in Turkey, which revealed the movement's power—its ability to destabilize a government elected with a large majority in 2002, 2007 and 2011—the governing elites in Central Asia have significantly increased the control they already exercised over the schools and the educational and extracurricular activities of their Turkish and local teachers.

Examining the balance sheet of Turkey's religious policy in Central Asia and the Caucasus requires us to put the totality of Turkish influences in the region over twenty years in perspective. In political and geopolitical terms, there is no doubt that Turkey's influence was far less than Turkish leaders had hoped. The collective Turkic political union coveted by Ankara in the years following the end of the USSR has not materialized. Moreover, the region's geopolitical and demographic heavyweight—Uzbekistan—is a fierce opponent of Turkey's influence in Central Asia and of all the integrationist, inter-Turkic projects it proposes. In economic terms, Turkey's influence seems to have been more remarkable thanks to the large number of medium and small enterprises that have put down roots in the region, but without always being able to compete with the economic presence of great powers like China in particular. In reality, it is in the cultural and religious spheres, which are closely linked, that Turkey's influence is most striking. We lack concrete indicators by which to measure it, despite the existence of some serious but incomplete work on religious cooperation between Central Asia and several Muslim countries. For example, there are no comparative official statistics on the number of Central Asian imams trained by Turkey and other Muslim countries. Nor do we possess reliable data on the quantity of religious books distributed by Turkey in the region. Thus, for want of precise tools for assessing Turkey's religious impact, we must resort to a combination of data collected by me on the ground and an analysis of the relations between state and religion where *Diyanet*'s inspiration can be felt.

The fact that *Diyanet* still has offices in most of these countries attests to the importance of Turkish Islam's influence in Central Asia. Turkish religious affairs attachés continue to administer Islamic cooperation on a considerable scale. To this it might be objected that *Diyanet* has closed its missions in Turkmenistan and Azerbaijan. But these closures are not the sign of a crisis comparable to that experienced with Uzbekistan. On the contrary, they demonstrate that Turkey has trained sufficient religious cadres and that such cooperation does not need to be maintained by a specific body. Moreover, it indicates that thanks to Turkey these states are now in a position to train their own Islamic elites.

Turkey's religious influence is also felt in the creation of State Committees for Religious Affairs in all the post-Soviet countries. These structures for regulating the relations between the state and Islam are based on the Turkish model of *Diyanet* and its *modus operandi* as a Ministry of Religion devised by a highly secular republican state. In fact, *Diyanet*'s activities in Turkey and the State Committees in Central Asia are comparable. In both cases, in Turkey as in Central Asia, religious personnel are treated as civil servants and, by virtue of ambiguous administrative embellishment, the majority religion—traditional,

Hanafi Sunni Islam—is *de facto* accorded the status of official religion. While it is difficult to quantify, Turkish influence is a marked reality and can be heard daily in the mastery of the Turkish language by a very considerable majority of the local religious elites and cadres encountered, who have mostly either lived in Turkey or studied at home but in Turkish establishments.

On the other hand, it is more difficult to assess the very particular impact of Gülen's movement in Central Asia, and even more difficult to determine whether this influence is genuinely religious. Gülen's schools have already educated thousands of pupils, some of whom are beginning to occupy important posts in the civil service, universities and the private sector. However, initial indications of their impact on young generations do not authorize us to speak of a fundamentally Islamic influence. In effect, the Islam developed and advocated by Gülen and his followers is more a synthesis of mystical Islam and Turkish nationalism. And the pupils emerging from these schools have a varying relationship to religion, some being religious while others are indifferent.

In the end, in almost twenty-five years of multi-sectoral cooperation between Turkey and the Central Asian republics, it is actually the religious dimension that has been most active and created the most links between Anatolian Turks and the Turkic populations of Central Asia and the Caucasus. To say the least, Turkey's participation in the revival of Islam in Central Asia is paradoxical and ironic, given that in 1991 the Turkish model was bruited and encouraged for Central Asia on the grounds of its lay character and secularism.

3

IRAN

A MINOR RELIGIOUS ACTOR IN CENTRAL ASIA AND THE CAUCASUS

Introduction: Interest and Anxiety about the Emergence of New Neighbours

Like most countries in the region, Iran was caught offguard by the unexpected disappearance of the Soviet Union in 1991. The empire's implosion shifted borders and disrupted bloc tectonics. It forced the mullahs' regime to reshape its regional diplomacy, opening up, with as much anxiety as hope, to these new territories, which were promising in terms of novel political and economic opportunities.[1]

As we shall see, the sources of anxiety were of various kinds. The first was purely political, for the regional upheaval weakened the young Islamic Republic, which was already ostracized by the international community. The second concerned geopolitics and security, as the conflicts over Nagorno-Karabakh and the Tajik civil war, in particular, shone a bright light on the discrepancies between the mullahs' ideology and higher national interests. The third was economic and decidedly strategic, involving exploitation of the Caspian's coveted resources.

At the same time, the end of the USSR represented a moment of euphoria and hope for Iranian diplomacy, given that the maritime and land borders shared with this vast region offered real opportunities for openness and cooperation.[2] Such hopes were all the more justified because these are regions where the Persian cultural heritage is still alive, especially in Tajikistan, but also in some regions of Uzbekistan and Azerbaijan, where significant communities survive who speak languages akin to Persian. From a religious perspective, which is our principal interest, Iran, where Shiism is majoritarian, can hardly expect to be influential in a Central Asia where a very large majority is Sunni. On the other hand, the Shia kinship between Iran and Azerbaijan, and even with some regions of Georgia, allows Iran to exercise undoubted religious influence in the South Caucasus.

The aim of this chapter is to assess the Iranian contribution, direct and indirect, official and private, to the religious revival and debate in the new Caucasian and Central Asian republics, by situating it in the political, geostrategic and economic context of the time. Thus, I shall examine Iranian policy in the ex-Soviet sphere in order to contextualize the religious dimension and assess the contribution of the mullahs' regime and the interaction between Iran's Islam and the traditional Islam of Caucasian and Central Asian communities.

The Ambiguity of Iranian Policy in the Caucasus and Central Asia

When the Soviet Union broke up, the politically fragile Islamic Republic had existed, uneasily, for a dozen years. Uneasily, because the trauma of the destructive war with Iraq was still present; the regime of the ayatollahs was a pariah on the international stage and moderate and Western Muslim countries feared its expansionist Islamist ideology, which they believed capable of influence, particularly in the new geopolitical zone of post-Soviet Central Asia and the Caucasus. In this context, the general but mistaken perception of Western observers was that the newly independent states of Central Asia and the Caucasus, vacated by vanquished communist ideology, would have no alternative but to turn to their Islamic and Turco-Iranian heritage for the purposes of reconstruction. Their only choice would be between the Iranian Islamist model and the Turkish secular model.[3] The historical sequel demonstrated how the West deluded itself out of ignorance and comparative disinterest in the historical and political processes at work in the new states.

In any event, Iran seemed a serious threat. And indeed the Islamic Republic's ayatollahs persisted with a logic of head-on opposition to the 'great Satans'—the USA and the USSR—and the 'little Satans'—a term which, in the new regime's official discourse, referred to the other 'imperialist' powers, France and Great Britain.[4] At the time, Iran's image was no better in its regional environment. Most regimes in the Middle East were secular and feared the possibility of contagion from Iran's intensely messianic Islamism on their oppositional religious movements.[5] Turkey, Egypt and Saddam Hussein's Iraq, which was emerging from a long, murderous war with Iran, feared the domino effect of the Iranian Revolution. At the other end of the spectrum, in non-secular countries like Saudi Arabia in particular, the government counterposed a Salafist or Wahhabi Islamism that is the antithesis of Iranian Shiism.

To this international and regional environment, which was hostile (or at least perceived as such), we must add the internal weaknesses of the regime in Teheran. The Supreme Guide of the Islamic revolution, Ayatollah Khomeini, died in 1989, and although his successor, Ali Khamenei, adhered strictly to his regime, internal factional struggles undermined the Iranian government.[6] Thus weakened, in a changing environment Iran was bound to display great caution when it came to understanding a whole new region and integrating it into its policy. For although it was a neighbour, it was unfamiliar and a source of concern because of its potentially destabilizing conflicts.

The emergent new region, whose borders from the Soviet era were problematic, was prey to armed conflicts. In Central Asia, the civil war in Tajikistan obliged Iranian diplomacy to position itself between the various local factions and foreign powers—Russia and Uzbekistan, in particular—involved in the conflict to different degrees.[7] Tajikistan is the country closest to Iran culturally. It explicitly and proudly affirms its Iranian cultural and linguistic heritage. But it was plunged into a civil war on the morrow of independence in 1992. In this unprecedented historical and geopolitical equation, there were too many unknowns for Iranian diplomacy not to be concerned about a general destabilization of the region. Although sheltered from any direct threat to its territory, Teheran did not take sides in the conflict, but stepped in to prevent the situation degenerating. In demonstrating a measured pragmatism, far removed from its ideological discourse, Iran cast itself as a stabilizing power in the region, which helped to improve its image.

In the Caucasus, even before their accession to independence, the republics of Armenia and Azerbaijan had embarked on a violent war for control of the autonomous region of Nagorno-Karabakh, largely populated by Armenians but located in the Republic of Azerbaijan.[8] The continuation of the war and the successive defeats of Azeri forces had a direct impact on Iran, which had to deal with a large influx of Azerbaijani refugees.[9] Iran already had a very strong Azeri minority, culturally very close to the neighbouring nation. Natural solidarity with the refugees and war victims led Iran to fear the whole country being dragged into the war between neighbours. The Nagorno-Karabakh conflict severely tested the diplomacy of the Islamic Republic, which, as self-proclaimed defender of Islam and Muslims the world over, found itself trapped between the support for the Azeri Shiites dictated by Islamic ideology and its divergent national interests, which suggested a much more restrained realpolitik.

Finally, another major concern for Iran was the alteration in the number of countries adjoining the Caspian,[10] and control of its fish stock, but especially its energy resources. Their exploitation was a significant source of bilateral and multilateral tensions. Its legal status, depending on whether it is a lake or a sea, continues to divide what are now five adjoining states: Russia, Iran, Azerbaijan, Kazakhstan and Turkmenistan.[11] Fixed by two bilateral accords between the Soviet Union and Iran in 1921 and 1940, the status of the Caspian as a Soviet–Iranian lake, exploited on an equal footing, was thus called into question. Until recently, Russian and Iran sought to retain the status of lake and its division into equal shares, which guaranteed them more of a hold than their linear coastal mileage would afford them if the international law of the sea were to be applied. Azerbaijan and Kazakhstan contest this position and are strongly opposed to it. The tensions, notably between Iran and Azerbaijan, are all the more acute in that the positions of both sides have developed with the continuing discovery of new fields for gas exploration. Thus, Russia has rallied by treaty to the position of Kazakhstan and Azerbaijan. The tripartite agreement of 2003 divides the north of the Caspian into territorial waters proportional to linear coastal mileage. This keeps Iran and Turkmenistan in a minority position and adds fuel to the fire in the already tense relations between Iran and Azerbaijan, in particular.

In this new regional configuration, at once changing and disquieting, Iran possesses strong advantages conducive to optimism. The first is the common cultural, linguistic and historical heritage linking Iran to Central Asia and the Caucasus.[12] In fact, a number of empires that once dominated today's Central Asia were Persian in culture, such as the Sassanids or Samanids, or Turco-Persian, like the Karakhanids or Timurids, and the latter's successors—the emirates of Bukhara, Kokand and Khiva.[13] Such dual Turco-Persian culture is characteristic of the region. Major intellectual and historical figures still venerated by the Turkic-speaking states, like Avicenna, Farabi, Biruni, Rudaki or Nizami, had Persian as their mother-tongue and made major contributions to Turkish and Persian culture alike.[14] This aspect of the Iranian heritage is still visible and tangible in the culture of the countries of Central Asia and the Caucasus. As well as Tajikistan, where the vernacular language is very close to the Persian of Teheran, there are several minorities who speak languages similar to Persian, like the various Tajik dialects of Samarkand, Bukhara and Termez in Uzbekistan, without forgetting the Talish and the Talishis in Azerbaijan.[15] Hence it was natural for Teheran to seek to improve these ties, establish good relations with these countries and enable Iran to escape, or at least reduce, its international isolation.

Thus in the early 1990s, for the mullahs in Teheran, Iran had every reason, given its strategic position and regional ambitions, to work for a rapprochement with the new republics of Central Asia and the Caucasus. In fact, its geographical position at the crossroads of the Middle East and Asia makes it an almost unavoidable hub, particularly for the Caspian's hydrocarbons[16] from Turkmenistan, Azerbaijan and Kazakhstan. Its know-how and long experience in oil extraction make Iran an attractive potential partner; this prospect fostered a number of hopes in Teheran, which were rapidly disappointed with the signature and implementation of the BTC,[17] to which I shall turn shortly.

In the end, conscious of its advantages, but with its weaknesses having soon caught up with it, Iranian diplomacy pursued a measured, pragmatic policy often very far removed from the Islamic Republic's founding ideological principles. In the face of vital economic interests and geopolitical security considerations that were a national priority, the messianic endeavours of the mullahs' Islamic regime did not impact as powerfully as was feared in the West. All the more so given that caution and realpolitik did not have the desired results in either the Caucasus or Central Asia.

The State of Relations between Iran and the Caucasian and Central Asian Countries

For the Iranians, the Caucasus is not a foreign region. The South Caucasus region long formed part of the 'Iranian domain'.[18] It freed itself from direct domination under the Qajars, in particular following the Russo-Persian Treaty of Turkmenchay in 1828, which fixed the River Aras as the border between the two empires.[19] Of the three post-Soviet republics in the Caucasus, Iran has had, and still has, the most complicated relations with the country closest to it, paradoxically: Azerbaijan. The disputes concern very different issues. Firstly, the two countries have divergent interpretations of their history and identity, which are, however, closely intertwined. For many Iranians, modern Azerbaijan remains part of the naturally Iranian territory seized by Russia in the nineteenth century. For the most nationalistic of them, it should on principle be restored to the Iranian fold.[20] In Baku, a number of nationalist circles, some of which are close to the government, regard the partitioning of the Azeri nation by two imperialist powers as intolerable,[21] and demand the reunification of occupied southern Azerbaijan with free Azerbaijan. The more or less intense activism and demands of nationalist groups either side of the border poison official bilateral relations, which are already very tense. Let us also signal that during the Soviet period the communists of Moscow and Baku exhibited irredentist tendencies towards Iranian Azerbaijan, to the extent that a brief Socialist Republic of Azerbaijan was created in 1946, in the hope of a future definitive annexation to the Soviet Union. This attempt, regarded as one of the first acts of the Cold War between the USSR and the West, was a major event in the history of Iran; the Iranians have not forgotten it.[22]

The two countries are also engaged in a purely ideological quarrel. In Azerbaijan, where the elites were heavily secularized by the Russian and Soviet legacies,[23] identification with the West is nothing new, because it was already an integral premise of the very short-lived Democratic Republic of 1918–20. It was therefore perfectly natural for the independent Azerbaijan of 1991 to unfurl this banner once again. Baku's pro-Western orientation assumed an institutional texture with the country's adhesion to the Council of Europe in January 2001 and the establishment of very good relations with most of the Western countries reviled by the Islamic Republic—at their head, the United States. This clearly pro-Western and *de facto* anti-Iranian position even applies to 'hydrocarbon diplomacy'. Thus, for the transport of petrol and gas from the Caspian to international markets, a Western alliance headed by the United States and Britain has done everything it could to exclude Iran and Russia from the various pipeline projects.[24] Whereas at the outset Iran was to be associated with the 'contract of the century'—the Baku Tbilisi Ceyhan (BTC) international consortium—Teheran was soon excluded from it, following American pressure.[25]

Over and above the ideological dispute and oil interests, Iran's position on the Nagorno-Karabakh issue probably weighed most heavily in Azerbaijan's decision to exclude it from the BTC. A province with an Armenian majority but forming an *oblast*—an autonomous region—in the Republic of Azerbaijan, Nagorno-Karabakh embarked on a secessionist war against Baku with decisive support from Armenia. Baku reckoned that Iran's position tended to favour Armenia in a war culminating in the defeat of Azerbaijan, from which Nagorno-Karabakh and several adjoining districts were amputated. Teheran denied having played any role other than that of mediator to halt hostilities, whereas Baku criticized the Iranians for having helped Armenia by extending economic support.[26] Baku would doubtless have preferred Iran to adopt as supportive an attitude as Turkey, which sealed its border with Armenia until after the end of hostilities. The difficult issue of Nagorno-Karabakh is in fact central to the new state's policy of national reconstruction, and influences Azerbaijan's regional positioning. It divides Iranians and Azeris much more than their shared affiliation to Shiism unites them.

As for Iran's relations with the other two countries in the South Caucasus—Armenia and Georgia, which occupy a secondary position in this analysis given the small size of their Muslim populations—they are generally good and enable Iran to be a not insignificant regional actor, almost as important as Turkey. Iran has excellent relations with Armenia, Christian in culture and very largely orientated to the West but also Russia, based on old ties that pre-date Russo-Soviet domination and the Islamic revolution in Iran. The presence of an Armenian minority in Iran, which is small but well-integrated and influential, has been conducive to the establishment of good relations between the two countries.[27] But good relations are explained in the main by geopolitical considerations. Anxious about the new regional configuration with the end of the USSR, Iran felt more 'threatened' by Azerbaijan, to which it is culturally very close, than by Armenia. In fact, for Iran, good relations with Armenia are a way of reducing the room for manoeuvre of the Ankara–Baku Turkic axis, which could form a pan-Turkist arc from Ankara to Central Asia, whither Turco-Iranian rivalry also extends. Above all, though not easy for an Islamic republic to admit, it has occurred to Iran's leaders that for the sake of the country's security and stability it is more useful to have good relations with Armenia than with Azerbaijan, which is a source of greater risks to Iran's security and territorial integrity.[28] Iranian leaders fear that Baku, particularly under the presidency of Ebulfeyz Elçibey, who is well-known for his pan-Turkism, will encourage the national sentiment of Iran's Azeris, propelling them into a form of irredentism that threatens Iran and its national unity. Furthermore, Armenia, on very good terms with Russia, practically finds itself in the Teheran–Moscow axis, whose main rationale is to reduce Western interference in regional affairs.

Although Iran does not share a border with Georgia,[29] they have good relations, which allows Iran to play a full part in the regional geopolitical game in the South Caucasus.[30] Despite the pro-Western leanings of post-Soviet Georgia, accentuated under the presidency of Mikhail Saakashvili and continued under Ibidza Ivanishvili, the political relations remain good with that republic, where a partly Shia sizeable Muslim minority lives. Georgia is thus the focus of particular attention in cooperation policy as well as of interest from private Iranian religious foundations active in the region.

Iranian policy towards Central Asia is manifestly determined by the same factors and expectations as in the Caucasus: the desire to utilize its geographical and cultural advantages, which nevertheless come up against neglected local realities, like a powerful secularism coupled

IRAN

with rejection of any foreign messianic influence, Iranian or otherwise, but also the counterweight of American pressure aimed at isolating Iran internationally.

Iran's main advantage in the region is unquestionably its geostrategic position. Unlike Turkey, which is linked to these countries by language, culture and religion, but does not share a border, Iran borders on Turkmenistan, Kazakhstan in the Caspian, and Azerbaijan. As such, Iran could have played a crucial role in transporting gas and oil from Turkmenistan and Kazakhstan, had it not been excluded from the BTC. As we have seen, Iran's second advantage is that it has close ties with other Central Asian countries—above all, Uzbekistan and Tajikistan—through language and cultural and historical heritage, in particular. Thus, Tajikistan is Iranian by language and culture; its founding myths are part of Persian civilization, for example, reference to the Samanids; and intellectual figures from Persian civilization—Rudaki especially—play a key role in the new Tajik national identity.[31] In Uzbekistan, where Turkish-speaking rather eclipses the Persian heritage that is equally constitutive of the country's culture, there are a number of regions where Tajik dialects, variants of Persian, are spoken. In addition to Samarkand and Bukhara, other regions of Uzbekistan, like Termez, and even some districts of the Fergana valley—Kasansay, for example—contain a number of speakers of these dialects. Moreover, Persian is part of the whole region's intellectual inheritance, inasmuch as the three states of importance in the region prior to the Russians' arrival—the emirates of Bukhara and Khiva as well as the khanate of Kokand—were ruled by governments and elites whose culture was both Turkic and Persian.[32]

However, these advantages have not cancelled out weaknesses in the Iranian approach, and indeed have sometimes harmed its interests. Iran's first disadvantage is that, in the dual Turco-Persian culture peculiar to Central Asia, Turkishness is widely preponderant. With the exception of Tajikistan, it is majoritarian in Uzbekistan, Turkmenistan, Kyrgyzstan and Kazakhstan. And this preponderance of traditional culture is strongly encouraged and promoted today, in the context of new national identity policies, at the expense of components deemed secondary. The distorting prism of such national ideologies thus debunks the Turco-Persian heritage, artificially extracting the allegedly pure

Turkic element. Thus, the new propaganda and reinvented historiography elevate heroic figures whose membership of the Turkish ethnic group they foreground, while ignoring their contribution to the Persian language and high culture. This is the case with Nizami in Azerbaijan, Avicenna in Uzbekistan, al-Farabi in Kazakhstan, and Mahtumkuli in Turkmenistan. The case of Uzbekistan is particularly striking. This is the country where Turco-Persian cultural hybridization is most significant and most enduring today. But it is also the one where denial and active erasure of the Persian heritage is most damaging, both to the country's tradition and ancestral culture and to its foreign relations with its Tajik neighbour. And, in fact, Tajikistan—in accordance with the same logic but conversely—exaggerates the extent of its Persian culture to the detriment of the Turkic heritage and its large Uzbek Turkic population. Thus, national policies colour historical reinterpretations and reveal many divergences in the appreciation of a common past, particularly in Samarkand and Bukhara, where the Turkic and Persian cultures lived in symbiosis. The ethno-nationalism of the titular nation that grounds the national policy of the five states in post-Soviet Central Asia, aims to reinforce national sentiment and, above all, legitimize a political entity with borders inherited from the Soviet regime, but artificially drawn by it. We need to remember that before the 1920s the Uzbek, Tajik, Kazakh, Kyrgyz and Turkmen nations did not exist. They were fostered by the Soviet nationalities policy. Having become independent in 1991 against their own wishes, the countries of Central Asia, in order to ensure their survival and sovereignty, therefore had to construct an identity for themselves. They opted to base themselves on their membership of the majority Turkic ethnic and cultural group, or Persian in the case of Tajikistan. But this preferred 'Turkishness' or 'Persianness' did not afford Turkey or Iran a genuine advantage, for the reconstructed national identities sought to differentiate themselves from one another and, above all, declined to accept supervision from any 'big brother',[33] Turkish or Iranian.

Iran's second disadvantage is the thorny issue of the status, and therefore the division, of the Caspian's waters and resources—a source of tension and disputes between the five adjoining states. With oil exploration and discoveries of new deposits and reserves of hydrocarbons, the position has developed since 1991. As we have seen, Iran, and

Turkmenistan in its wake, favours preserving the equal shares inherited from the Soviet–Iranian accords of 1921 and 1940, whereas in 2003 Russia rallied to the camp of Kazakhstan and Azerbaijan, favouring a proportional division of territorial waters and their resources in accordance with coastal linear mileage. The Iran–Azerbaijan crisis of July 2001, verging on escalation into open military conflict, marked the confrontation between the two. Iran regarded oil exploration in a zone more than 90 miles from the coast of Baku as illegal, making known its disapproval of what it regarded as a violation of the treaty in force since 1940, and sending a warship to intimidate the BP oil company commissioned by the Azerbaijani government. The crisis was ratcheted up when Turkey openly expressed solidarity with Azerbaijan, exasperating Teheran, which did not appreciate Ankara's interference in its relations with its neighbours.[34]

Iran's third major handicap in Central Asia is an economic weakness that is both circumstantial and structural. On the morrow of the USSR's implosion, the Iranian economy seemed too weak and too centralized to hope to be able to equip Iran with the tools for powerful influence in the region.[35] Cooperation in the energy sector might still result in it beating the odds. At the same time, however, Iran lacked economic logic in the market, which, following the collapse of the Soviet *dirigiste* system, was sought after by the new republics as if it were the Holy Grail of a successful liberal conversion.

However, Iran's greatest handicaps abroad in general, and in Central Asia in particular, are in terms of ideological values and political norms, as well as positions on the global stage. The very fact of the USSR's implosion, which concluded the trial of strength between the two blocs and sealed the victory of the Western camp headed by the United States, also signified the defeat of Iran in its anti-American orientation internationally.[36] To varying degrees, and with the exception of the deterioration in Uzbek–American relations after the Andijan tragedy,[37] most countries in Central Asia adhered to a pro-Western line that prevented them from developing close relations with Iran.[38] It would be more accurate to say that these countries were unable to keep out of the quarrels between the United States and Iran. In fact, the Central Asian republics have been subjected to all sorts of pressure from Washington to prevent an unwelcome rapprochement with

Teheran, which would reduce Iran's international isolation. That said, the Central Asian states did not have to force themselves unduly, for they are not naturally attracted by the mullahs' regime. The ruling elites are, and wish to be, fundamentally and structurally secular, even anti-religious—something that effectively shields them against any inclination on the part of the Islamic republic to promote its model among them. All the more so in that Iran is a large country with a Shia majority in a region where Sunnism is predominant. Inter-faith bridges being quasi-non-existent, Teheran had little chance of developing a policy with powerful influence in the region.

Conscious of its advantages and its weaknesses, Iran's policy in Central Asia therefore stuck to a pragmatism that has not been without relative success with some countries, like Turkmenistan and Kazakhstan, but especially Tajikistan, which is connected to it by Persian culture. With neighbouring Turkmenistan, relations have been good since the start of the 1990s, and the change of president in Ashgabat in December 2006 has not had any negative impact on bilateral relations.[39] Home to a significant Turkmen minority, Iran initially feared that its neighbour was developing particular ethnic and cultural relations with it, which threatened the balance and integrity of the Iranian nation. But this was not the case. Turkmenistan has shown very little interest in its co-ethnics in Iran, preferring a policy of economic cooperation with Teheran, especially on energy.[40] On the other side of the country, Teheran feared that Azerbaijan might similarly rekindle irredentist sentiment among Iran's Azeris. But this did not transpire either. Iran's ties with Kazakhstan are purely economic. There too, despite US hostility, Kazakhstan has developed economic relations in the oil sector that are not insignificant,[41] though doubtless insufficient for Teheran, which would have liked to play a greater role in accessing Kazakh and Turkmen energy resources and transporting them to international markets via its territory and the Persian Gulf. In the case of Uzbekistan, whose diplomacy has oscillated between East and West ever since it attained independence, depending on the momentary fears and anxieties of its president Islam Karimov, relations with Teheran are superficial.[42] More than anything else, Tashkent fears destabilization of its regime and strict social control by any oppositional Islamic influence, and this naturally impedes the development of close relations with the Islamic Republic of the mullahs.

IRAN

Of all the region's countries, Tajikistan is the one with which Iran has had the best relations since independence. They are based more on cultural and linguistic proximity than any religious affinity, which does not in fact exist. Iran has enjoyed a certain prestige and political credibility in Tajikistan since Iranian diplomacy at the height of the civil war displayed moderation and acted as a mediating force between the parties.[43] Iran did, indeed, play a major role in calming the situation. Sharing Moscow's view, it was easier for it to secure an end to hostilities and set the various protagonists on the road to national reconciliation. Good relations between Teheran and the Party of Islamic Renaissance—the main component in the Tajik opposition and a major actor in the conflict—were placed in the service of the peace concluded in 1997, after more than five years of violence and fighting.[44] Since the end of hostilities, Iran has figured among the most influential countries in Tajikistan, where Teheran enjoys a positive image despite the ideological and religious differences between the two countries.

In Iran's general policy towards the Caucasus and Central Asia, what, then, is the role of the religious dimension? What is its weight in the current context of a restructuring and reconstruction of the local Islam? To assess Iran's direct or indirect contribution to the revival of Islam in the Soviet sphere, a very clear distinction must be made between Iranian commitments in Central Asia, where the Shia factor is marginal, and the Caucasus where, on the contrary, the local Islam, essentially in Azerbaijan, is majority Shia.

The Islamic Dimension of Iranian Policy in the Caucasus and Central Asia

Before examining Iran's role in the restructuring of Islam in the post-Soviet sphere, it seems useful to recall briefly the history of the links between successive Iranian states and religion. More particularly, what is the position and perception of Iran in the Muslim world in general and the Shia universe in particular? Although the direct inheritor of the Pahlavis' Iran, characterized by a political regime attached to militant secularism,[45] the Islamic Republic of Iran has registered its break with it, realigning itself as an extension of older dynasties, notably the Qajar[46] and Safavid,[47] which aimed to be protectors of Shiism throughout the world.[48] The whole Qajar period was punctuated by recurrent

81

religious conflicts between the Persian and Ottoman Empires, respective defenders of Shiism and Sunnism.[49] Protectors of Shia and other communities similar to Shiism in the Ottoman Empire, the Safavids played the same role in Central Asia, where the sixteenth- and seventeenth-century conflicts pitting them against local dynasties, Uzbek and Afghan, had religious foundations. By this token, it is legitimate to consider the Islamic Republic in 1979 as having to a certain extent closed the Pahlavi parenthesis opened in 1925, repositioning itself at the heart of the Muslim world in general and the Shia world in particular, although the *ummah* is much more fractured and fragmented than it seemed then and the Shia community is far from homogenous. In truth, there exists not one but several Shia worlds, which do not necessarily accept the patronage of Iran, including spiritually.[50]

However, as emerged from examination of its general foreign policy towards the Caucasus and Central Asia, the Islamic Republic is quick to modulate its initiatives depending on the geographical areas targeted or the causes and interests defended, sometimes displaying blinkered ideological dogmatism and sometimes great pragmatic flexibility. Thus, the Islamic factor does not play the same role in Iranian policy in the Middle East as in Central Asia, just as Iranian diplomacy since 1979 does not defend the Shia of the Middle East and those of the ex-USSR or Afghanistan with the same fervour.[51] Iran's Shia connections are much stronger in Iraq and Lebanon than they are with Shia in the rest of the world. Furthermore, though complex and difficult to decode, Iranian diplomacy has been tracing a gentle curve from a fundamentally Islamist dogmatic line to a more realist and pragmatic line since the death of its founding father, Khomeini, in June 1989. In fact, in contrast to the early years of the Iranian regime, with the presidencies of Rafsanjani but especially Khatami from 1997, Iranian foreign policy seemed to wish to demonstrate greater flexibility and openness. The much harder, conservative parenthesis of Mahmud Ahmadinejad's presidency, and then the arrival of Rouhani in power in August 2013, should not be allowed to mask the fact that Iran has remained faithful to the realpolitik it has adopted.[52] On several subjects, like the thorny issue of nuclear power, and in various areas of foreign relations, notably with the West, Iran stands firm in its traditional dogmatic, intransigent positions. The regime does not seem to wish to give way on anything, whereas in other areas, where there is less pressure, Iranian diplomacy seems disposed to greater flexibility. This is true of Iran's religious policy towards Central Asia and the Caucasus. Thus, religious cooperation with Shia communities plays a marginal role in Iran's foreign policy. However, a distinction and qualification are in order. Just as Iran's influence is insignificant in the restructuring of Islam in Central Asia, so it is essential in the revival of Islam in the Caucasus and, more especially, Azerbaijan. This reality, which we shall detail later on, is not the result of a proactive policy of cooperation emanating from Iran's state and ideological apparatus. It derives more from the fact that Shiism does not exist on the same scale, and is not possessed of the same influence, in the two geographical zones—Central Asia and the Caucasus. In fact, although the Islamic Republic declares itself indifferent to the Shia–Sunni cleavage, in the eyes of the Muslim world it remains *the* Shia power, with a capacity for influence and inspiration throughout the world. To be persuaded of this, let us look in more detail at Iran's influence and impact on Islam in Central Asia and then in the Caucasus.

Iranian diplomacy's ambitions of religious influence in Central Asia seem to have encountered several obstacles since the end of the Soviet era, forcing Teheran into modesty and prompting it to forsake the religious dimension for an approach based more on cultural cooperation and soft power.

The first impediment to Iranian influence on Central Asian Islam is the profound gulf between the Islam of the two regions. Whereas Shiism is overwhelmingly the majority form in Iran, the Shia communities in the five Central Asian republics are extremely small. Moreover, Twelver Shiism, predominant in Iran, is Jafari,[53] whereas the latter is minoritarian in Central Asia. Furthermore, as well as being in a minority, Twelver Shia are divided into two distinct groups: those long settled in Uzbekistan and Turkmenistan, the Ironi, and the Azeri minority, whose recent migration to Central Asia dates only from the Soviet era.

The most significant Shia group in Central Asia is composed of an ethno-confessional group called Ironi—a population predominantly settled in the cities of Samarkand and Bukhara. The community, doubtless descendants of migrants or slaves from Iran—hence the name 'Ironi'—who came or were expelled to the region several centuries ago, is linguistically and ethnically difficult to define. We may say, how-

83

ever, that it belongs to the Turco-Persian family and speaks Uzbek and Tajik.[54] This Shia population is numerically small, not exceeding 300,000, and is almost exclusively concentrated in Uzbekistan. The group does not suffer major discrimination, political or economic. Quite the reverse, it is often highly influential. This was true of one of its members, Ismoil Jurabekov, who was a pillar of the Karimov regime, to which he was an adviser before falling out of favour in 1998. On the other hand, from a community, cultural and religious standpoint, because it does not fit with the new ethno-national ideology, the Shia minority can be at best ignored and at worst persecuted.[55] The secular republic of independent Uzbekistan has in fact restructured its Islamic apparatus to prioritize *Maturidiyyah*,[56] a school of Hanafi Sunnism that has historically been very influential in Central Asia. The new regimes sought to revive it to satisfy the population's desire for spiritual reference points and to counter any form of invasive foreign religious influence. In this context, with the foregrounding of a kind of Sunni official religion that does not speak its name, but is moderate in intent and under control, the Shia element is excluded. In fact, Twelver Shia are not recognized by the Uzbek Directorate of Spiritual Affairs. They can just about practise their form of worship, in three or four closely monitored mosques, one of whose imams has been imprisoned for what were deemed to be unduly close links with Iran.[57] Whether for Ashura or pilgrimage to the holy cities of Shiism in Iran, the community experiences the utmost difficulty in practising its religion unchecked. It is often harassed by the authorities, who interfere in religious matters much more than the sham secularism would suggest. They develop, run and control the promotion of official traditional Sunnism, formatted to conform to the values of the young Uzbek nation, but above all to the interests of the state and current regime.[58]

The other Shia group in Central Asia comprises the Azerbaijani 'diaspora' found in Turkmenistan, Uzbekistan and, to a lesser extent, Kyrgyzstan. Their number is difficult to calculate, for censuses in these countries do not record affiliation. But it is estimated that the size of the Azeri community in the whole of Central Asia is around 200,000. Most hail from Soviet Azerbaijan and migrated to the Soviet East to work in various sectors, particularly oil in Turkmenistan, at a time when these republics formed a single state. In Turkmenistan, the community is consequently most visible in Krasnovodsk, a port city on the Caspian renamed Turkmenbashi after independence. As in the other republics, it exists predominantly as a cultural and ethnic community, without making reference to its religious specificities, so secularized has it been. Foregrounding its Shia identity, by displaying religious particularism, would be a bad move, because it is inevitably suspect and deemed subversive by the regime. It would run the risk of exposing the community to collective repression for harming the official Sunni Islam controlled and promoted by the state. Its links with its country of origin—Azerbaijan—have developed, but once again cooperation is based more on cultural and linguistic solidarity than specific affiliation to Shiism, which in any event plays no role in Azerbaijan's foreign policy.

Thus, just as there are few Shia mosques run by Ironi, so the Azeri communities possess very few specific places of worship. However, there are a limited number of mosques or *Hussainiya*.[59] During my various visits to these countries, I was able to meet the often self-proclaimed imams of small Shia mosques in cities such as Tashkent, Merv, Turkmenbashi and Bishkek.

In the Islamic relations between Iran and Central Asia, special mention should be made of the Isma'ilis of Badakhshan.[60] This is a minority akin to Shiism, since it worships the figure of Ali in particular.[61] The community nonetheless differs from the majority Twelver Shia in Iran, who believe in the existence and recognize the hierarchy of twelve imams. The Isma'ilis, also called Seveners, venerate seven imams. Although they belong to two distinct branches of Shiism, Iran and the Isma'ilis of Tajikistan have developed and maintain a certain religious collaboration.[62] In addition to the cultural and linguistic dimension, this religious proximity has made it possible for a number of Ismaili students to pursue their studies in the madrasas of Qom or Mashhad, where they form the largest contingent of Tajik students. During my research in Qom, I met several Ismaili students who, with a few dozen comrades, were following theology courses there. Before the end of their studies, most became Twelvers. Few of the converted returned to Tajikistan; most remained in Iran, where they became permanent students.

Apart from the presence of Tajik students, in their great majority Tajikistan's Isma'ilis steer clear of close religious cooperation with Iran. They prefer to worship Agha Khan Shah Karim Hussaini IV, the

49th imam of the Ismaili branch. They are well rewarded, for the extremely wealthy prince finances an international development programme which is generous and multifaceted, not restricted to religion—far from it.[63]

Since attaining independence, most of the states of Central Asia have proved generally distrustful of religious states, regarding them as too Muslim, like Saudi Arabia, but especially Iran, whose image on the international stage has instilled caution. In this respect, particular attention must be paid to the triangular relationship between Central Asian states, the USA and Iran. The last has been the US *bête noire* since the advent of the Islamic Republic; the Teheran regime has been reviled by Washington since it sought to equip itself with a nuclear programme. In its strategy of isolating Iran internationally, Washington has no hesitation in pressurizing its allies in Central Asia to limit their cooperation with Iran. For example, Washington strongly encouraged Kazakhstan to refuse the cooperation of Iranian firms, although they were well-placed to renovate the maritime port of Aqtau on the Caspian.[64] For want of means to counter this negative image and these strategic options, Iran has preferred cultural, academic and educational cooperation programmes to the religious variety, because they assure it of much more rewarding levers of influence.

Iran thus uses its cultural links with Central Asia to forge relations that would be more difficult to establish politically and religiously. In practically every country in the region, institutes of Oriental Studies dependent on academies of sciences are the agencies of cooperation regularly solicited by Iran.[65] Thus, for example, the Department of Persian Studies at the Institute of Orientalism cooperates on a regular basis with Iran's embassy in Tashkent for the purposes of teaching Persian—a precious language for Uzbekistan, whose libraries are full of ancient manuscripts. Elsewhere, the Iranian embassy in Bishkek offers its support to two Kyrgyz universities—the University of Human Sciences and the Slav University—where departments of Persian Studies have been created. Similarly, the Orientalists of Kazakhstan's Academy of Sciences, as well as the National Library of the Republic of Kazakhstan, regularly cooperate with Iranian partners via the Iranian diplomatic mission in Almaty and Astana. Thus, an Iranian bookshop chain called al Hoda, dependent on the regime, has opened branches in Baku—understandable given the significance of Shiism—but also in Bishkek, where the readership is much smaller and mostly uninterested in religious literature promoting the image of the Iranian regime. In Kyrgyzstan, the al Hoda bookshop distributes more general literature, rather than the purely religious variety, and also concerns itself with teaching Persian.[66]

In addition, cooperative programmes exist whereby Iran hosts Central Asian students in various Iranian establishments. Albeit in small numbers, students from Central Asia enrol at the Imam Khomeini International University in Teheran to pursue their studies there, which are not exclusively religious. In the theological domain, a restricted number of Central Asian students go to Mashhad and Qom. During my inquiries on the ground, it was above all Tajiks and some Ironi from Uzbekistan whom I met and interviewed. Finally, let us not forget that in Shia Iran there are Sunni universities which accept students from Central Asia, albeit in very limited numbers. Not very widespread, the phenomenon exists and is worth mentioning.[67] In Zahedan and Mashhad, two madrasas with a Sunni programme attract Central Asian students, whose influence and impact on the societies of Central Asia is relatively limited, but often singled out by the authorities in their struggle against radical Islamism.

In addition to limited educational and cultural cooperation, a number of influential figures in Central Asia are said to have sentimental ties with Iran. These are more a matter of allegation than observation, but even were they to exist, they would weigh comparatively little in Iranian influence. Thus in Tajikistan, the Islamic Renaissance Party supposedly has a Shia branch personified by Akbar Turajanzade, who was one of the party's pillars. The Turajanzade family, notably through one of its eminent members, Eshoni Turajanzade, is reputed to carry the torch for Iranian Shia influence in Tajikistan.[68] Moreover, it would appear that in recent years Tajikistan's southern region has seen the development of some Shia proselytizing. The number and scale of the conversions is, however, difficult to estimate. Among influential local figures with a notable pro-Iranian orientation, we may mention Tursunbai Bakir Uulu in Kyrgyzstan. A former ombudsman and ex-ambassador of Kyrgyzstan in Malaysia, he leads the *Erkin* party, which openly advances an Islamist ideology. With one of his close collaborators, the businessman Nurlan Matuev, he created the Congress of Muslims in Kyrgyzstan, which however does not enjoy much popular support in the country. In Uzbekistan, Iran had a friend at the heart of the regime, in the person of Ismoil Jurabekov. A member of the Ironi minority, he succeeded in becoming a key element in Karimov's presidential apparatus, before falling out of favour in 1998.[69]

In the end, the religious and, *a fortiori*, Shia factor plays an extremely marginal role in Iranian policy in Central Asia. Iran endeavours above all to cooperate in the economic domain—without much success—but also in the cultural sphere, here too with only very limited success given the significant legacy in common. Generally speaking, Iran aims to protect itself against the anti-Iranian influence disseminated by the United States in Central Asia; in its turn, it tries to foment a certain anti-Americanism that resonates in Central Asia, above all among nostalgic old Soviet elites. Held in a vice by the dual US invasions of Afghanistan in 2001 and Iraq in 2003,[70] Iran gravitated towards Russia, once again displaying geopolitical pragmatism rather than religious dogmatism and messianism. It could not be otherwise for its approach in Central Asia. Things were very different in the Caucasus.

As we have seen, Iran is most influential in the South Caucasus, mainly for historical reasons. For centuries, much of the South Caucasian region lived under the political domination and cultural and religious influence of the Iranian empires, Safavid and Qajar in particular. Then came the Russians, descending from the north in search of access to the southern seas. Russian conquest of the Caucasus was definitively sealed in 1828 with the Turkmenchay Treaty, which put an end to Qajar domination on the northern banks of the Aras River. This liquid frontier, which flows towards the Caspian, still divides the Azeri nation today, which is likewise distributed over the two banks. This Turkic-speaking people, the majority of them Twelver Shia, remained under Iranian domination in the south and Russian and then Soviet domination in the north.

The Islamic Republic's attempts at cultural and religious cooperation have, therefore, focused in the main on a now independent Azerbaijan. In fact, in Armenia the percentage of Muslims in the national population is negligible.[71] Following the Nagorno-Karabakh war with Azerbaijan, which did not assume a religious character, the only Muslims in the country—a small Azeri minority long settled in the Christian country—preferred to leave and take refuge in Azerbaijan. Added to them were some even smaller groups in Georgia or in Dagestan in the Russian Federation. Overall, however, the Shia factor in the South Caucasus is very largely an Azerbaijani phenomenon. As for the Azerbaijani diaspora in Russia, we shall not neglect them when it comes to Shia interaction between Iran and the Caucasus.

We may add to these preliminary remarks that it is often very difficult to make out the actual role of a proactive Iranian policy in developing Shiism in this region of the world. Here as elsewhere, any religious phenomenon related to Shiism is rapidly and wrongly associated with the hand of Iran, even when it is nothing of the sort. In my analysis, I shall therefore try, so far as is possible, to distinguish between the influence directly promoted by the Iranian state and the institutions of the Islamic Republic, on the one hand, and on the other hand, the multiple, varied influences that may be attributed to private Iranian foundations, or initiatives by ordinary individuals who travel from Azerbaijan to Iranian cities in search of knowledge of Shia Islam.

The Development of Islam in Azerbaijan since 1991

We saw in Chapter 1 that Azerbaijan has not escaped the 'return' of the religious witnessed in the post-Soviet sphere since 1991. In the guise of a general spiritual and identitarian quest, encouraged by the relative vacuum left by the chaos and collapse of the Soviet ideology and nation, a significant religious effervescence and revival of Islam have occurred in Azerbaijan. Within the traditionally Shia community, certain forms of worship have re-emerged that were hitherto confined to the private sphere and individual consciences, because state atheism prohibited public expressions of them and repressed those who still dared to practise them in public view under the nose of the communist government. In the Shia tradition, certain public and collective forms of expression are fundamental. This is particularly true of Ashura, the tenth day of the month of Muharram, when Shia the world over commemorate the killing of Hussain, son of the first imam, Ali. Under the Soviet regime, it was very rare, because risky, to participate in public in the passion of Hussain, a historical tragedy constitutive of Shia Islam.[72] Thus, minor pilgrimages to the tombs and mausoleums of figures descending from Shia imams—the *imamzades*—became greater centres of attraction of popular religious sentiment.[73] The revival of interest in religion, and the Shia revival in particular, has created a strong demand for religious education, which has offered Iran a chance, in state cooperative structures as well as private initiatives, to develop tools for influencing the new Azerbaijani Islam. This demand is all the stronger in that it emanates both from various components of society and a state intent on redefining its relations with religion.[74] And despite the distrust it inspires internationally, rendering any messianic policy counterproductive or even impossible, Iran tends to encourage the Islamic and Shia revival in certain countries. Obviously, there is no comparison between this and the operations and alliances of its diplomacy and secret services in the Middle East, where Teheran is closely linked to the Damascus regime, Hezbollah in Lebanon, Shia forces in Iraq and, more generally, to all the countries that form the 'Shia crescent'.[75] Less visible than elsewhere, official Iranian incentives for strengthening Shiism in Azerbaijan were above all offered during the initial years of independence. In the context of the Nagorno-Karabakh war, between 800,000 and 1 million Azeri refugees had to leave Armenia and the territory occupied by Armenia to seek refuge in areas of Azerbaijan.[76] Accepted as a matter of urgency in more or less temporary camps throughout the country, they put economic and social pressure on the young Azerbaijani state, which was not in a position to meet the urgent needs of people without gainful employment. This was the context in which Iran, via its official humanitarian organization (*Imam Khomeiny Komiteti*), embarked on significant programmes of humanitarian aid, accompanied by various religious educational programmes. Iran's official contribution to the revival of Shia Islam via aid programmes for refugees is often evoked by the Baku authorities to highlight and condemn Iranian religious propaganda, even though the latter actually remained rather marginal.

In addition to occasional humanitarian activity on behalf of refugees, the Islamic Republic of Iran's diplomatic missions administer cultural centres, one of whose main tasks is disseminating the ideas of the guide of the revolution. Thus, the director of the Iranian cultural centre in Baku, Ahmad Ojak Najad, actively participates in furthering Iranian influence in Azerbaijan. He does so in the form of public seminars and lectures, but he also preaches regularly and during the major ceremonies of Shiism, such as Ashura. In so doing, he performs his diplomatic duties as authorized by the Azerbaijani authorities.

In tandem with this exclusively religious activity, Iran also undertakes cultural and educational activities, in cooperation with Azerbaijani universities or the Academy of Sciences, to strengthen ties with its northern cousin.[77] Emulating its policy in Central Asia, where it is seeking to shed its image as a militant Islamic regime, Iran tends to consolidate relations with its immediate neighbours to the north by prioritizing shared cultural aspects other than religion. Thus, the Iranian regime's proactive religious influence in the Caucasus is marginal, even insignificant. By contrast, that of private organizations or initiatives outside the control of Iranian officials is much less so.

If Iran moderated its official activity in the Islamic revival in Azerbaijan, it is predominantly because the authorities, inheritors of certain Soviet reflexes of self-protection, proved averse to any form of Islamic influence and interference from without. In fact, as we saw in Chapter 2, the defence of secularism remains a safeguard to which the authorities are attached. At the same time, it justifies state control of religious affairs. Iran finds itself explicitly excluded from the policy of religious cooperation conducted with other countries—particularly Sunni Turkey—by Azerbaijan. This option indicates that national interests and political, ideological and strategic considerations basically take priority over traditional religious solidarities.[78] During an interview on his country's religious policy, the chairman of the State Committee for Religious Affairs made it very clear to me that, notwithstanding the community of fate between Azerbaijani Islam and Iranian Islam, his country much preferred to cooperate with Turkey in establishing a secular Islam subservient to the government. He justified acceptance of Turkish influence by its innocuous character of political institutions and its compatibility with the new state's identitarian and national objectives.[79]

However, despite the Azerbaijani state's resistance to any form of Islamic influence from Iran, and notwithstanding Teheran's realpolitik, a strong resurgence of Shiism in Azerbaijan has its sources in Iran.

In the event, as one of the historical cradles of Shiism, whose key cities it contains, the Islamic Republic of Iran remains the reference point for Shia communities throughout the world. Since the Safavids established Shiism as the official religion, it has been rooted in Iran. From the Shia institutions and holy cities of Mashhad and Qom, Shiism expanded and won over the faithful, and Azerbaijan is no exception to this rule. Several tendencies in Azerbaijan identify with Shiism in a political or cultural form, in varying strength, and are influenced in some way by Iran or by private Iranian foundations. What are these Shia currents, and what are their relations with Iran?

We may first of all note that it is not easy to identify with clarity the Shia religious organizations directly influenced by Iran in Azerbaijan, for they rarely advertise themselves as such. In an ultra-secular country, which has serious political and ideological differences with Iran and is sometimes cast as a historical enemy, it is not unusual for the pro-Iranian label to serve to denigrate currents running counter to the line of the official religious authorities—that is, an institutionalized Islam wholly subject to the government. Thus, when reference is made to Iran's religious influence, we must distinguish clearly between the influence directly and deliberately exercised by the Iranian authorities, and forms of influence, political or cultural, which manifest themselves in connection with Iran, without being an official tool of the mullahs' regime, contrary to what is often thought by the Baku authorities.

The Shia political current most often accused of collusion with Iran is the Islamic Party of Azerbaijan (the *Azerbaycan Islam Partiyasi*, AIP), which merits a particular place in the debate on Iran's religious influence in Azerbaijan. The party's history is closely bound up with that of the village of Nardaran, an Islamic enclave on the edge of Baku. There we find one of the cradles of the country's popular Shia religiosity: the mausoleum of Rahima Khanim, daughter of the seventh imam, who is the object of a particular cult among Shia. For this reason, Nardaran has always been one of the centres of militant Islam in Azerbaijan,[80] including in the Soviet era, when central government control of religion was weak. But the history of the Islamic Party of Azerbaijan is also linked to the Popular Front (*Halk Cephesi*), a socio-political movement composed of nationalists and religious activists, which was one of the first political forces to denounce the Soviet system with *perestroika*. Led by the charismatic ex-dissident Abulfez Elchibey, briefly president of independent Azerbaijan from June 1992 to September 1993, the movement was known for its pan-Turkism and hostility to Iran.[81] It was precisely its anti-Iranian orientation that caused it to split, prompting the departure of the Islamists. Under the direction of Haji Alikram Aliyev, the latter created the Islamic Party of Azerbaijan, officially recognized by the authorities of the time. However, the deterioration in relations with Iran, but also the reorganization of the Azerbaijani state, which had been highly unstable during the early years of independence, compelled Heydar Aliyev's new regime to tighten control over society from 1993 onwards. Thus, the Islamic Party of Azerbaijan was refused renewal of its legal registration. Underground since 1995, it continues to pursue political and publishing activities, but without being able to present itself at elections. Its activists are regularly accused of spying for Iran, and several of its members have been pursued by the justice system and imprisoned. Its current leader, Movsum Samadov, was arrested with several other of the party's cadres in January 2011; all of them have since been in prison on the grounds that they worked for Iran's intelligence services.[82] The proscription of the party and the repression to which its activists are subject demonstrate the extent to which Azerbaijan vehemently rejects any Islamic political opposition of the Iranian variety. The facts indicate that, despite their Iranian affinities, the party's cadres have a very low level of political education and that Iran itself has hardly invested in supporting this political current, which it knows lacks a strong social base. We are far removed from anything resembling the relationship between Iran and certain Shia forces in the Middle East, like Hezbollah in Lebanon.

In the relations and interaction between the Islam of Azerbaijan and the Islam of Iran, Ilgar Ibrahimoglu's religious community plays a special role. Born in 1973, this imam is among the most influential, and turbulent, of the country's young religious authorities who have entered the lists against the official Islam embodied by the Shaykh al-Islam, the chairman of the Directorate of Spiritual Affairs. Trained in Iran, where he was a student for six years at Qazvin and Teheran, Ilgar Ibrahimoglu followed an advanced religious programme during ad hoc seminars and sojourns in various madrasas in Mashhad and Qom. Having returned to Azerbaijan in 1998, he became imam of the Friday mosque, one of the oldest and most prestigious in the country, situated in the old city of Baku, which had been led by Haji Azer since the end of the Soviet Union. At this time, when appointments were still made by informal circles affiliated to some particular mosque and the official politico-religious authorities, Haji Ilgar signed up against official Islam, whose rights and legitimacy in imposing a norm on the all the country's Muslims he challenged.[83] A young, influential religious figure, Haji Ilgar is also a human rights activist who campaigns for respect for religious freedom. For this reason, he enjoys genuine support from international bodies for the defence of religious liberties, like the IRLA—International Religious Liberty Association—whose representative he is in Azerbaijan.

Frequently turbulent, a firebrand even, Haji Ilgar is very openly involved in politics. On the morrow of the November 2003 presidential elections, he took part in several public protests to denounce the irregularities in the electoral process whereby Ilham Aliyev succeeded his father Heydar. Having taken up the cause of the oppositional party *Yeni Musavat* (New Equality), on account of his participation in street demonstrations he was arrested and sentenced to several months in prison and thereafter forbidden to leave Azerbaijan for several months. Since then he has been under constant surveillance by the authorities; despite having expelled him from his mosque, they have not managed to silence his anti-government rhetoric. One of the reasons invoked for sidelining him is, once again, suspicion of collusion with Iran. It is an accusation that warrants clarification.

Having lived for more than eight years in Iran, Haji Ilgar has obviously been marked by his Iranian experience, like any student who has lived abroad and assimilated another culture. However, the accusation of being an 'agent of Iran' often levelled at him by the government is greatly exaggerated and aimed at discrediting any domestic opposition. That said, in the numerous interviews he granted me between 2003 and 2006, as well as in December 2012 and October 2013, the positions he took on political and religious affairs appear to be very close to Iran's. But it would be unjust to claim that he is subservient to the views of the Islamic Republic. At most, he shares a community of lived experience and an interpretation of current affairs, above all regional ones. While he shares Teheran's opinion on the Palestinian issue or the civil war in Syria, his vision for Azerbaijan is original and singular.

The case of Haji Ilgar is, in fact, illustrative of a reality often ill-interpreted by Azerbaijani officials and analysts of Azerbaijani Islam.

Since the end of the USSR, many students have travelled to Iran to study, but this does not necessarily make them agents of the Islamic Republic of Iran. Several hundred Azerbaijani students have stayed in various Iranian madrasas and have had an impact on the development of religious relations between Iran and Azerbaijan. Highly attractive theological centres like Qom and Mashhad are also veritable *hawzas*, which in Persian refers to the world and the educational system peculiar to Shiism.[84] A *hawza* is an Islamic campus where intellectual life is organized and where thinkers who help develop global Shiism are trained. As important as Karbala and Najaf, the *hawza* of Qom attracts students from all over the world thanks to two madrasas—*Madrasat ul-Hujjatiyya* and the *Madrasa Imam Khomeiny*—which specialize in receiving foreign students. Because of the shortage of Shia educational structures in Azerbaijan, but also because it is highly prestigious to study in these institutions recognized throughout the Shia world, hundreds of Azerbaijani students have begun to converge on them since the opening of the border between Iran and Azerbaijan. Their motives vary and it would be wrong to regard them as a homogenous group of dissidents divorced from their native country. Nevertheless, this bad reputation is fuelled by the official authorities, who take a dim view of any strong educational bond with the outside, especially Iran. Furthermore, the students' motives differ. They do not go for the teaching of a single spiritual authority, but often to learn Persian, to expose themselves to another culture and to the world, while receiving the basics of Shiism by following the courses of several different Shia spiritual authorities. It is a personal choice, made on their own initiative, and often financed by their family or by private Iranian charitable foundations. In all instances, the minor jobs done during their residence enable them to pursue their studies *in situ* for several years.[85] Without a doubt, it is these students who do most to further the expansion of Shia links between Iran and Azerbaijan. They are involved in an abundant exchange of religious literature. Thus, most of the religious books, notably the treatises of the grand masters of Shiism—the famous *Risale*, the master work that every major figure in Shia Islam has a duty to produce—are translated by them, before being distributed in Azerbaijan. Above all, they play a crucial role in the development in Azerbaijan of an institution central to Shiism, the *marjaiyya*.

For Shia Muslims, the depository of authority, political and spiritual alike, is the imams, successors of the Prophet who by definition are infallible. Having gone into minor occultation since 874 and major occultation since 941, the hidden imam has, according to Shia belief, left the community of Muslims without a spiritual and temporal guide. In order to settle the issue of authority, in 1864 the principle of *marjaiyya* was initiated by one of the highest religious authorities in Iran at the time, Murtada al-Ansari.[86] According to him, pending the return of the Mahdi, the hidden imam, the way to settle political and religious issues was to trust in the authority of a supreme religious figure, who is to be regarded as a source of imitation, *marjaal taqlid*. Thus, all believers have a duty to trust this authority, who will guide them in the performance of their religious duties. Consequently, in the Shia world—especially Iran, Iraq and Lebanon, which may be considered the main bastions of Shiism—since the introduction of the *marjaiyya*, various religious authorities have acquired the title of *marja'al taqlid*, and by this token are at the head of a large community of followers. At the present time, there are twenty *marja'al taqlid* throughout the Shia world, the majority based in the most important cities of Shiism: Qom, Najaf and Karbala. The *marja'al taqlid*'s appointment does not follow specific rules, but emerges in accordance with well-established customs,[87] with his spiritual influence and with the quality of his courses and number of his followers; it has the power to rally an exclusive community of the faithful around him and his precepts. Thus, he is obliged to publish his religious treatise—the *Risale*—and maintain one or more *daftar*, representative offices where his followers propagate his ideas. Finally, the *marja'al taqlid* alone is authorized to collect the *khoms*—the tax peculiar to Shiism, which is distinguished from the *zakat*, a tax common to all Muslims. This tax represents one-fifth of what remains to the believer once he has purchased life's necessities.[88] An influential *marja'al taqlid* can thus raise an enormous sum, which he generally devotes to financing the construction and administration of religious establishments, health clinics and hospitals, but also study grants for the least well-off. The institution of the *marja'al taqlid* is completely independent of the political authorities, which nevertheless seek to control and limit its influence, especially if the *marja'al taqlid* is highly popular and influential.

IRAN

As a result of prolonged Russian and Soviet domination in Azerbaijan, the principle of the *marja'iyya* has always been insignificant among Shia in the Caucasus and Central Asia. However, from the 1980s, some echoes of Iran's Islamic revolution developed the influence of the *marja'iyya* among a handful of religious 'professionals', particularly in the village of Nardaran, where levels of religious observance have always been very high. As the founder of the Islamic Republic, Ayatollah Khomeini enjoyed a certain popularity among Azerbaijan's religious elites. The development of exchanges with Iran and, to a lesser extent, other Shia countries like Iraq or even Lebanon, and the sending of students to Iran, furthered the development of the *marja'iyya* in Azerbaijan after independence. Obviously, because they remained secular in their daily life, most Shia Muslims in Azerbaijan were completely unaware of the existence of the *marja'al taqlid*. However, for every Shia Muslim who observed the basic principles—in particular, daily prayers—adhesion to the precepts of the *marja'al taqlid* assumed a particular meaning. It is difficult to say precisely which *marja'al taqlid* has most influence in Azerbaijan. The Iranian embassy and, more particularly, the director of its cultural centre, Seyyid Ali Akbar Ocaq Nejat, are involved in disseminating the ideas of the official *marja'al taqlid* in Iran, Ali Khamenei, the guide of the Islamic Republic. This work is performed officially. Yet it would seem that he is far from being the most prestigious Shia authority in Azerbaijan. Ali Sistani is doubtless more so, as indeed he is throughout the Shia world.[89] He is particularly well-known in Azerbaijan, where his books are very much present in the bookshops of the capital and the provinces. Two other *marja'al taqlid* exercise a notable influence in Azerbaijan, or at least did so until their recent decease. Fazil Lenkerani, based in Qom, attracted many Azerbaijani students, who attended his courses assiduously during their studies in the Imam Khomeini or Hujjatiyya madrasas. Much of his *oeuvre* has been translated by his students from Persian into Azeri and distributed in Azerbaijan. Similarly, Jevad Tabrizi, likewise an Iranian Azeri based in Qom, enjoyed a certain influence in Azerbaijan. After their deaths—Tabrizi in 2006 and Lenkerani in 2007—their followers began to reorient themselves towards other *marja'al taqlid*, notably Mekarim Shirazi and Vahdi Khorasani.

Although it has developed considerably since the end of the USSR, the *marja'iyya* in Azerbaijan is not as vigorous as it is in Iran and other countries where Shia are dominant. Thus, collection of the 'Shia tax'—the *khoms*—is hardly practised in Azerbaijan. For a start, the faithful are not sufficiently attuned and converted to such ways. Secondly, the secular authorities would take a very dim view of such competition as a challenge to state authority. Consequently, to avoid incrimination, in Azerbaijan identification with a *marja'al taqlid* pertains to the private sphere and is hardly exhibited publicly. For this would be to evince a form of sectarianism, even division of the community—something severely condemned by all *marja'al taqlid*.

The issue of the development of Shiism in Azerbaijan and its links with Iran also arises in Georgia and Russia, where sizeable Azeri communities live, a majority of whom are Shia. In the Georgian capital Tbilisi, which was a major centre for the Azeri intelligentsia, but above all in the villages of Marneuli and Dmanisi, Azeri communities have been settled for a very long time.[90] Moreover, not very far from there, in Gori, the '*gorniy seminar*'—the Gori seminary for training South Caucasian elites—was created and educated Azeri elites on the eve of the Bolshevik Revolution. Mirza Fatali Akhundov, one of the great Azeri intellectuals, lived all his life in Tbilisi.[91] Finally, that was where the famous satirical Azerbaijani magazine *Molla Nasraddin* was published between 1906 and 1917. Known throughout the Muslim world, one of its missions was attacking the mullahs' role in society.[92] Thus, the presence of Azeri Muslims in Georgia is nothing new.

During the Soviet period, the administration of Islam in Georgia was carried out from Baku. The authority of the Shaykh al-Islam based in Baku extended to Georgia, because it was up to him to appoint the religious personnel in the neighbouring Soviet republic.[93] With the end of the USSR, this continued thanks to the good relations between Baku and Tbilisi. However, the development of religiosity among Muslims in Georgia, in awakening consciences—Shia on one side, Sunni on the other—led the two communities to take divergent paths. Thus the Shia, who are all Azeri, were administered for a time by the Shaykh al-Islam from Baku. In 2011, Georgia put an end to this situation and created its own administrative structure for Islam, the Administration of All Muslims of Georgia. The new body also administered the affairs of Sunni Muslims—essentially the Kists of the Pankisi Gorge and the Muslims of Adjara.[94] Although a majority of Georgia's Azeri Shia accepted being subject to Baku and administered by the Shaykh al-Islam, and then since 2011 by Tbilisi, a number of them identify instead with more independent imams, who are not necessarily appointed by the Shaykh al-Islam of Baku or approved by Tbilisi. Above all, we note the existence of two cultural and religious associations with well-nigh identical names—*Ahlu Bay* and *Alu Bayt*—which are supported by the Iranian Embassy in Georgia or private foundations based in Iran.[95] As in Azerbaijan, these associations rekindle spirituality within the population by celebrating the main events specific to Shiism, such as Ashura during the month of *Muharram* or other religious feast days.

Larger than Georgia's, the Azeri Shia community in Russia is several hundred thousand strong.[96] Already during the Soviet period, but especially since the end of the USSR, when a large diaspora of Azerbaijani workers migrated to Russia's major industrial cities, a significant Shia presence developed in Russia, affording Iran's Shia authorities a certain base. Moreover, although a figure cannot be put on it, we note the phenomenon of conversion to Shiism in the Russian Federation,[97] where traditionally Sunni Islam—among the Tatars, Bashkirs and North Caucasians—is in the majority. Less tense than relations between Iran and Azerbaijan, Russo-Iranian relations afford means of influence to certain Shia authorities based in Iran. Thus, whereas in Azerbaijan the authorities do not allow the *marja'al taqlid* to set up a representative office (a *daftar*), Russian legislation is more liberal and authorizes it. So, for example, Ali Sistani has a representative in Russia to advise and guide those of the faithful who identify with his ideas.[98]

Regardless of whether it derives from the Iranian Islamic Republic, the development of Shiism in Azerbaijan, in the form of politics, culture or worship, is associated with Iran, whose role in Shiism's global development is very often exaggerated. In the case of Azerbaijan, a series of remarks are required to get a sense of proportion about the Shia revival and Iran's role in it.

Iran's encouragement of Shiism among the Nagorno-Karabakh refugees during the early years of independence was often distorted and exaggerated by the political authorities in Baku, whose relations with Iran have always been difficult. Attached to the secularism inherited from the Soviet period, these elites are hostile to the emergence of any form of religious opposition with political ambitions that might compete with the regime. Moreover, the fact that post-Soviet Azerbaijani historiography rewrites the country's history, holding Iran and Russia equally responsible for the country's division, says a lot about the dispute and perceptions. Teheran is repeatedly blamed for the emergence of any form of Shia movement that refuses to recognize the authority and legitimacy of official Islam, established by the government and the Directorate of Spiritual Affairs under Allahshukur Pashazadeh. Characterizing any dissident religious authority as an accomplice of Iran is sufficient to cast opprobrium on it. Thus, although the Islamic Party of Azerbaijan's cadres openly identify with the Islamic Republic of Iran, acknowledging it as a model and source of inspiration, in Azerbaijan, oppositional Shia Islam as a whole is charged with being pro-Iranian. The media, oscillating between nationalist or pro-Western stances, or adopting both at once, systematically echoes this, forcing groups like the Islamic Party of Azerbaijan to tone down its pro-Iranian line and gloss over its revolutionary approach. Despite this, when the party's leadership displayed growing interest in the Turkish experience of the AKP from the early 2000s, it was already too late for it to change course and free itself from the abiding image of Iranian religious and political influence.

The problem for unofficial Shiism in Azerbaijan and elsewhere is that it is caught in a dilemma. The inescapable Iranian source of inspiration that ensures its growth at the same time prevents it from being regarded as an indigenous element, worthy of Azeri national culture as minimally and exclusively defined by the new national ideology. It must therefore pledge unconditional allegiance to a regime that denigrates it and obstructs its development. The situation is particularly tense for the numerous Azerbaijani students in Iran who attend the establishments of Qom or Mashhad. The fact that access to other holy cities, like Najaf and Karbala in Iraq, is difficult renders the Iranian alternative even more unavoidable. Furthermore, the vast majority of *marja'al taqlid*, whose teaching they follow, emanate from Iran. But here too neither the option to study in Iran, nor the selection of an Iranian *marja'al taqlid*, entails pursuit of a political and oppositional Islam to challenge the established order in their country. Shiism is often imagined as a monolithic bloc subservient to the guide of the Islamic Republic for the purposes of disseminating the ideology of political

Islam, Shia if possible, throughout the world. Yet the Shia world is highly fragmented and disparate. The supreme authorities whose teaching attracts students the world over to Qom or Mashhad do not all relate to politics in the same way, and some of them are far removed from it. As for the dissemination of the mullahs' political ideology, Azerbaijanis do not need to go to Iran to be inspired by them. They need only follow the religious and cultural activities staged for them by Iran's cultural centre and embassy in Baku, whose mission is precisely to disseminate the ideas of Ali Khamenei.

Iran has an openly pro-Shia policy in the Middle East, where it supports Hezbollah in Lebanon and Shia parties in Iraq. Similarly, it extends its support to Bashar al-Assad's regime, whose survival, despite four years of war, it aids (albeit less for religious reasons than political ones). As the case of Azerbaijan indicates, however, the cradle of Shiism it finds itself taxed with propaganda and interference even when it is not guilty of them. The Islamic Republic has opted not to play the religious card in its relations with the states that emerged from the USSR. Yet it is demonized there as if it were doing so. This negative image spills over onto Azerbaijani students and all those who derive Shia instruction from Iranian sources.

Conclusion: A More Significant Influence in the Shia Sphere

Despite initial expectations and assumptions in various quarters, Iran's Islamic influence on the post-Soviet sphere has been very limited. It has been well-nigh absent from Central Asia, though more significant in the Caucasus, where the Shia factor, common to Iran and Azerbaijan, has facilitated genuine religious cooperation between the two banks of the River Aras. Compared with Turkey, however, where we have seen the pursuit of a genuine religious policy aimed at the post-Soviet sphere, Iran is a minor Islamic actor. This has not prevented analysts and political actors, both in these countries and in the West, from entertaining a whole host of fantasies about its capacity for religious ascendancy in the region. In truth, there has been an instrumentalization of the potential and risk of religious influence from Iran, both in the post-Soviet sphere and in Western academic circles.

In Central Asia and the Caucasus, the myth of the threat of fundamentalism, the fear of the erosion of a secularism inherited from the

Soviet period, which is constitutive of national identities, has led the post-Soviet ruling elites to overestimate the risk of Iranian-style Islamic fundamentalism. Likewise, there has been a kind of instrumentalization of the threat for domestic political purposes by ruling elites unwilling to make concessions to civil society on religious liberty and diversity. The fundamentalist risk has too often, and incorrectly, been associated with Iran—an association and amalgam facilitated by Iran's image and conduct internationally, that is, Teheran's defiance of the West.

In fact, the international posture of Iranian diplomacy, the fact that Iran has operated to protect the Muslim and/or Shia world in several regions—notably the Middle East—has ruined its soft power potential throughout the post-Soviet sphere. Although the Islamic Republic is, as its name indicates, Islamic, it is also the inheritor of several empires with an Iranian culture, which spread over the whole Caucasian and Central Asian zone. The Islamic and messianic discourse of Iran's current rulers, even when actually accompanied by a certain pragmatism and marked capacity for adaptation, ruins this heritage and scares off Central Asia elites, who are afraid of Islam and Islamism. Thus, on account of its discourse and image internationally, Iran has divested itself not only of its capacity for religious influence, but also—even more so—of considerable soft power that extends well beyond the Islamic dimension, particularly in literature, art and culture.

4

INFLUENCES FROM THE ARABIAN PENINSULA ON THE REVIVAL OF ISLAM IN CENTRAL ASIA AND THE CAUCASUS

Introduction: Pilgrimage and Diaspora as Sources of Revival

Crucibles of Turkic and Persian culture, Central Asia and the Caucasus naturally became Turkish and Iranian zones of influence once again in 1991. The symbiotic character of the two traditions led to talk of the region's Turco-Persian heritage. In the realm of ideas, particularly religious ideas, the influence of a third Islamic space was also fairly decisive in the revival of Islam throughout the post-Soviet sphere. This third tradition or source of influence derived from the Arab world in the broad sense, but more especially from the Arabian Peninsula, whose core is Saudi Arabia, and also Egypt and, more specifically, Al-Azhar University. In 1991, when the Muslim zone of the ex-USSR opened up to the world, it was commonplace to hear political analysts and decision-makers claiming that the new religious arena was going to be an area of contention between Turkey, Iran and Saudi Arabia—the respective centres of the Turkic, Persian and Arab worlds. Almost a quarter-century after the 'liberation' of these forgotten Muslims from the Soviet yoke, this trilinear interpretation, which seemed rather schematic, is nevertheless correct, because each geographical space—Turkish, Iranian, Arab—has indeed had its share of influence in the reconstruction of post-Soviet Islam. Just as Turkish and Iranian influence is easy to identify, because it is confined to a given area and responsibility for it is assumed by the Turkish and Iranian authorities, so the Arab influence is more difficult to characterize. In fact, the Arab world is far from homogenous and the countries that comprise it do not share the same approach to their Muslim brothers of Central Asia and the Caucasus. Furthermore, the fact that Islam was revealed in Arabic and initially confided to an Arab people adds to the conflation of Islam and being Arab.

The aim of this chapter is to describe the Arab contribution to the revival and reconstruction of Islam in the post-Soviet sphere. For the purposes of clarity, and because they are crucial issues in the Islamic exchanges and interaction between the Arab world and the post-Soviet sphere, the chapter is organized around three axes. After a brief historical reminder of the relations between Central Asia's Muslims and those of the Arab world, we shall reflect on the role of pilgrimage to Mecca and Medina—the *hajj* and *umrah*—in reactivating Islamic links between Central Asia and the Arabian Peninsula, and then study the neglected subject of migratory and diasporic links between Central Asia and Saudi Arabia, and their impact on the Islamic revival in Central Asia. While their number is limited, Uzbek and Uighur migrants, who settled in Saudi Arabia from the 1930s and 1960s respectively, have acted as vehicles of communication and influence of Arabic Islam on that of the peoples of Central Asia and the Caucasus.

General Considerations on the Intellectual Dynamics between Central Asia and the Arab World

Historically, Central Asia and the Caucasus received Islam from the Arab world, not the Turkish or Persian world. It was from the Arabian Peninsula, birthplace of Islam, that the first conquerors set out to Islamize the Caucasus and Transoxiana. Historical sources testify to the presence of Yemeni tribes in the first waves of Arab conquest, which reached Derbent in the Caucasus in 733 and the oases of present-day Central Asia during the Battle of Talas from 751.[1] Along with the Arab conquest, the Islamization of Central Asia and the Caucasus also resulted from the development of brilliant indigenous Islamic civiliza-

INFLUENCES FROM THE ARABIAN PENINSULA

tions, Turco-Persian in character. In a short space of time, the first Arab conquerors had merged with the local masses, and the Arabs of Central Asia soon ceased to form distinct communities. Although a population called Arab still exists in the Karshi region in Uzbekistan,[2] this community—the *Jawna*—has been completely assimilated; the only Arab thing about it now is its name. However, though rapidly indigenized, Islam in these regions has remained under the influence of various currents in the Arab world. In the domains of science, medicine, philosophy, mathematics and Islamic jurisprudence, the ties between the zones forming present-day Central Asia and the Arab world have been very strong throughout history, like trade via the Silk Road. This intercourse and interaction encouraged the permeability of Islamic mysticism to external influences. Central Asia was the birthplace of some of the most illustrious scholars in Arab–Islamic civilization. Avicenna in medicine, Ahmad Muhammad al-Farghani in astronomy and astrology, Muhammad al-Farabi and Muhammad ibn Ismail al-Bukhari in the sciences of the *hadith*, to look no further, these figures played a key role in the circulation of ideas between the Asiatic and Middle Eastern worlds.[3]

However, the slow but decisive decline of Islamic civilization, which coincided with the emergence of the European imperialist powers that dominated the whole Islamic zone, was a powerful impediment to the intellectual dynamics between the various Islamic regions. In the case of the Caucasus and Central Asia, the emirates and khanates had already loosened their ties with the Arab world well before the region's conquest by Tsarist Russia. Russian domination in Central Asia and West European domination of the Arab–Islamic sphere, wrested from the declining Ottoman Empire from the nineteenth century onwards, also impeded intellectual dynamics between the various Islamic zones, especially Central Asia and the Arab world. When the Russian Empire's Muslims were aroused and sought to reform their societies in the context of the so-called Jadid reformist movement, they looked more towards the Turkish or Persian world, to Istanbul or Teheran.[4] In fact, as we have seen, the Uzbek Jadid reformists, particularly the *Yash Buharilar* (Young Bukharians), were inspired more by Istanbul's Young Ottomans than the Arab reformist movement in Cairo or Damascus. Thus, the literature (including religious literature) read by them was generally published in Istanbul and Teheran, even Delhi. At the time, more texts were written in Turkish and Persian than Arabic. In the Caucasus, the Azerbaijani reformers around the *maarifçilik* movement—a Turco-Arabic term that might be translated as 'national intellectual enlightenment' or 'reawakening'—had close links to Ottoman and Iranian reformers, as well as Russian modernist currents.[5]

The fall of the Russian Empire and the construction on its ruins of a new international power—the Soviet Union—were no more conducive to the exchanges of ideas, particularly religious ideas, with the Arab world. While the Soviet Union was keenly interested in the Arab world when it came to disseminating its own ideological influence, by adopting a militant stance against the colonial countries' hegemony in decolonizing Arab countries, its endeavours were generally not very successful. They were even less so with the Arab countries that count in the formation of a global Islamic consciousness: the Egypt of Al-Azhar University and the twice holy Saudi Arabia of Mecca and Medina. Naturally, the USSR was more influential in Arab countries identifying with socialism, like Gadhafi's Libya or Hafez-al-Assad's Syria, complicity with which lasts to this day in the shape of strategic Russian support for Bashar al-Assad's regime. Similarly, the USSR supported the establishment of a pro-Soviet regime in North Yemen in 1962,[6] and cooperated closely with Algeria, where it despatched large numbers of collaborators in a whole range of fields.[7] Given the ideological context, however, such economic, scientific and technical exchange did not result in the circulation of religious ideas. And this for two reasons. Firstly, the framework of any cooperation between the USSR and these countries in the name of socialism did not contain a significant cultural and religious dimension. Above all, they were not the most important countries in the religious sphere, especially in training Islamic cadres. Obviously, a country like Syria attracted Sunni as well as Shia students. But if there are countries that really count for their role in training Islamic elites throughout the world, they are Saudi Arabia and Egypt. What, then, was the state of Soviet–Egyptian and Soviet–Saudi relations at the time?

Born, we must remember, into a relationship of mutual contempt and hostility with the European powers, the Soviet Union's vocation was confrontation with its Western ideological opponents. In the Arabian Peninsula, this translated into fierce Soviet opposition to any

INFLUENCES FROM THE ARABIAN PENINSULA

colonial and post-colonial presence, especially by Britain. Thus, the Soviet Union was the first to recognize the independence of the Kingdom of Saudi Arabia and would remain a close supporter of the house of Saud between 1926 and 1938, when tensions between the nascent kingdom and Britain were high, before ceding its place to the United States. There are several reasons for the Soviet Union's lack of interest in building good relations with Saudi Arabia. While the first Soviet leaders still believed that good relations with the masters of Mecca and Medina could help them control their own Muslims more effectively in Central Asia, the Caucasus and Siberia, they fairly soon realized that the guardians of the holy cities were weak and mediocre in this regard and turned away from them.[8] Moreover, the kingdom, branded by Soviet propaganda as a symbol and embodiment of obscurantism and feudalism, already exhibited a pro-Western orientation, which was confirmed with the installation of a US military base in Dhahran in 1955.[9] The Soviet Union's atheistic ideology was soon regarded by the kingdom as its antithesis, because its own legitimacy derived from religion, as the guardian of Islam's holy cities. The invasion of Afghanistan by Soviet troops consummated the breach between the two countries, now engaged in open warfare on Afghan soil, since the mujahidin enjoyed considerable Saudi support.[10] At the same time, the Soviet Union no longer hesitated to extend support to forces liable to destabilize the kingdom. Thus, without any real success, Moscow supported a Saudi Communist Party, which sought to use the marginalized Shia minority as a tool with which to destabilize the Saudi government. Likewise, Moscow's agitprop encouraged oil workers, employees of ARAMCO, to rebel against the Saudi authorities. But these workers, most of them migrants from the Yemen, Egypt or the Indian subcontinent, were too submissive, too uneducated and too politically unaware to make a socialist revolution in the Saudi desert.[11] In the end, the non-existent or extremely turbulent relations between Saudi Arabia and the Soviet Union did not favour cooperation—*a fortiori*, Islamic cooperation. Only with the collapse of the Soviet system and the USSR's disappearance did a new dynamic emerge.

With Egypt, the other country of Islamic scholarship, relations were more substantial, but changeable and irregular. In fact, Soviet policy towards independent Egypt was marked by distrust from the outset.

ISLAM IN CENTRAL ASIA AND THE CAUCASUS

Even with the arrival in power of free officers under the leadership of Gamal Abdel Nasser in 1952, the Soviets hesitated to engage massively with Egypt.[12] However, Stalin's death initiated a change in Soviet policy, which, with the intensification of the Cold War, turned more towards non-aligned countries, including Egypt. Nasser's anti-colonial and anti-British options, at a time when other Arab countries like Iraq remained pro-Western, led Moscow to create close relations with Egypt. However, they remained predominantly military and geostrategic. They scarcely involved ideas, still less religious ideas, flourishing Arab socialism being very different from the Soviet version.[13] Nasser's successor, Anwar al-Sadat, initiated a pro-Western turn that culminated in the signature of the Camp David Accords and Egypt's conversion into a pro-American satellite. Egypt now became one of the bases of the US presence in the Middle East. Whatever its alliances, Egypt did not have strong Islamic relations with Moscow. Al-Azhar University certainly hosted Soviet students, but their number was very small and marginal, and while more than 20,000 Soviet advisers came to work in Egypt under the Nasser and Sadat governments,[14] very few Egyptians went to the Soviet Union as part of this policy of cooperation. Islamic links between Central Asia and Egypt developed predominantly after the dissolution of the Soviet Union.

Thus, Islamic links between Central Asia and the Arab world experienced a comparative renaissance towards the end of the Soviet era and in the early stages of independence. Long inaccessible, the Arab world and, more broadly, Arabs enjoyed a certain prestige among religious elites in the ex-USSR. In fact, unlike in Turkey or Iran, where Arabs are generally regarded unfavourably, their image in Central Asia was positive. For in the view of the Uzbek, Tajik, Kazakh, Azeri and other Islamic elites, they were associated with Islam itself, with the language of the Koran, with the custodianship of the holy cities. With the independence of the new states, dozens of young students from Central Asia spontaneously departed for Saudi Arabia, Egypt and other countries to receive an Islamic education in Arabic. Al-Azhar University, but also that of the city of Medina, received most of them. However, those who travelled to the Arab world were not always overwhelmed by their experience in the land of Islam,[15] and those who returned did not necessarily bring back radical Islamic ideas, discor-

INFLUENCES FROM THE ARABIAN PENINSULA

dant with or foreign to the local Islam. But one thing is certain: it was this spontaneous student phenomenon that laid the basis for Islamic cooperation between the two geographical areas. New-found interest in the Arab world was not confined to students, for in a climate of openness to the world, including the Muslim world, Central Asia's governing elites sought to diversify their international partners. Thus, diplomatic relations were established with a fair number of Arab countries, particularly the most significant, such as Egypt and Saudi Arabia, but also the United Arab Emirates or Qatar. While the religious factor was not the main motive in this rapprochement, the Islamic sphere indirectly benefited from it. In any event, the creation of an Islamic university, Nur-Mabarak, was a good example of Islamic cooperation between Kazakhstan and Egypt.[16] In addition, with their accession to independence, the new states, anxious to promote their past and their relationship to Islamic civilization, gravitated towards certain international Islamic organizations. Institutional links were created with Arab or international Islamic organizations, such as the Arab League but especially the Organization of Islamic Cooperation. The latter took a very close interest in the new republics via two foundations affiliated to it. The first is ISESCO, the Islamic International Educational, Cultural and Scientific Organization, whose headquarters is in Morocco.[17] The second organization, which engages in Central Asia in the same domain, often in cooperation with the first, is the IRCICA, the Research Center for Islamic History, Art and Culture, based in Istanbul.[18] The latter has bestowed on Tashkent, Baku and even the young city of Astana (just built in the arid steppes) the honorific and symbolic title of 'capitals of Islamic culture'. This has resulted in international conferences and facilitated the development of closer cultural links. Over and above such diplomatic gestures, however, it was the reopening of the routes of pilgrimage to the Muslims of the ex-USSR that promoted genuine contacts between post-Soviet Islam and that of the Arabian Peninsula.

Pilgrimage to Mecca and Medina as a Source of Islamic Revival

Partially converted almost from the infancy of Islam and the Arab conquests, the peoples of Central Asia and the Caucasus assign great significance to the pilgrimage to Mecca, from which they were debarred for so long under the Soviet regime. But at a time when it is enjoying a resurgence of interest, what was the practice of the *hajj* in Central Asia prior to the Soviets?

All historiographical work on the pilgrimage from Central Asia to the Hejaz indicates that its practice, from organizing it to securing its routes, has always played a considerable role in diplomatic relations between the political authorities that control the territories crossed by pilgrims. Before the conquest of Central Asia and the Caucasus by Tsarist Russia, relations between the Ottoman Empire and the khanates of Central Asia were largely determined by the pilgrimage and the way the political authorities had to cooperate to facilitate its performance by the faithful in Central Asia. As Suraiya Faroqhi shows,[19] and as is also highlighted by Audrey Burton in her works on Bukhara,[20] the *hajj* is what most connected the sultans of Istanbul with Central Asia's political authorities. To enhance their prestige and aura among Muslim populations throughout the world, especially since their appropriation of the title of Caliph from 1517, the Ottoman sultans assigned considerable significance to the *hajj*. They portrayed themselves as protectors of the holy cities—a prerogative taken over by the Saudi sovereigns, who officially regard themselves as the 'servants' of the two holy cities, the *haramayn*.[21] Similarly, thanks to pilgrims passing through Istanbul before going on to Mecca, Central Asian pilgrims developed a number of spiritual links with the Ottoman Empire. Thus, Uzbek monasteries, including the most famous *özbek tekkesi*, situated in the hills of Üsküdar in Istanbul, played a sizeable role in disseminating Sufism between Central Asia and Anatolia.[22] The Ottoman sultans were not alone in assigning such importance to the pilgrimage. Other Islamic powers, like the Mughals,[23] endeavoured to make its routes easier, safer and more comfortable, with a view to enhancing their reputation among their subjects. The same applied under the various Iranian dynasties. However, with the advent of the Safavid dynasty and the adoption of Twelver Shiism as the official religion, against a backdrop of Iranian–Ottoman rivalry from the sixteenth century onwards, the *hajj* was voided of its substance.[24] The number of Iranian pilgrims to Mecca decreased significantly and the Shia *ulama* decreed that Shia pilgrimages to Mashhad, Najaf and Karbala were equivalent. This period left lasting

INFLUENCES FROM THE ARABIAN PENINSULA

traces in today's Iran, which still sometimes boycotts the *hajj* against a backdrop of rivalry with the Saudis,[25] the Ottomans' successors in controlling Mecca and Medina.

With the development of European colonization, especially Dutch, British and French, in Asia and Africa, the *hajj* and its organization became a matter of concern to the colonial powers. Controlling the circulation of their subjects, but also minds and interaction, justified policies to administer the *hajj*. Officially, this involved checking that the pilgrims were not carrying contagious diseases injurious to health in the colonies. Particular attention was paid to the contagion of subversive ideas.[26] The Netherlands was the first to open a pilgrimage office in Jeddah and even in Mecca to facilitate the pilgrimage of its subjects, most of them from Java. France was slower to become aware of the need for an active policy and the creation of a dedicated service. In fact, like other colonial powers, it did not know whether to ban the *hajj* or to supervise it, to reduce health risks and prevent its subjects being tempted by subversive ideas, which were thought to be in plentiful supply in Mecca, supposed site of the creation of an international Muslim public consciousness.[27] Russia, also a colonial power and Muslim in a different fashion, similarly equivocated over ways of administering its Muslims' pilgrimages.

Russia was already possessed of a sizeable Muslim population in the seventeenth century and became a veritable Muslim power between 1828, the date of the Turkmenchay Treaty with Iran, and 1881, the date of Battle of the Göktepe in the Turkmen steppes. Thereafter, the whole of the Caucasus and Central Asia were under the Tsars' heel. Like France, Britain or the Netherlands, Russia became a front-rank Muslim colonial power, obliged to confront the tricky issue of administering Islam on the southern edges of its vast empire. Along with building and running mosques, the pilgrimage was the most urgent issue and the one most difficult to handle. Our knowledge of the Russian Empire's relationship to it has been greater since the work of Daniel Brower,[28] but especially Eileen Kane, who has published a monograph[29] and a remarkable work on Russian administration of the pilgrimage to Mecca and Medina.[30] What do we learn from these works? First and foremost, it seems that, like a number of Christian colonial powers, Russia was initially distrustful and resistant, even opposed, to the *hajj* and any encouragement of it. Like other powers, it feared that pilgrims would return ill, infected by contagious diseases like the plague and cholera, and fanaticized by the pan-Islamist ideas fashionable at the time. However, it would appear that the Russian colonial government fairly quickly changed its mind and attitude towards the pilgrimage. Doubtless following the liberal Dutch example, devised by the parliamentary representative and Orientalist Christiaan Snouck Hurgronje,[31] Russia implemented a policy of supervision and facilitation of the pilgrimage. According to Eileen Kane, its precise objective was to use Islam as a political resource to compete with its European rivals. This can be observed at several levels.

In the Russian Caucasus, from 1840 the Tsar abolished the visa charges that had previously been imposed on pilgrimage applicants. The same year, almost exclusively for the purposes of the *hajj*, a Russian consulate was opened in Damascus. Similarly, between 1860 and 1890 several other Russian consulates were opened on Ottoman territory to facilitate the passage of Muslim pilgrims from the Russian Empire. This liberal policy, coupled with the development of novel means of transport—the steamship and railway—multiplied the number of Russian pilgrims. Thus in 1910, a direct link was opened between the Red Sea and Odessa, which had become a veritable crossroads and compulsory stage en route to Arabia. It was also in Odessa and Astrakhan that public services were set up for the pilgrimage for the first time in the Russian Empire. Thus a *khajikhana*, house of the *hajj*, was created in the context of a public–private partnership between the Russian state and a rich businessman from Tashkent, Said Saidazimabev.[32] Inspired by a similar experiment by Thomas Cook between British India and the Hejaz,[33] logistical support for the pilgrimage consisted in establishing centres for pilgrims between some of the Empire's Muslim cities, in Central Asia, Siberia, the Caucasus and the port city of the Black Sea, to enable them to travel in better conditions. In Odessa, a health centre, travel agencies and 'Islamic' restaurants emerged thanks to the *hajj*. The experiment started by Saidazimbaev, who had strong support from the political authorities, was repeated after him by other entrepreneurs, who expanded the maritime links and connections, albeit more for profit than out of any sense of duty. The economic dimension was fundamental in Russian motives for supporting the pilgrimage. Added to it was a wholly political motive, since the consulates and pilgrims' centres were tremendous sources of intelligence on Russia's Ottoman neighbour.[34]

In the ageing Russian Empire, the *hajj* was democratized thanks to the steamship and the railways with the opening of the Trans-Caspian. The mobility of Russia's Muslims vis-à-vis their brothers in the rest of the world increased and encouraged an opening of minds, particularly through access to Turkish, Arab and Indian publications, but also and above all meetings and interaction with other Muslims—Turks, Arabs, Indians—encountered on the route of the pilgrimage or in the holy cities. These relations were brutally interrupted by the advent of the Soviet Union, which shut itself up in an anti-religious ideology that was especially strict and intransigent under Stalin, before becoming slightly more flexible thereafter.

As we saw in the introductory chapters, the Soviets pursued a relatively repressive policy towards Islam, even if it involved accommodation and compromise on the ground. On the other hand, as regards pilgrimages—the *hajj* and *umrah*—prohibition was the rule and, apart from a few religious dignitaries still granted the right to travel to the holy cities, ordinary Soviet Muslims had little chance of being able to perform the fifth pillar of Islam. As a result, in some countries, Slimane Zeghidour explains in his book on everyday life in Mecca, Soviet Muslims were called 'four pillar Muslims'.[35] The story is anecdotal, but is nevertheless true; Soviet Muslims, unable to observe tradition, had to invent substitute minor pilgrimages inside the sealed borders of the USSR. Local religious authorities sanctified visits to mausoleums (*ziyarat*), putting them on a par with pilgrimage to Mecca, although they do not figure in the Koran, the *hadiths* or Islamic traditions. Thus the mausoleum of the mystic Ahmad Yassawi, but especially the tomb of Bahauddin Naqshband in the Bukhara region, were among the main sites of these substitute pilgrimages.[36] Added to this improvization was repetition, because no *ziyarat* could be altogether equivalent to Mecca and Medina. So depending on the figure for whom a mausoleum was constructed, or the injunctions of some particular religious authority, the *ziyarat* had to be performed three or seven times over a believer's lifetime. Substitute pilgrimages were not specific to the ex-USSR, because the same beliefs and practices existed in other parts of the world—the Balkans, the Middle East and the Indian subcontinent.[37] But they assumed particular significance in communist countries subject to more or less vigorous atheistic propaganda and denied any possibility of travel to Saudi Arabia. There were a few exemptions to the limitation, even prohibition, of the pilgrimage by the Soviet government. This was for the purposes of propaganda addressed to Muslim countries, which Moscow sought to convince of peaceful cohabitation with Islam in communist countries.[38] They involved small groups of seven or eight hand-picked pilgrims, loyal to the regime and probably tasked with espionage, gathering information on Islam outside the borders of the USSR. Not until the *perestroika* and *glasnost* introduced by Gorbachev in the late 1980s, and then the advent of independence, did believers experience the opening of Soviet borders and set out on the roads of the *hajj* once again.

The change was profound, individually and at state level, and brought with it a new perspective on the pilgrimage, which becomes the defining moment of a rediscovery of identity and/or reinforcement of faith for millions of more or less pious, practising Muslims. Here, as elsewhere, motives varied and fluctuated. An authentic act of faith, the pilgrimage is also the expression of a desire to enhance social prestige within the family or community. It also frequently has something of an entrepreneurial initiative about it, aimed at developing trade and exchanges with Saudi Arabia. The individual pilgrimage is therefore often at once an access of faith, social ambition and economic calculation. As for the authorities, authorizing or even encouraging the pilgrimage to Mecca is part of their new identity policy, taking advantage of people's quest for meaning after the destruction of Soviet dogma, which left a gaping void. This policy consists in incorporating religion into the formation of the new identity of country, state and nation. Uzbekistan, with its sizeable population and self-proclaimed Islamic identity, is an interesting case study. During the early years of independence, between *perestroika* and 1993, making the journey to Mecca was an individual undertaking that was neither obstructed nor encouraged by the political authorities. Gradually, however, as the country rediscovered or, rather, reconstructed its ideological and identitarian reference points, the government, still composed of cadres formed under the old regime, took back control and organization of society—and this in all areas, including the religious domain. Soon it was paying particular attention to the pilgrimage. From 1993 onwards, quotas were fixed in the framework of an agreement between Uzbekistan's Directorate of Spiritual Affairs and the Saudi Pilgrimage Ministry.[39] The pilgrimage was democratized and no longer confined to a tiny handful of wealthy Uzbeks or those sufficiently famous to be invited at the Saudi King's expense. Thus, in the initial years of this arrangement, around 1,800 pilgrims journeyed to Mecca each year, but in recent years the figure has oscillated to between 4,000 and 5,000 for the *hajj* and a similar number for the 'lesser pilgrimage', the *umrah*.[40] Emulating Turkey, which has extensive experience of organizing the *hajj*, an organization committee was set up to supervise groups of Uzbek pilgrims, with doctor, translator, cook and, of course, religious guide. Like other countries before it, Uzbekistan thus seeks to monitor its pilgrims during the *hajj* and *umrah*, to prevent them succumbing to the sirens of bad preachers spreading 'bad Islam'—an issue to which we shall return.

The other ex-Soviet countries deal with the issue of the pilgrimage in pretty much the same way. Thus, the number of Azerbaijani pilgrims varies. After 1991, it was in the region of 2,000 pilgrims per annum; it grew rapidly in subsequent years, with a peak of 6,000 pilgrims in 2009. This was when the Azerbaijani authorities decided to restrict the number of pilgrims so as to achieve firmer control over religious affairs throughout the country. Thus, in accord with the Saudi authorities, the quota for Azerbaijan was negotiated downwards and a number of private companies specializing in organizing tours to Mecca and Medina were forced to close down. In 2015, only 3,500 Azerbaijanis performed the *hajj*.[41] In the case of Azerbaijan, the sole country of the ex-USSR to be majority Shia, mention must be made of the significance of pilgrimages to Shia sites in Iran and Iraq, such as the cities of Mashhad, Karbala and Najaf. This Shia specificity explains why there are relatively few Azerbaijani pilgrims to Mecca and Medina. In Kyrgyzstan, the organization of the *hajj* is an annual source of controversy. Between 1990 and 2001, the country had a quota of 1,500 pilgrims; it has since been 4,500 per annum. This figure is not enough to satisfy total requests, which far exceed it.[42] Thus, the lucky applicants are selected by drawing lots—a method that fails to scotch rumours about cases of corruption bound up with the pilgrimage. In effect, like the Olympic

Games with which it is often compared by some researchers,[43] *de facto* restriction by quotas for the *hajj* causes frustration and results in cases of embezzlement and corruption. Every year, these countries' media broadcast accusations, which are difficult to prove, of instances of personal enrichment by organizers of the *hajj* or *umrah*. However that may be—it is a side issue for our work—for thousands of pilgrims the *hajj* is a new reality and major experience, whose meaning and impact we must now assess, particularly for the influence on traditional local Islam. To what extent does the *hajj* make it possible for religious ideas to circulate between the Arabian Peninsula and Central Asia and the Caucasus? Does its importance justify separate treatment in studies? How does it connect with the reality, neglected by researchers, of migratory and diasporic links between the post-Soviet sphere and the Arabian Peninsula?

The Circulation of Religious Ideas between the Arabian Peninsula and Central Asia

Isolated from the rest of the world for decades, Soviet Islam revived with the independence of the ex-Soviet states, thanks largely to the ties created or recreated with the outside Muslim world. While the initial sources of revival were internal and generated by local dynamics, the foreign factor was decisive. The Arabian Peninsula, birthplace and cradle of Islam, was bound to play a role in this revival. In addition to the *hajj* and *umrah*, which were now open to Central Asian and ex-Soviet pilgrims generally, there is a factor ignored by analysts despite its critical importance in the dissemination of ideas: migration and diaspora. The literature has demonstrated the link between migration and the circulation of ideas, including religious ones.[44] As regards the migratory and diasporic link between the Arabian Peninsula and Central Asia, it is threefold. The first, which we shall cite without lingering over it, involves refugees and migrants from Afghanistan who settled in Saudi Arabia following the invasion of their country by Soviet troops in 1979. This topic has not thus far been researched, but given that the interaction it created between Saudi Arabia and Central Asia is limited to Afghanistan, it falls outside the present work. We should, however, note that a number of Afghan refugees came from Turkmen and Uzbek minorities who fled the towns of Central Asia at the time of the Soviet conquest in the 1930s. The issue of Afghan refugees, who are settled but poorly integrated into Saudi society, warrants a separate study aimed at a clearer understanding of the way that Afghanistan benefits from funds repatriated by migrants working in various Saudi cities. Our study of Islam between Central Asia and the Arabian Peninsula is more concerned with two other communities: the Uighurs, who are natives of China, but also and above all the Uzbek community, who have been settled in various Saudi cities for some decades.

The Uighur community of Saudi Arabia is estimated at nearly 50,000 people, mainly settled in Mecca, Medina, Jeddah and Ta'if. It comprises the descendants of Uighur migrants who left Chinese Turkestan in the 1960s just after the Maoist revolution had imposed an assimilationist policy in the autonomous Uighur region. Formerly known as eastern Turkestan, the region found itself stripped of its Turkic identity and was renamed Xin Jiang, 'new frontier', by the Chinese government. Those who decided to flee to escape religious persecution, naturally looked to the holy places of Islam and Saudi Arabia, regarded as a haven of peace. Thus, after years of travel, many Uighur families found refuge in Saudi Arabia. Like the Uzbeks before them, they worked hard to get themselves accepted and to integrate into Saudi society.[45] To that end, they tended to eliminate their affiliation to eastern Turkestan and instead to sensitize the Saudi host authorities to their fate as *Muhajir* migrants—refugees—forced into exile (*hejira*) simply because they were Muslims. The parallel with the Hegira of the Prophet Muhammad, who was also forced to flee Mecca and seek refuge in Medina, compelled Saudi Muslim solidarity with the Uighur migrants, for it is the duty of the Saudis to receive and aid migrants, whoever they are, from wherever they hail, and who have been persecuted on account of their faith.[46] Thus, the settlement and integration of the Uighurs was relatively easy at the time, in strong contrast to the Saudi state's current practice towards migrants from the Arab world, the Indian subcontinent and elsewhere.

Although it has been difficult for the Uighurs to maintain links with their native country because of Chinese repression in eastern Turkestan, where they were no longer welcome, the migrants have played—and continue to play—a key role in the Uighur national movement in exile.

Thus, the Uighur National Congress, which seeks to unify the Uighur diasporas in order to defend the national cause, includes important, influential figures living in Saudi Arabia—in particular Rahmatullah Turkistani, who has managed as a non-Arab Saudi to rise to the top of an international Saudi organization, a tool of the Saudi kingdom's policy of global influence: the Muslim World League, or *Rabita*. Such stature has afforded him prestige and courses of action that he has not hesitated to place in the service of the Uighur cause. Generally speaking, however, the mobilization of Saudi Arabia's Uighurs is of more benefit to the brothers who have remained in the country than to the numerous diasporic groups living in the other Central Asian republics, where their presence is long-standing, dating back at least to the creation of the Soviet Union, when the border between Russian Turkestan and Chinese Turkestan was still porous.[47] In fact, sizeable Uighur communities survive in Uzbekistan, but especially Kazakhstan and Kyrgyzstan, under the watchful eye of the local authorities, who are more fearful of their formidable Chinese neighbour than they are capable of supporting the cause of an oppressed Turkic people. In fact, these communities, which are obliged to keep a low profile, have only slight contact with the Uighur diaspora in Saudi Arabia. Despite everything, exchanges and meetings occur regularly. Uighur national congresses make it possible to forge ties between the two groups. However, when it comes to religious cooperation, the influence of the Saudi Uighurs extends to their brothers still in China; it is often through Islamic taxes—particularly the *zakat* collected with the help of Islamic foundations in Saudi Arabia—that the Uighurs send aid and study grants. Thus, Saudi religious activism is counted in cold, hard cash in Kashgar, Turpan, Yarkant and elsewhere throughout Xin Jiang, whereas it is well-nigh absent in the revival of Islam in the post-Soviet sphere. Things are different when it comes to the Uzbeks of Saudi Arabia.

During my inquiries on the ground, I often crossed the path of representatives of Uzbek communities scattered throughout various countries of Central Asia, but also Turkey, Afghanistan and to some extent the world. Along with Russia, Uzbekistan is the country that has the most co-ethnics outside the national boundaries assigned to it at the end of the USSR. But I was interested in the Uzbeks of Saudi Arabia not so much to understand the diffusion of the Uzbek ethnic group

INFLUENCES FROM THE ARABIAN PENINSULA

throughout the world, but rather the mutations of Islam in Central Asia, its internal and external dynamics. Their trajectory, their life in the diaspora, their reconnection with their native country—Uzbekistan—on account of its independence, form part of an assessment of their contribution to the local Islamic revival.

At present, there are 50–100,000 Uzbeks, or people who claim to be, living in several cities in Saudi Arabia. They are the descendants of migrants who left various towns in what is today Uzbekistan in the 1930s and 40s, when the Socialist Republic of Uzbekistan was established on bits of territory that previously formed the Emirate of Bukhara and the khanates of Kokand and Khiva. Their exile in the harsh years of Stalinist repression was prompted by political and economic motives as well as religious ones.[48] Those who left were often political figures, sometimes engaged in the resistance to Soviet power and belonging to so-called *Basmachi* organizations.[49] Unable to fend off Soviet power, which in their view was illegitimate, the only alternative was to leave. Economically, a fair number of the heads of families or clans belonged to a privileged section of society. In fact, the family narratives collected as interviews with the oldest members indicate that these families belonged to the class of wealthy landowners, who were particularly hit by the collectivization measures introduced by the Soviet government in the 1930s and 40s. Finally, departure was also motivated by the impossibility of living one's faith under an impious, atheistic and repressive regime. For these migrants, the fatherland they left behind was still called Turkestan or Bukhara. They did not as yet identify as Uzbeks, since Uzbekistan was nothing but a recent, unassimilated Soviet construct. They mainly fled south, towards Afghanistan, whose border with the Soviet Union remained porous. The northern region of Afghanistan, already populated in part by Uzbeks, was familiar to them, because flows of migrants in both directions had long been commonplace.[50] Some of the migrants remained there, merging with the local Uzbek population. Today, they are to be found Afghanized and their condition locally has radically altered their mentality and identity compared with their northern brothers, even if they still speak the same language and share certain cultural characteristics. Afghanistan's Uzbeks did not undergo Russification—something readily apparent from their accent and conservative mindset. Other Uzbek émigrés from the Soviet Union, uninterested in Afghanistan, preferred to continue their journey and seek refuge in Turkey, but also Saudi Arabia, or rather the holy cities of Mecca and Medina.

As with the Uighurs, according to testimony collected from migrants or the descendants of migrants during field work, settlement on holy land—initially in Jeddah, Ta'if and Yanbu'—was facilitated by foregrounding their status as refugees—*Muhajirs*, victims of religious oppression. Whereas local identity took priority over any other affiliation at the time, so that among each other they were identified as *Ferghani*, *Kokandi*, *Tashkenti*, *Marghilani* and so on, once they arrived at the gates of the Saudi kingdom they highlighted their affiliation to the historical province of Turkestan, which was more meaningful to their hosts and more likely to elicit their solidarity. Also utilizing the historical prestige of the emirate of Bukhara, they cast themselves as *Bukhari*, which conferred a certain nobility on them, because it linked them to Ismail al-Bukhari—a major intellectual figure in the history of Islam, respected throughout the Muslim world for his work compiling and authenticating the Prophet's *hadiths*. Recognized as *sahih*, authenticator of the Prophet's utterances, the name *Bukhari* helped the migrants to get themselves accepted in their host country. The status of *Mujahirs*, immigrants in Arabic,[51] also won them recognition wherever they settled in the kingdom, which has built its political legitimacy on protecting the holy places and oppressed Muslims. Thus in 1986, the kings of Saudi Arabia accorded themselves the title of 'protectors of Muslims throughout the world and servants of the two holy cities, Mecca and Medina'.[52] Comparatively well-established and integrated in several Saudi cities, Uzbek migrants gradually lost contact with their friends and relatives in Central Asia on account of the Cold War.[53] However, despite this rift, a certain sense of identity was preserved among Saudi Arabia's Uzbeks, partially preventing dissolution into Saudi identity. The word 'partially' must be stressed, because the younger generations have been largely Arabized. Often, all that remains of their original identity is their name, since knowledge of the mother tongue has not been handed on and social practices, culinary and other, have changed markedly. By contrast, elderly people still speak Uzbek and continue to call themselves *Turkistani* or *Buhari*. Uzbeks owe the relative preservation of identity to two things. Firstly, since Saudi law does not allow

INFLUENCES FROM THE ARABIAN PENINSULA

the creation of associations, schools or cultural centres peculiar to a community in exile, the community, to preserve its particularisms,[54] depended on a different type of institution, the *ribats*. The term has several meanings in Arabic, but generally refers to reception centres for pilgrims on the road to Mecca, caravans or pious foundations, where pilgrims stop to rest, recuperate or educate themselves before arriving in the holy cities.[55] Other *ribats* receive them *in situ* and, even before the phenomenon of mass migration, generous patrons from Central Asia had established *ribats* to facilitate the reception of pilgrims from Turkestan. This tradition continued and developed after the settlement of Uzbeks in Arabia. It has facilitated the reception of Uzbek pilgrims from other cities in the Arab world, Turkey or elsewhere. Above all, however, the *ribat* has played the role of cultural and community association where Uzbeks come together to exchange views and to maintain and reinforce their identity. Moreover, links with Turkey also helped them to avoid merging completely with the host Saudi society. In addition to Arabia's Uzbeks receiving a visit from those of their brothers who had found refuge in Turkey, the hundreds of thousands of annual Turkish pilgrims enabled Uzbeks in the Arab world to preserve a strong bond with Turkishness, as a supra-national identity syncretic of Central Asian and Anatolian ethnic elements. In accordance with this logic, self-identification as *Turkistani* assimilates them to Anatolian Turks, in the sense that they share a common ethnic destiny, reinforced by numerous instances of matrimonial exchange. The situation developed radically with the break-up and opening of borders in 1991 and the appearance on the international scene of an independent country that called itself Uzbekistan and identified itself as Uzbek.

The psychological and emotional shock among diasporic communities was considerable. For the first time in two generations, the iron curtain was lifted and made it possible to recreate links with family and fatherland. The old migrants and their descendants discovered that they were Uzbek and the young independent state did not fail to take an interest in these communities, who are so many bridges to the outside world, especially countries that might be good international partners for Tashkent. Thus in the early years of independence, Uzbekistan prized and interacted with the Uzbeks of the diaspora and Saudi Arabia. Exchanges multiplied. Official delegations despatched by President Islam Karimov came to meet brothers hitherto reviled as traitors to the fatherland.

During his own pilgrimage to Mecca, the Uzbek president made sure to meet the leading figures in Saudi Arabia's Uzbek community and had himself guided by Saudi Uzbeks. They, in turn, made the reverse journey, returning to the towns and villages where they or their parents were born. These renewed relations nurtured novel forms of exchange, particularly in the intellectual sphere, including religious ideas.

The Effects of the Hajj and Migration on the Development of Religious Ideas between Central Asia and the Arabian Peninsula

Both the local media and authorities in Central Asia and the Caucasus, and international research into Islamism in all its forms—Salafism, Wahhabism, even Jihadism—attribute a particular role to Saudi Arabia in the spread of ideas that challenge the established order. Indeed, even before the development of an oppositional Islam in Saudi Arabia, the emergence of a Saudi sphere of influence in the Muslim world, boosted by the sacred attributes enjoyed by the kingdom, was announced in the West and locally. Somewhere between myth and reality, the Arabian Peninsula has indeed contributed to the revival of Islam in the post-Soviet sphere. With the establishment of diplomatic links with Saudi Arabia, the development of the pilgrimage, and the encounter between pilgrims and migrants, Saudi Islamic influence, rightly or wrongly characterized as Wahhabism, has been registered in Central Asia and the Caucasus. However, it has remained limited.

The establishment of diplomatic relations and air links with the countries of the Arabian Peninsula, especially Saudi Arabia, encouraged forms of economic and religious exchange, so that in Central Asia religious tendencies of a Saudi variety—i.e. conservative and fundamentalist—have been able to develop in their turn, contributing to the revival of Islam and, to a lesser degree, of Islamism in Central Asia. The testimony of migrants on returning to their homeland indicates that the chance to return was experienced as a favour from Allah, an unexpected gift from Heaven. Gratitude has been expressed by building and financing mosques in their native town or village, out of their own resources or with the aid of Saudi charitable foundations. According to

INFLUENCES FROM THE ARABIAN PENINSULA

migrants, it was a question of thanking Allah for the opportunity to see their country freed from communist tutelage, rather than exporting a Saudi Islam opposed to the existing Uzbek government. In fact, to these migrants it was self-evident that they must respond favourably to requests for financial aid, so urgent was the desire to reconnect with religious tradition and practice on the part of populations that were confused and bereft of identitarian reference points. Thus, in the initial years of independence, there was a religious frenzy among the rural and urban communities of Uzbek Fergana in particular, verging on rivalry over who would boast the region's first, most beautiful minaret. There was no urgency about building mosques; the existing infrastructure was more than adequate to meet new needs. If there was Saudi influence on Central Asian Islam, it was in the construction of mosques left, right and centre, rather than the transfer of ideas peculiar to official Saudi Wahhabism—and this via the intermediary of wealthy Uzbek patrons making the pilgrimage and of Uzbeks from Saudi Arabia returning to Uzbekistan.

Uzbekistan being the only country in Central Asia to possess a diaspora in the holy cities of Arabia, the diasporic factor was not operative in the neighbouring states of Kazakhstan, Kyrgyzstan or Tajikistan. Cohorts of pilgrims from these countries came into contact with Saudi charitable foundations, but the incidence of aid and exchanges was not major. Thus in the case of Kazakhstan, most of the religious ties with Saudi Arabia are essentially diplomatic in kind. Furthermore, while the pilgrimage played a role in developing links between post-Soviet Muslims and the Muslims of Saudi Arabia, other possibilities for meeting existed. Thus, Saudi charitable foundations—particularly the International Islamic Relief Organization and the Al-Haramain Foundation—made connections with believers in Azerbaijan outside the framework of the *hajj*.[56] At the same time, a unique Islamic organization played a considerable role in spreading Saudi Islam throughout the world and, to a lesser extent, the post-Soviet sphere. This was the Muslim World League, more commonly called *Rabita*.

The League is at the heart of the Saudi apparatus of soft power. It was founded in 1962 at the height of the 'Arab Cold War', under the impetus of the then Crown Prince. At a time when Saudi Arabia was tussling with Egypt for leadership of the Arab and Muslim world, the

League's mission was to counter the influence of the Nasser regime and block the spread of Arab revolutionary socialism. Although it employs an international workforce drawn from the whole Muslim world, its leadership and religious and political orientations are entirely under Saudi control. Officially, it has the status of an NGO, but is in fact a Saudi para-state structure.[57] Its various activities include building, running and financing places of worship throughout the world, humanitarian aid, research into Muslim law, and training preachers of the Koran. Engaged in a strategy of voluntary sector training on a global scale, it is active in 100 countries and controls large mosques in Africa and America, but especially Europe, where it is most heavily invested. Since its creation, it has assisted Saudi diplomacy in spreading Salafism—a rigorist Muslim conservatism, one of whose variants is official Saudi Wahhabism. Although concerned about the fate of 'forgotten Muslims'—in particular, those of the Soviet Union and China—the League never embarked on concrete initiatives to come to their aid, for this vast region was not at stake in its struggle for influence with Egypt, likewise absent from that zone. On the other hand, when the iron curtain fell, and the Muslim countries of the former USSR became independent, they acquired a not insignificant value as a new strategic pawn on the chessboard of religious influence for several Islamic currents in Turkey, Egypt and elsewhere. A virgin space suddenly emerged in which to disseminate Saudi influence and serve its aspirations to grandeur. Despite everything, the League's nascent interest in this space remained weak, much inferior to the ambitions on display in Europe, for example. In its few initiatives, it relied on the old Turkestanis of the Central Asian diaspora, Uzbek and Uighur, going to spread the Good Word in their native countries, distribute copies of the Koran, support the construction of new mosques, and proselytize in line with the rules and interests of the League and Saudi Arabia. However, the impact of such endeavours was limited. For a start, the preachers were too few in number to make a difference. Above all, however, the local authorities, becoming increasingly distrustful of any outside interference and influence, did not allow them the liberty to preach freely in the mosques that they had themselves financed. The region's states, first and foremost the Uzbek government, very soon reinstated strict control of public and private religious matters to

INFLUENCES FROM THE ARABIAN PENINSULA

check any form of Islam from abroad, particularly Saudi Arabia, which was perceived as the original home of all radical Islamist currents.

The name of Saudi Arabia recurs in analyses of radical Islamism in Uzbekistan and, more particularly, the support enjoyed on the ground by the Islamic Movement of Uzbekistan (IMU), an archetype of radical, jihadist Islam in Central Asia. This is a tricky issue and difficult to analyse, because concrete data are lacking. One thing is certain: IMO cadres have taken an interest in Saudi charitable foundations, but also in the Uzbek community in Saudi Arabia. Tahir Yoldashev, the MIU's military head, is said to have travelled to Arabia to raise funds, including from wealthy Saudi Uzbeks.[58] An influential figure in the Uzbek diaspora in Saudi Arabia, Maqsud Marghiloni (d.2007), allegedly gave financial support to this radical party in its guerrilla campaign against the Uzbek regime. Hard to prove, such support does not reflect the general feeling among Arabia's Uzbeks towards Uzbekistan and the terrorist movement led by Namangani and Yoldashev. The debate on the character of Islam in Uzbekistan was invariably at the centre of my interviews with influential figures in the Uzbek diaspora in the holy cities. And the general sense is that Saudi Islam is not suitable for export as such to a still fragile Uzbekistan, which is undergoing renewal and reconstruction of its identity, but possessed of a very different traditional heritage. Aside from any political considerations, Uzbeks in the diaspora observe with some sympathy the onerous task that falls to President Islam Karimov, scarcely a religious enthusiast, in establishing and strengthening Muslim national identity as the basis of the new state's legitimacy. The visible signs of Saudi influence in Central Asia are therefore counted more in sacks of cement than in converts to Wahhabism. The rest is mere myth or fantasy, for the reality indicates a failure in the renewed ties between the Uzbeks of Uzbekistan and the Uzbeks of the diaspora in Saudi Arabia.

Like other post-Soviet republics, particularly Azerbaijan[59] and Kazakhstan,[60] in the early stages of independence the Uzbek regime sought all kinds of support to reinforce itself and assert its existence internationally. Via policies aimed at co-ethnics abroad, to associate them with the construction of a new nation-state, Uzbekistan took a strong interest in Uzbeks abroad. President Karimov even devoted a presidential decree to them to demonstrate Uzbekistan's interest in the

Uzbek 'diaspora' throughout the world. However, as the Uzbek regime became stronger, it gradually changed direction and priorities vis-à-vis Uzbeks abroad.[61] Promoting exchange encouraged the import of foreign ideas, regarded as fundamentally subversive and contrary to efforts at nation-building. Thus, the aim of generating a diasporic policy to strengthen links with Uzbeks abroad was gradually forgotten.[62] Unlike its neighbours, Uzbekistan has gradually de-solidarized and disinterested itself in the fate of Uzbek minorities in several countries in Central Asia and elsewhere, as attested by the Karimov regime's relative political abandonment of the Uzbeks in neighbouring Kyrgyzstan during the inter-ethnic clashes of which they were the victims in June 2010.[63] As regards the Uzbeks of Saudi Arabia, initial lively interest has given way to distrust, even hostility. Uzbekistan's consulate general in Jeddah has significantly limited the issue of visas to restrict contacts between the diaspora and the native country. At the same time, Uzbek pilgrims are more closely supervised and monitored by state structures than they used to be.

In their turn, Saudi Arabia's Uzbeks have become disillusioned with the native homeland. The romantic, nostalgic vision of the old migrants has gradually vanished, unable to withstand the shock of the observed alterity. In fact, the two communities have developed separately and differently. The Turkestani, Bukhari or Muhajir of the Arab world do not identify with 'Uzbek' national identity. Beyond respect for the term 'Uzbek', they are not far from regarding this identity as a fiction, an invention of the Russians in their enterprise of colonial division and then communist domination under the Soviets. They left Turkestan in the 1930s and discovered an Uzbekistan in the early 1990s that is in many ways foreign to them, with which they do not identify. As for the young generations, they are so disconnected from it that they are ignorant of the language and therefore the culture.

This mutual lack of interest has influenced the weak religious interaction. It has remained limited, mainly to a plentiful literature that is intellectually mediocre. The idea that Saudi Arabia has been a source of significant Islamization in Central Asia thus derives from the West's fantasies about it, as well the real value that people place on the pilgrimage.

INFLUENCES FROM THE ARABIAN PENINSULA

Conclusion: Saudi Arabia as Scapegoat for Bad Forms of Islamism

In the Arab world, Egypt and Saudi Arabia have been the predominant sources of Islamic inspiration and influence in the ex-USSR—something we find in other regions of the Muslim world, given the exceptional role played by these countries in the Arab–Islamic universe. Yet their influence on Central Asia is often exaggerated. Official Wahhabi and Salafist Saudi ideology is decried among Central Asia's governing elites, marked as they are by a strong secularism inherited from the Soviet period and an obsession with security that proscribes any outside interference in the control of people and popular consciousness. The fact that Saudi Arabia conducts an official policy of exporting its rigorist form of Islam by various means—diplomacy and soft power, but also via the intermediary of an organization like the Muslim World League—does not prevent us from registering a marked discrepancy between wishful thinking and the reality of resistance in Central Asia. Firstly, in the post-Soviet countries, all Islamist movements or individuals who do not conform to the official religious line fixed by the government are pejoratively labelled Wahhabi or Salafist. Thus, a number of religious currents that are simply oppositional are taxed with Wahhabism and Salafism, even when they are not, in fact. How many opponents of the Uzbek regime are rotting in prison on the unanswerable charge of supporting Wahhabi ideas, when they actually belong to Hizb ut-Tahrir or some other movement that has nothing to do with Saudi Salafism? Not all the rigorist and fundamentalist behaviour discernible in the post-Soviet sphere is necessarily the product of Saudi influence. People often forget it, but the desire for a return to the origins in order to purify Islam of the influences which have, over time, 'perverted' the religion of Muhammad, severely condemns *bid'ah*, or innovation. This obsession with original authenticity is not exclusive to Saudi Wahhabism. A determination to live the Islam of the Prophet and his first companions, the *Sahabah*, has always existed in Central Asia. Moreover, at the height of the Soviet period, germs of Salafism already existed in and around several intellectual cells or circles set up by followers of Damullah Hindustani, to whom we referred in the first chapter. We should therefore not be surprised by the existence of such currents and the rigorist return to the sources advocated by them. Similarly, in neighbouring British India, different rigorist and fundamentalist currents developed in the same era among local men of letters.[64]

After a few initial attempts to spread a rigorist Islam in Central Asia, Saudi Arabia itself downgraded its religious ambitions in the region. Thus the *Rabita*—Saudi diplomacy's main tool for spreading Islam—reduced its activities in the post-Soviet sphere. While it runs mosques and Islamic centres throughout the world, particularly in Europe (including France, where it is highly active), all in all the *Rabita* has appointed a handful of old Uzbeks to carry out *da'wah*—proselytizing—in their native country. The results have been mediocre, for the discrepancy between the two traditional Islams is far too great to be effective in any way. At all events, the tendency to return to the sources has not hailed exclusively from Saudi Arabia. With the development of means of communication, travel and new media, the post-Soviet authorities cannot prevent the propagation of some form of rigorism, which, in the final analysis, is an almost inevitable result of the globalization of religion.

As regards the role of the *hajj* in the spread of a certain kind of Islam in Central Asia, let us deconstruct the myth. On the issue of the *hajj*'s possible influence on pilgrims, research divides into two schools of thought. The first, inherited from the work of Victor Turner, believes that the *hajj* and Mecca are the occasion and site of every plot and the development of a militant Islam that leaves its mark on pilgrims and alters their religious viewpoint once they have returned home. This alarmist view was popular among a number of colonial officials, just as today many countries seek to supervise their pilgrims to prevent them being tempted by a deviant Islam that is a danger to their country.[65] The second school, which relativizes the *hajj*'s influence on pilgrims' consciousness and behaviour, is inherited from the work of the Orientalist Christiaan Snouck Hurgronje.[66] The case of pilgrims from Central Asia and the Caucasus rather vindicates the Dutch scholar's position, in the sense that they are no more radicalized than they are changed. On the other hand, he warned, their contact with compatriots who had long been settled in the holy cities could have a negative influence. Thus, in the case of Dutch Muslims of Indonesian origin, he recommended to his country's authorities that they accompany and supervise Dutch pilgrims so that they had minimum contact with the Javanese community settled in the places of pilgrimage. One has a sense that the attitude of the Uzbek authorities is inspired by this school. In fact, the Uzbek pilgrims are accompanied and supervised so that contact with the Uzbek community in Saudi Arabia is minimal. Thus the Uzbek pilgrims, of whom there are actually very few—on average 4,000 per year—return from the pilgrimage just as they embarked on it, neither more nor less converted to Saudi Wahhabism or any other form of rigorism, whose promoters in Central Asia they are alleged to have become.

When all is said and done, the establishment of diplomatic ties with the countries of the Arabian Peninsula, combined with the pilgrimage and the migratory link, are not the major factors behind the emergence of Salafism in Central Asia and the Caucasus. This remains limited, but it results from the general crisis of Islam throughout the world. Since the shock of the encounter with the West and its modernism, the Muslim world has constantly interrogated itself about the reasons for its retardation. The sense that a return to the sources, the true foundations of Islam, might be a solution and remedy for this crisis is widespread among Muslims, including those of the ex-USSR who posed the issue before being subject to influence from Saudi Arabia or elsewhere.

The interest in the Arabian Peninsula shown by post-Soviet Muslims is, in reality, prompted by the opening it offers onto the Muslim world as a whole and the curiosity it arouses about the Islamic influences and tendencies that come together there—things they had been cut off from for decades—whether from the Arab, Turkic or Iranian world, or even from the South Asian world that is the subject of the next chapter.

5

SOUTH ASIA'S INFLUENCE ON THE REVIVAL OF ISLAM IN CENTRAL ASIA

Introduction: South Asia's Influence in Central Asia

Whereas Turkish, Iranian and Arab influence is easy to explain and contextualize historically, South Asia's influence on Central Asia is less obvious, but no less dynamic. The two regions likewise have a rich past in common, even though it is possibly more remote and more difficult to discern today. This connection, which became looser after Central Asia fell into the lap of the Tsars and then the Soviets and after India became British, today takes the form of Tablighi Jamaat's unprecedented penetration of Central Asia.

This pietistic, proselytizing Islamic movement, which is representative of South Asian Islam, has singlehandedly disrupted the local religious order, and its impact on religious reconstruction in Central Asia justifies the attention that will be given to it in this chapter. Study of Tablighi strategy and preaching methods in Central Asia led me to trace the origin of their engagement to India. The case of Tablighi Jamaat is all the more interesting in that it is the only one of numerous Islamic movements originating in the Indian subcontinent that not only selected Central Asia as its terrain for expansion, but also succeeded in growing there. Its influence is confined to Central Asia, because it is absent from the Caucasus. And, insofar as Central Asia's Tablighi are not linked in a network with Afghanistan's, this study will not deal with the Afghan Tablighi. For all the talk and the fantasies it generates in research on Central Asian Islam, particularly because of the presence of radical Central Asian jihadists on the ground, Afghanistan in fact has little influence on the new Islam in Central Asia.

South Asian influence, from a region containing India, Pakistan and Bangladesh, is basically down to Tablighi Jamaat. The preachers who are present in Central Asia come from these three countries and take on young Central Asians who have come to receive further training in the precepts of their philosophy and Tablighi preaching, the *da'wa*. We shall first situate relations, especially intellectual and religious relations, in the historical context of Central Asia and South Asia. Next we shall study the strategy and motives that govern Tablighi Jamaat's activities in Central Asia, especially Kyrgyzstan, but also Kazakhstan and Tajikistan.

The Historical Links between Central Asia and South Asia

The mountain chains of the Hindu Kush and Tian Shan that delimit present-day Central Asia and the Indian subcontinent have never really represented an insurmountable obstacle or check to the development of the most diverse ties between the two regions. Since deepest antiquity, forms of exchange have been dynamic and varied, especially in the sphere of trade, but also intellectually, as is demonstrated by the work of, among others, Edvard Rtveladze.[1] Caravan trade is particularly well-documented thanks to the works of Mansura Haidar,[2] but more especially courtesy of those of Scott Levi[3] and Kulbhusan Warikoo.[4] One of the important axes of the Silk Road, so the works of Levi and Stephen Dale inform us,[5] linked Central Asia to India; the thriving trade, which was not confined to silk, but also involved tea, coral, indigo, fabrics and furs, horses and slaves, forged a multiplicity of close ties between the two regions. The Silk Road's gradual decline, on account of the discovery of new maritime routes, did not completely stifle commerce between the two regions, particularly due to the maintenance of trade between Russia and India that had to pass through Central Asia. Thus, the works of Scott Levi[6] and Razia Mukminova[7] indicate the presence of whole colonies of Indian traders in various Central Asian cities. The caravan trade employed numerous people and fostered an intermingling

SOUTH ASIA'S INFLUENCE

of ideas and cultures as well as the distribution of merchandise. Thus in the intellectual sphere, the discovery of Buddhist paintings on archaeological sites, notably Termez in present-today Uzbekistan and in Chinese Turkestan,[8] like the famous reclining Buddha in the museum at Dushanbe in Tajikistan,[9] attest to the development of Buddhism as a vehicle of communication between India and Central Asia[10]—and this well before the Arab invasions and the advent of Islam. From time immemorial, travellers, vagabonds, adventurers and mystics, from all walks and with no clear distinction between them, travelled through the two regions and made a major contribution to the exchange of ideas.[11]

The links became closer still in the Mughal era—a golden age of exchange between the two Asias. Remote descendants of the Timurids, the Mughal sovereigns maintained close relations with their native county; their exercise of power in Delhi bore strong similarities to that of their peers in Samarkand or Herat. Added to the dynastic ties were intense cultural links. The practice of the *mujavaba*, for example, consisting in a verse dialogue between poets, formed part of the literary promotion of Mughal poets in Central Asia and of Central Asian poets in the Mughal Empire. The Emperor Babur himself was among these recognized poets and devoted himself to the *mujavaba*, exchanging views from Delhi on what was amiss with the country for Central Asian poets. Further as regards literary exchanges, let us mention the role of Maulana Samarqandi in the court of the Mughal King Akbar, or the role of Mushfiq,[12] or that of another poet marked by India, its culture and music, Mahmud Amir Wali, a native of Andijan.[13] Finally, of the Central Asian men of letters who travelled to India, Abdul Qadir Bidil (1644–1721) remains one of the most highly regarded today.[14]

Literary exchanges were also enriched by exchanges in the arts and publishing. The art of the miniature in the Mughal or Safavid style, called Bihzad[15] after the name of a great Persian master of the art, spread over a vast region. In Herat, Tabriz and Bukhara, Turkish, Persian and Indian cultures were mutually influential. In academic painting, the master Mir Musavvir, a native of Termez, made himself famous through his time at the court of Tahmasp. Cultural reciprocity extended to astronomy, mathematics and other sciences. The Samarkand school had a particular influence on scholars in India. Thus, copies of *Zij-Ulugbek*, its astronomical tables, have been found in India. Similarly, we know that works of astronomy were translated into Sanskrit from Persian, the language of scholars and learned men in Central Asia. Finally in architecture, whether palaces, places of worship, funerary monuments or mausoleums, Central Asian borrowings and influences are clearly visible in India.[16]

As for religion, the Mughal emperors regarded themselves as admiring devotees of the Naqshbandi sheikhs, following Babur who, like his father, was influenced by the great spiritual masters of the Naqshbandi. The memoirs of Babur (1483–1530)[17] proudly highlight Transoxiana's contribution to Islamic civilization. The first Islamic links are old, dating back to the epoch of the sultanate of Delhi.[18] But it is thanks to the Mughal intermediary and, more particularly, the incredible activism of the Naqshbandi brotherhood that we can speak of enduring, reciprocal Islamic influence between the two regions.

From the time of its creation by Babur Shah until its dismantling by the British colonial power, the Mughal dynasty represented an extended period of intense communication between India and Central Asia. For this reason, Richard Folz is right to argue that the Mughals—Muslims descending from Central Asia who founded a new, brilliant civilization—never really broke with their Central Asian roots. Attachment to the native country, its values and customs, remained very strong, including in exile.[19] It is acknowledged that the Mughals never swapped their Central Asian identify for a different—specifically Indian—one. Loyal to their roots, the Mughals (in Foltz's estimation) favoured a 'cross-fertilization' of the arts, culture, music and, obviously, religious ideas between India and Central Asia. In his essay on the Timurids, Stephen Dale maintains that Timurid high culture to a certain extent united Mughal India with Central Asia, but also with the Safavid and even the Ottoman world. This unification of a vast Muslim zone is well-illustrated in literature by the *oeuvre* of Ali-Shir Navai, in miniatures by that of Bihzad, but also in architecture and music by the proximate styles to be found from one end of this vast area to the other.[20] According to Jo-Ann Gross, well before Muslim India bore the stamp of the Timurids and Mughals, hence from Islam's initial expansion into India with Mahmud Ghazni and the Delhi Sultanate, the elites of the region's various political and geographical entities shared the same culture of governance and were unified by the same codes, values and references. We find these elites spread over a vast geographical zone comprising Central Asia and South Asia, but also Iran and beyond.[21]

When it comes to religious ideas, the strongest bridge between the two zones was the one constructed by the Naqshbandi brotherhood. Trivially but symbolically, the native village of Bahauddin Naqshband (1318–89), founder of the order that bears his name, is called Qasr-i Hinduvan, which means 'Indian castle' in Persian and Turkish.[22] And the mystical order founded by him rapidly captured minds beyond the borders of his native country. On his death, another key figure in the order, Khwaja Ubaydullah Ahrar (1404–90), took up the torch and developed the brotherhood to the extent of establishing influence over the Timurid sovereigns of Samarkand and Herat. In the brotherhood's expansion to India, mention should made of the historical roles played by Baqi Billah and Ahmad Sirhindi. Initiated in Ubaydullah Ahrar's time, a certain spirit of exchange existed between various Naqshbandi groups from India to Central Asia. However, it was under the auspices of Baqi Billah that spiritual links were strengthened between India and Central Asia. Born in Kabul in 1563, he journeyed to Delhi in 1598, whence he crisscrossed several Indian cities to carry out his mission of preaching and training new disciples in Naqshbandi teaching. In the history of Islamic and brotherhood relations between India and Central Asia, Baqi Billah's ideas and expeditions in Asia helped propagate the ideas of Naqshbandi Sufi doctrine to such an extent that he is still regarded as the first, most emblematic of the spiritual connections between the two regions.[23] Having died in 1603, he was replaced by an Indian Ahmad Sirhindi (1564–1624). The latter is celebrated in the history of the brotherhood for having worked on its extraordinary modernization, which earned him the nickname 'reviver of the second millennium'. At his meeting with Baqi Billah in Delhi in 1599, he received the *ijaza*—official authorization to preach[24]—and embarked on this mission from Asia to the Middle East. Naqshbandi spiritual interaction between Central Asia and India possesses the historical peculiarity of having occurred in both directions. When the Naqshbandi brotherhood, now very influential in India, virtually became an Indian phenomenon, whereas it tended to decline in Central Asia, the proselytizing movement reversed, returning to the native country. Thus, the brotherhood was reintroduced into Central Asia from the seventeenth century onwards. This episode of its redeployment in Central Asia is more familiar to us thanks to the archival labours of Bahtiyar Babadjanov and Anke von Kügelgen.[25] According to these authors, the Naqshbandi, renamed the Mugaddidiya ('the revived'), returned in two successive waves. Haji Habibullah Allahyar, born in 1700, was one of the first to lead the brotherhood in its revived form back into Central Asia, at a time when successive wars in Bukhara and Samarkand had dragged the region into a phase of quasi-depopulation and moral and intellectual decline. The second wave of resettlement of the Naqshbandi occurred in the mid-eighteenth century, but this time thanks to Central Asian spiritual authorities who had come to India in search of resources to study Naqshbandi doctrine and train new disciples.

The Russo-Soviet Period and the Decline in Spiritual Interaction between India and Central Asia

From the nineteenth century onwards, Central Asia, weakened by disinterest in the Silk Road, continued to decline and was prey to its powerful neighbour Russia. The Tsarist Empire thirsted after territory and access to the seas to the south. The city of Tashkent, today capital of Uzbekistan, was captured in 1865, marking the start of the region's conquest by the Russian army. The Battle of Göktepe in 1881 sealed complete Russian mastery of the region. In the same years, South-East Asia, prey to the imperialist designs of the British Empire, was deprived of control over its own destiny and passed under the yoke of the crown. Prior to its submission to the Russians and British respectively, the great Central Asian region had already begun to be the stage for an intense war of influence and espionage—the Great Game, in which Afghanistan had become a buffer zone between the two rival empires.

It would be an exaggeration to speak of a complete rupture in relations. Commercial, cultural and spiritual forms of exchange persisted between Muslims who were subjects of the crown and Muslims enfeoffed to the Tsars. Merchants and dervishes were able to continue to circulate between north and south. The holy road between Ush, Kashgar and Srinagar, so well described by Thierry Zarcone,[26] continued to be taken. But European colonial power over Asia significantly affected the development of links between Indian and Central Asian

Muslims. Attempts at cooperation and mutual inspiration between the Muslim reformers of Central Asia—the Jadids—and those of India were not lacking, however. Thus, the reformation of India's Muslim society advocated by an Indian Muslim like Abu Kalam Azad was not dissimilar from the reformist debate agitating Muslims in the Russian Empire in the same years. Its journal *Al-Hila* possesses a number of distinguishing features that are similar to various Jadid publications in Central Asia. Communication and intellectual exchange occurred not so much directly as via the intermediary of Turkish intellectual circles in Istanbul. At the time, the capital of the Ottoman Empire was a highly attractive hub for Muslim intellectuals the world over. Thus, it was on his return from a stay in Istanbul that one of the greatest Jadid reformers in Central Asia, Abdulrauf Fitrat, published his book on India's revolutionaries, *Hind Ixtilolchilari*, in Bukhara. Another intellectual from Central Asia—Furqat—spent time in exile in India, whence he derived some of his ideas about emancipation. The latter were not without an impact on the intellectual life of his country, the emirate of Bukhara. Selection of India as a model and source of inspiration for the anti-colonial struggle of the peoples of Central Asia was therefore no accident. However, few research works have documented this phase of cooperation between reformers from Central Asia and India (still less have they explored the links that developed with intellectuals in the Arab world, Egypt or Syria). Consequently, today it is difficult to disentangle their influence from an indigenous intellectual and historical process. In any event, such intellectual cooperation was restricted, stifled and cut short by the appearance of the Bolsheviks, whose progressive stranglehold over all intellectual life in Turkestan and Bukhara signalled the start of an ossifying isolation for the local intellectual and religious scene. The establishment of the USSR's sealed borders behind the 'iron curtain' later confirmed the rupture between the Muslims of Central Asia and the rest of the world, and reduced reciprocal influence between local Islam and Turkish, Arab, Iranian and Indian Islam almost to zero.

Prior to the Soviet break, cooperation between reformists and revolutionaries from Central Asia and India was fostered by mutual emulation against a background of struggle against British and Russian imperialism. In Central Asia, Indian revolutionaries stayed in Tashkent in particular to make contacts with revolutionaries from Central Asia. But such collaboration did not involve any religious dimension—quite the reverse. At state level, the development of relations between the Soviet Union and India after Partition in 1947 was based on the ideological dimension of their historical experience, cemented by India's non-alignment and the Soviet Union's opposition to Western imperialism. Thus, the low level of relations at the time, official and unofficial, was not conducive to Islamic cooperation between the two countries.[27] Moreover, with Partition and the birth of Muslim Pakistan, the warming in relations between Soviet Muslims and Pakistanis that might have been anticipated did not transpire. In fact, from its birth, which coincided with the onset of the Cold War, Pakistan found itself in the Western camp, a US ally. This inevitably rendered any prospect of cooperation, Islamic or otherwise, with Central Asia highly unlikely.

Yet, in a period unconducive to any religious interaction between Central Asia and South Asia, there was a significant exception. In a context of ideological and religious stasis, a religious figure emerged and entered posterity having created links between the Deoband School in Uttar Pradesh and several Soviet cities in Central Asia, where Islam survived in the private sphere and underground notwithstanding repression. This was Domullah Hindustani, who, despite difficulties in leaving the Soviet Union, was able to reside in several madrasas in India. This training enabled him to introduce religious ideas into Central Asia, where he in turn trained followers, some of whom laid the basis for a Salafist current that developed after the Soviet period.[28] But for this exception, the whole Soviet period was meagre in spiritual interaction between the Indian subcontinent and Central Asia. And from 1979 onwards, the Soviet invasion of Afghanistan made relations between Muslims on either side of the Amu Darya even more difficult, though some argue that part of radical Islam in Central Asia was fuelled by the war in Afghanistan. It remains the case that the development of genuine, substantial Islamic relations between the two regions occurred only after the end of the Soviet Union. In fact, it was thanks to the new states' independence that novel prospects for cooperation opened up for Central Asia and missionaries could embark on journeys of exploration and instruction.

These cooperative initiatives predominantly bore the stamp of Tablighi Jamaat, which warrants special treatment because of its exceptional role. But two other Islamic influences from South Asia are worth mentioning here: the Ahmadiyya and a branch of the Naqshbandi.

The Development of Religious Links between South Asia and Central Asia since the End of the Soviet Era

The Ahmadiyya is a religious movement founded by Mirza Ghulam Ahmad (1838–1908), who later portrayed himself as a new prophet and identified with Islam.[29] Messianic, he claimed to be the *Mahdi*, the long-awaited Messiah. Syncretic, he also asserted that he was the new incarnation of Jesus and integrated Hindu elements into his discourse, particularly the religious figure of Krishna. The new religion created by him at the start of the twentieth century emerged in the context of considerable pressure on India's Muslims. It was of two kinds: the pressure of Protestant missionaries, denigrating Islam for its violent character, and the pressure of the Hindu *Arya Samaj* sect, likewise involved in converting Muslims. It was then that Mirza Ghulam Ahmad launched his movement, which in a few decades assumed an international dimension. Its lightning expansion did not shield it from dissension, however. The new religion soon experienced a split: a majority branch, the so-called Qadiani, which stressed Mirza Ghulam Ahmad's prophetic status, and a minority branch, the so-called Lahore school, which remained closer to the Islam from which they both derived. Although separate, the two tendencies in the Ahmadiyya were harshly repressed in the Muslim world, especially Pakistan and Saudi Arabia. The obstacles put in its way did not prevent it from being exported throughout the world, including to the highly anti-religious socialist republic of Albania.[30] After several attempts to establish itself in Central Asia, the Ahmadiyya succeeded in getting itself known and creating some disciples in Kyrgyzstan, where comparative religious freedom contrasted with the rigidity of the neighbouring republics, generally more hostile to any form of proselytizing. Even so, its presence was limited and weak, because the country's political authorities, while agreeing to grant it official legal status, tended to harass it, making worship and conversion difficult.

At the same time, and given the historical importance of the Naqshbandi in Central Asia and India, Marth Brill Olcott[31] argues that from 1991 Sheikh Muhammad Zulfikar Naqshbandi Mujaddid, a Naqshbandi authority well-known in Pakistan, had created a circle of followers in Uzbekistan, notably in the Bukhara region, cradle of the brotherhood. This new Naqshbandi connection is difficult to confirm, but it would have been short-lived. From 1993 the Uzbek government, gripped by suspicion and fear of religious subversion, closed the lid on the religious revival by closely monitoring all Sufi mystical authorities likely to create autonomous circles. The only two identified cases attest to the weakness of the links and forms of influence between Central Asia and South Asia until the appearance on the scene of the Tablighi Jamaat,[32] whose activism and unexpected success disproved predictions of the failure of Indian initiatives.

Tablighi Jamaat as a Link between Central Asia and South Asia

To arrive at a clearer understanding of its activity in Central Asia, and to assess what it brings to post-Soviet Muslims, Tablighi Jamaat must be resituated in its original geographical and historical context. It is in fact a pure product of Indian thinking. Above all, it is an avatar of the prestigious Sunni Islamic school called Deobandi, referring to the city of Deoband where this reformist current emerged in response to British colonization in the 1880s. At once traditionalist and apolitical, the Deoband school has given rise to a large number of highly diverse religious currents, from the most pietistic like Tablighi Jamaat to the most radical like the Afghan Taliban. The origin of the Deoband School lies in a mere seminar, the *Darul Uloom*, which in the colonial context gradually developed into an Islamic university where the classical methods of the madrasa and the educational principles of a European-style university were combined. Success was immediate. From its foundation, the school was full and its renown extended throughout India and then beyond, wherever affiliates were created in its name.[33] The various currents born in the wake of the Deoband School share the same rigour, even an obsession for piety and the everyday practice of Islam—what Olivier Roy calls neo-fundamentalisms,[34] in the sense that the priority is not so much religious ideology as the rigorist practice of the faith.

Let us above all recall that Tablighi Jamaat owes its considerable expansion to the political context in which Indian Islam evolved. The latter experienced a serious crisis, simultaneously threatened as it was by Hindu nationalism and British colonialism.[35] Tablighi Jamaat's founder Muhammad Ilyas Kandhlawi (1881–1944), who laid the basis for the movement from the 1920s onwards, was anxious to equip his vision of Islam with the means to resist these two threats. The first was the *shuddi* movement—a Hindu nationalist current—which advocated purification and preached a return to Hinduism to rediscover and re-embody authentic Indian identity.[36] Muhammad Ilyas also endeavoured to organize Muslims against Christian missionary currents, aided by colonization, who arrived to convert Muslims, diverting them from their faith and identity. The resistance movement conceived by Ilyas would grow rapidly and become an Islamic current on an international scale. In so doing, it relied on a series of principles.

Firstly, *tabligh*, also called *da'wah* or preaching, aimed predominantly—even exclusively—at returning Muslims to the Islam from which they had departed. At the time, in the context of colonial India, it involved Muhammad Ilyas steering Mewat's Muslims towards not dissolving themselves into Hinduism and purifying their faith and practice of any pre-Islamic influence, especially borrowings from Hinduism. *Tabligh* also made it possible to struggle against Christian missionary movements. Muhammad Ilyas' teaching barely promoted scripture and the classical madrasa. Instead, it privileged oral preaching, the transmission of values and ideas through experience and the movement. He encouraged his followers to travel, to set out to meet believers. The mission of every Muslim, whether rich or poor, educated or uneducated, literate or illiterate, was to act in the here and now, enjoining the faithful not to neglect their faith and practice of their religion.[37] Gradually, a whole corpus of preaching rules was established. It fixed at three the number of days a month that every Muslim is required to devote to preaching. Then, with experience, the number increases to forty days a year and so on, to the point where four successive months are devoted to transmitting this teaching to those in need of it. The individuals involved or roped in to the *tabligh* generally carry out 'sorties'—*gasht* or *khuruj*—in small groups, visiting one another's homes, going door-to-door and inviting people to come and pray at the mosque and listen to *beyan*—sermons on various subjects that always focus on the importance of the faith and of practising religion.

Thanks to this method of preaching, which prizes the oral above all else and the establishment of direct relationships on the ground, Tablighi Jamaat rapidly spread throughout India and, following Partition, Pakistan and later Bangladesh. Decolonization largely served the movement's interests. In fact, Muhammad Ilyas' successors, who often derived directly from his original followers, were instrumental in globalizing the movement, which at present is probably the most transnational of Islamic movements, present and active on every continent.[38] It initially established itself in the United Kingdom at the time of decolonization,[39] in particular thanks to the South Asian diasporas that gravitated to Britain's industrial towns and cities. In Africa, it was exported to the Anglophone zone in the first instance, particularly the Gambia in the 1960s,[40] but also South Africa, where, though a minority religion, local Islam always had a strong relationship with Islam in the Indian subcontinent. But Tablighi Jamaat also took an interest in Francophone Africa and established itself firmly in Morocco in the 1960s, although it was only recognized in the kingdom from 1975 onwards.[41] In the United States, its presence was not insignificant, particularly in Chicago and New York.[42] In France, the *Foi et Pratique* association is an offshoot of Tablighi Jamaat and is particularly active in the suburbs, and in Paris itself, in the mosque on the rue Jean-Pierre Timbaud in the Eleventh Arrondissement.[43] Its expansion into Central Asia occurred after the end of the USSR.

This transnational expansion occurred despite Tablighi Jamaat's ambiguous relationship to politics and to Sufism. From 1991, the political authorities' control over religious affairs involved pressure on—even massive repression of—Islam in Central Asia and, to a lesser extent, the Caucasus. There was a strong general tendency to believe that good Islam is Sufi and apolitical (hence not subversive or threatening), whereas political Islam is inherently bad and its prohibition legitimate.

Tablighi Jamaat was born nearly eighty years ago and has been studied in detail by international researchers, but there is no consensus in the scholarly community as to whether it belongs to the Sufi movement. The issue is not easily settled, because the movement has evolved and changed radically since its emergence. It is an established, undeniable fact that Muhammad Ilyas was a Sufi, practised the doctrine, and was a follower of the Chisti,[44] a well-known brotherhood in India.[45]

Thus, Tablighi Jamaat's headquarters is opposite the *dergah* (mausoleum) of Nizamuddin, who was a major mystical authority. This has led a specialist—Barbara Metcalf—to argue that the movement pertains to a reformed Sufism.[46] It is true that all Tablighi leaders share the same doctrinal tradition. Some were supporters of the Chisti,[47] others of the Suhrawardiyya,[48] and still others of the Qadiriyya or Naqshbandi. Muhammad Ilyas himself was initiated by Rashid Ahmad Gangohi,[49] a well-known doctrinal authority and founder of the Deoband School. Furthermore, Tablighi Jamaat's literature makes frequent references to Sufism. Certain technical terms specific to Sufism are invoked and re-used in Tablighi discourse. And Muhammad Ilyas himself referred to his movement as a *hanaqa*—a mobile hospice, an institution peculiar to Sufism.[50] Yet these attributes and influences are insufficient to make Tablighi Jamaat a Sufi movement in the true sense of the term, for it lacks key features of Sufism. First of all, absent from *tabligh* as defined by Ilyas, and then practised by all groups identifying with his movement, is the principle of initiation—that is, a ritual of entry into the movement, consecrating the master-disciple bond. Adhesion to Tablighi ideas does not entail any commitment. People come and go as they please.[51] Secondly, the practice of visitation does not exist in *tabligh*, whereas it is central in the mystical Sufi currents. In Central Asia, where there are numerous places of pilgrimage very popular with local populations, I have never seen any Tablighi stop to say a prayer or perform an act of meditation. On the contrary, visiting popular religious sites is forbidden. Finally, Tablighi do not engage in the Sufi practice of *zikr*, the rhythmic evocation or chanting of God's name in a ceremonial form, sometimes accompanied by singing and music.[52] While some observe it, the *zikr* is internalized and altogether marginal. The performance of prayers or ecstatic dances is inconceivable among Tablighi. Setting aside these elements of practice, Tablighi Jamaat might at a pinch be characterized as a reformed or derivative Sufism, having generated an intermediate stage of evolution between Sufism and conservative fundamentalism.

We also encounter Tablighi Jamaat's problematic link with Sufism in its relationship to politics. It is important to clarify things here, for in India, as everywhere else to which it has emigrated, the movement, because it remains unknown, arouses fear and suspicion of its goals. Is it a politico-religious organization concealing its societal ambitions? Is it the long-term vehicle of particular political aims? Does it directly or indirectly serve international jihadism?[53] One way of bringing out the political character of Tablighi Jamaat consists in analysing how its activity is organized in several countries, how it behaves towards the state and its governance, but also how Islam is administered.

Let us start with what the hierarchy of the Tablighi organization has to say about politics. A movement of individual faith and practice, Tablighi Jamaat originally professed and intended itself to stand aside from politics. Its founders did not advocate joining a political party to win power. This initial focus exclusively on issues of faith, education and practice has led some analysts, like Faruqhi,[54] to claim that it is completely apolitical. In the same vein, Sadowsky believes that for Tablighi there is no confusion between religion and politics.[55] It is true that by comparison with Jama'at i Islam, born in the same context, Tablighi Jamaat has hitherto shown no sign of any political aspirations or ambitions. However, such is the thesis defended by Yoginder Sikand, that while not a political organization in the strict sense, Tablighi Jamaat defends a political view of society and religion. But this is not set down in texts and the hallowed literature. Consequently, without advocating specific political positions, Tablighi Jamaat is a product of its time: an organization of community solidarity and resistance in the face of an invader and hence an essentially political movement. Thus, reckons Yoginder Sikand, Muhammad Ilyas Kandhlawi's family was influenced by the politico-religious thinking of the family of Shah Waliullah (1703–62), particularly Ahmad Shahid (1786–1831), which sought to encourage a regeneration of Islamic faith with a view to restoring the political supremacy lost by Islam during the final years of pre-colonial India.[56] Thus, although focused on faith and practice, the goal of *tabligh* preaching as defined by Muhammad Ilyas, his descendants and their followers was to prepare people mentally for Islam to recover its political grandeur and strength in the long run. As a result, there is (according to this author) a tacit division of labour between Tablighi Jamaat, whose mission is to prepare and consolidate bases, educate and re-Islamize, and other, more openly political Islamic currents—particularly Maududi's Jamaat i Islam—in Islam's ultimate mission to recover its erstwhile supremacy.

Tablighi Jamaat displayed this ambiguous approach to politics following Partition. Muslims became a minority in India, and Tablighi Jamaat adopted a rather balanced strategy, favouring official state secularism in order to defend Muslim rights and interests against the nationalist drift of Hindus, who formed the overwhelming majority in India.[57] In Pakistan, the state largely supported, or even instrumentalized, Tablighi Jamaat's apolitical discourse to weaken openly Islamic political parties. We find this attitude in other countries where states often appreciate the Tablighi for their concentration on faith and practice, ensuring that youth enrolled in Tablighi structures do not end up swelling the ranks of oppositional political parties.

Furthermore, in a number of countries, intellectual figures who have been through Tablighi Jamaat have gone into politics and occupied senior positions. This does not reflect its hidden political ambitions, but reveals the ease with which it is joined and left. Similarly, some jihadists, certainly marginal, have a Tablighi background, as in the case of the alleged authors of a thwarted bomb attack in Spain in 2008.[58] These isolated facts do not demonstrate that Tablighi Jamaat is a terrorist organization, defends terrorist positions, or supports the violent acts that follow from them. But it does indicate that loose ties, or an absence of organic ties, with its members facilitates defectors, who emerge in spite of its ideas.[59] In any event, even if it is not comparable to an Islamic organization with a political project, still less a jihadist one, because of political and security concerns its establishment in Central Asia has been difficult everywhere except Kyrgyzstan.

Tablighi Jamaat's Uneven Settlement in Central Asia

Let us first note that Tablighi Jamaat is conspicuous by its absence in the Caucasus. Years spent on the ground and on regular assignments in Azerbaijan and Georgia indicate that not only is it still not active there, but it remains completely unknown or ignored by believers, including 'professionals'—that is, analysts, servants and functionaries of Islam. However, during individual interviews conducted at Tablighi Jamaat's global headquarters in Nizamuddin, on the outskirts of New Delhi, I did meet an Azerbaijani. This young man came from the Azerbaijani diaspora in Russia, not the South Caucasus itself. The geographical remoteness of the Caucasus from India is a poor explanation, because the movement has a global presence. Consequently, it is not being inhibited by miles, oceans and mountains, but more likely by the fact that in the South Caucasus the majority Islam is Shia, whereas Tablighi Jamaat is Sunni. By contrast, it is known throughout Central Asia, but its actions and actual presence on the ground vary from country to country, as does its reception.

Tablighi Jamaat made its first appearance in Central Asia, in Uzbekistan, just after the end of the Soviet Union. The choice was not insignificant, because Uzbekistan was—and remains—not only the most populous country in the region, but also the most Muslim in terms of the number of religious establishments and the significance and density of the Islamic heritage in a country at the heart of Central Asia. During the brief period when Uzbekistan was liberating itself and allowing scope for greater freedom—religious, in particular—between the end of *perestroika* and 1993, a plethora of religious tendencies seized the opportunity to come and test their attractiveness to Uzbek Muslims. Faced with the arrival of Tablighi missionaries in Uzbek cities, the country's most charismatic and influential religious figure, the mufti Muhammad Sadik Muhammad Yusuf, issued a positive fatwa on Tablighi Jamaat, whose character and objectives he was quick to understand.[60] Such approval of the movement's ideas and objectives by the country's most respected religious authority, who enjoyed great prestige throughout Central Asia, transcending political or confessional cleavages, did not enable the Tablighi to establish themselves firmly in Uzbek territory. The country soon sealed itself off again, and its legal institutions and security forces proscribed, and began to track, any form of religious influence deemed inappropriate in Uzbekistan. Tablighi missionaries were expelled. In passing, comportment and dress in the public sphere were subject to particularly strict and restrictive decrees, so that it rapidly became impossible for Tablighi and other Islamic religious currents, notably Turkish ones, to pursue their activities in Uzbekistan.

In neighbouring Turkmenistan, hostility towards Tablighi Jamaat was even more violent, but almost beside the point. For the country, closed to any outside influence, was scarcely likely to arouse missionary enthusiasm on the part of Tablighi Jamaat or other Islamic currents. The situation scarcely developed or altered after independence, either under Turkmenistan's omnipotent first president, Sapar Murad Niyazov, or under his successor, Kurbanguli Berdimuhammedov, who has run the country since 2007.[61] Few diplomatic or consular stations abroad granted visas; the country preferred not to attract attention and did very little to promote itself. Finally, as regards Islamic revival,[62] we note that in the mosques the dictatorship imposes not a particular national vision of Islam, but the cult of the president's personality. Alongside the Koran, every mosque is obliged to display a copy of Niyazov's compendium, *Ruhnama*, a kind of moral guide for the whole country, mosques and schools.[63] *De facto* inaccessible, Turkmenistan eludes the expansionist strategy of transnational groups like Tablighi Jamaat.

Kazakhstan and Tajikistan represent an intermediate state of affairs, which oscillates between outright proscription and liberalization. For a long time, the two countries tolerated Tablighi Jamaat's presence and activism, without going so far as officially recognizing it, which is an indispensable step for anyone or anything wishing to survive and prosper. This singular position has its own springs in each instance.

Kazakhstan, the economic giant of Central Asia, open to the outside world in order to make the most of its economic potential (especially in energy and mining), has always striven not to deter investors. To that end, it must demonstrate a minimum of openness and political and social liberalism. But the old Soviet reflexes of control still constrain the system. The country barely tolerates the existence of an opposition and controls religious liberty with a firm hand. In other words, the latter is not wholly guaranteed. In this strange pseudo-liberal atmosphere, relations have been established between Kazakhstan and the Indian subcontinent. For several years, young Kazakhs have travelled to India, but also Pakistan and Bangladesh, to take part in major Tablighi gatherings. This freedom of movement and Islamic cooperation between Kazakhstan and South Asia have allowed Tablighi Jamaat to develop its proselytism throughout the country. Without enjoying formal legal authorization, and hence legal protection from the Justice Ministry or the State Committee for Religious Affairs as required by law, hundreds or even thousands of young preachers influenced by Tablighi thinking and methods regularly roam the roads of Kazakhstan to meet the faithful, to exhort them to believe and practise. But these activities, which were just about tolerated, came to an end in 2013, when the country tightened up its legislation on the registration of religious organizations, and Tablighi Jamaat, hitherto ignored, is now included on a list of proscribed radical organizations.[64] Since its prohibition, it has not operated in Kazakhstan, or only marginally and clandestinely, risking prosecution. The mere fact of being suspected of proselytizing and being Tablighi is sufficient to trouble innocent parties, who are arrested, fined or even imprisoned for offences that are unproven and which they have not in fact committed.[65] Thus, few brave the arbitrariness of religious repression in Kazakhstan.

In Tajikistan, the government's attitude to Tablighi Jamaat was likewise ambiguous, before becoming openly hostile and even repressive from 2009 onwards.[66] In the years when it was permitted to preach openly, groups of Tablighi made regular tours, or *gasht*, in various cities. They then extended their operations to Central Asia, but also India, to the Nizamuddin Markaz headquarters, and Deoband and Lucknow, where I was able to interview them. Despite the movement's proscription, some Tablighi still engaged in proselytizing expeditions, leading to their immediate arrest by Tajik security forces. Here too, as in Kazakhstan, suspicion can drift into arbitrariness and the harassment of individuals unconnected to Tablighi Jamaat. The distrust of the country's leaders has become such that even the Party of Islamic Renaissance—the sole legal Islamist party because it has been associated with the government since the end of the civil war—was harassed for some years before being banned in July 2014, on the pretext that it serves as a breeding ground for terrorism.

There are several reasons for the outright or relative proscription of Tablighi Jamaat in the countries of Central Asia, with the exception of Kyrgyzstan, which will be treated separately. Some are specific to the movement, while others are more general in scope and include everything regarded as incompatible with official religious norms. Since independence, all these countries have implemented policies for the regulation of religious affairs that distinguish 'good' Islam from the 'bad' variety, without always clearly defining the boundary between them. Generally, with a few divergences depending on each country's interpretation of it, the traditional Islam favoured and encouraged among the faithful is Sunni Islam, of the Hanafi School, as promoted by the organs of the official religious apparatus.[67] In other words, 'good' Islam is that defined and controlled by the Directorates of Spiritual Affairs charged with appointing imams, running schools, organizing worship and banning unauthorized preachers. Thus, the regime ensures that it retains control over minds and prevents the opposition instrumentalizing religion for the purposes of political destabilization. The authorities' anxiety to control any form of foreign Islamism answers to concerns about security and stability. The proximity of Afghanistan, the existence of a jihadist threat that is certainly real but often greatly exaggerated, and fear of the country becoming a breeding ground for radical Islamism are the main reasons invoked for controlling the religious scene. The risks are often overestimated and, in reality, measures to proscribe and control are primarily geared to sheltering official power from any internal threat—even if, with their bans, the authorities create more dissatisfaction and frustration, hence more risks and threats, than they realize. Political and economic reform, or the organization of free, transparent elections, although fundamental and a priority for these states' democratization and consolidation, always take second place to the threat of so-called 'radical Islam' and are constantly being postponed—which represents an even greater risk to the country's stability.[68]

In this respect, Tablighi Jamaat arouses fear that is all the more alarming because it gives every appearance of being a dangerous organization. Its methods, and, above all, the dress code of its preachers in Pakistani *shalvar kamis* or *jellaba*, frighten the Uzbek, Tajik and Kazakh authorities and are regarded by the population as signs of a radical religious militancy. Recalling dress codes in Afghanistan, this style is therefore associated, rightly or wrongly, with the despised Taliban; this is enough to discredit Tablighi further in countries where public opinion is still largely shaped by the Soviet secular heritage. Thus over time, Tablighi Jamaat has found itself stigmatized as a radical, or even terrorist, organization, put in the same basket as Hizb ut-Tahrir or the Islamic Movement of Uzbekistan and banned throughout Central Asia, with the notable exception of Kyrgyzstan, where it is very active and so well-integrated that the mufti of the Kyrgyz Republic is a well-known Tablighi. Why this exception?

ISLAM IN CENTRAL ASIA AND THE CAUCASUS

Kyrgyzstan: Tablighi Jamaat's Positive Exception in Central Asia

Tabligh Jamaat is ubiquitous in Kyrgyzstan. It is enough to visit any town or city to register the movement's remarkable presence and visibility. In every town, whether in the urban zone or the rural, at the exit of mosques or in the public sphere, Tablighi are often to be seen roaming the streets and travelling the roads to preach the virtues of the Muslim faith and practice. However, their task has not always been easy. During the early years of independence, they suffered their share of abuse and harassment, like any other foreign missionary movement. In fact, the original missionaries came from Pakistan and it took time and perseverance for them to be accepted in Kyrgyzstan. Hostility emanated from all sides and for all sorts of reasons. As has been noted, their dress and beards shocked both the elites and the urban and rural populations. Wearing a beard was restricted to the elderly in Central Asia. As for wearing the long robe called a *kurtan* or *kamiss* in Urdu, but also sometimes the *jellaba*, which surprised Central Asians unused to this predominantly North African costume, it created an initial negative prejudice towards them, which they found difficult to overcome, including in Kyrgyzstan.

For a number of elites, during this phase of rediscovery and redefinition of national traditions which they were seeking to cleanse of Russo-Soviet influences,[69] such foreign sartorial customs—especially the wearing of the veil—represented a challenge to their traditions and national identity.[70] Very soon, however, Tablighi leaders succeeded in invoking the same principle of tradition and national identity to their advantage and to counter supporters of the new post-Soviet Kyrgyz identity. Thus, by their sartorial behaviour or by wearing beards, Tablighi advocated a kind of return to, a restoration of, Muslim traditions, shared by the Kyrgyz, which were said to have been perverted by prolonged Russo-Soviet domination.[71] They argued that, prior to the Russians' arrival, Kyrgyz dressed in long shirts and baggy trousers and official historiography vindicates them. All the *batirs* (legendary heroes of the past), intellectuals, singers and popular story-tellers, poets and writers of the pre-Soviet period dressed in a style closer to Tablighi styles than the Western variety imposed by the Soviets. As regards the veil, wearing it was associated with the *elechek*,[72] a national female head-dress greatly prized among Kyrgyz and Kazakh nomads before the Russians' arrival. To illustrate their point and reinforce their argument, Tablighi appealed to the mythical figure of Kurmanjan Datka[73]—a female leader of the Kyrgyz tribes in the country's south in the nineteenth century, who was well-known for fighting against enemy forces. A historical figure mythologized both by Soviet propaganda and by the new government since independence, Kurmanjan Datka is today the object of a virtual cult. Her portrait, in which she is wearing the *elechek*, is honoured in a number of official sites, and a large statue has been erected to her in Osh. For Tablighi, the *elechek* worn by this venerable ancestor is proof that the veil is not foreign to the national traditions perverted by Soviet domination. Equipped with such arguments, they have succeeded in imposing their style and establishing themselves in the country to spread Tablighi practice. But style is not everything. In their endeavours, they have received approval and support from the Kyrgyz authorities. Why and how has the Kyrgyz state participated in reinforcing Tablighi Jamaat in Kyrgyzstan?

Tablighi Jamaat unquestionably owes its astonishing expansion in Kyrgyzstan to its missionary expertise, but also to a remarkable capacity to adapt. However, it was aided in its missionary work by the Kyrgyz state. At the outset, the state apparatus, controlled by elites formed and fashioned by the atheistic Soviet mentality and ideology, did not particularly appreciate the arrival of very foreign-looking religious figures. But out of pragmatism, the state allowed the movement to take root. Lacking oil wealth and natural resources, with nothing but beautiful mountains to attract foreign visitors and manual labour to despatch to Russia in exchange for remittances, Kyrgyzstan opted for openness, democratization in the absence of democracy, to attract international investment and aid. Such a policy involved making an effort in the direction of liberties, including religious freedom.[74] And Tablighi Jamaat proved adept at exploiting the breach, just as the Kyrgyz state demonstrated opportunism in banking on Tablighi pietism against other, more politicized movements. Killing two birds with one stone, it got Tablighi Jamaat to assume the mission of supervising youth. *De facto* legalized to play the role of mediator and pacifier of youth, Tablighi Jamaat thus performed a buffer role, absorbing the frustrations and dissatisfaction of Kyrgyz youth, who were unemployed, without prospects, and suffering amid the country's economic difficulties.

In order to administer and supervise its work more effectively, the Directorate of Spiritual Affairs, in agreement with the State Committee for Religious Affairs, created a specific department within itself, dedicated to *da'wah*—that is, spreading the faith. It was entrusted to an active figure in Tablighi Jamaat, Rawshan Eratov, who was credited with great experience thanks to eight years spent studying Islam in Pakistan. His role consisted in overseeing Tablighi Jamaat's activities so that its proselytizing was organized in accordance with the state's needs and interests. This clearly involved control of the former by the latter. The monitoring was conducted as follows. As is the case wherever Tablighi Jamaat is established, there are regular *ijtima'*, local, regional and national meetings. They decide the destination of expeditions (*khuruj*), which are responsible for preaching (*da'wah*), and their duration—three days or forty days. All this work on planning and organizing travel, with a list of participants, is supervised by the *tabligh* department of the Directorate of Religious Affairs. The latter reports to the State Committee for Religious Affairs, predominantly composed of bureaucrats who rarely have religious competence. Such supervision goes beyond sheer control, because candidates for embarking on *tabligh* are supposed to provide written proof that they have the agreement of their local police chief and also, especially, of their wives. This is intended to ensure that a candidate does not pose a security threat to the community and that his family can provide for itself in his absence. Thus, Tablighi Jamaat is not wholly free in its movements and proselytizing strategy. To a certain extent, there is an instrumentalization, even recuperation, of Tablighi Jamaat by the state, which utilizes it as a tool of ultra-controlled re-Islamization. This manifestly symbiotic relationship, at once ambiguous and completely systematized, directly challenges the lay character of the secular state, which in principle should not intervene in the religious domain. It also raises the question of the putative apoliticism of Tablighi Jamaat, which, in openly collaborating with the Kyrgyz state, becomes an instrument of its policy of forming good Muslims subservient to the state's religious prescriptions.

The collaboration took an even more marked turn when the Directorate of Spiritual Affairs was entrusted to a Tablighi. In fact, as well as establishing a so-called department of preaching entrusted to Eratov, the republic's muftiate was entrusted to a Tablighi from 2015 onwards. Maksat Toktomushov, the most prestigious figure in the country's Tablighi movement, succeeded in being installed as mufti—the highest religious figure in the national hierarchy. But why choose this movement, which is ultimately new in the country and not representative of local, Kyrgyz and Central Asian Islam?

Surprising as it may seem, the unnatural alliance between a secular state deriving from the USSR and a religious movement foreign to local Islamic traditions possesses a certain rationality. The Kyrgyz state seems to have found in Tablighi Jamaat a tool that answers to its needs. In effect, its Islam represents 'good' Islam—a minimalist, non-erudite form of it that energetically and enthusiastically takes on a not insignificant social role, since it protects the faithful from the evils that particularly plague youth in Kyrgyz society: first and foremost, unemployment and alcoholism. Tablighi Jamaat's expansion is also bound up with the fact that its Islam is well-adapted to Kyrgyz cultural traditions. This thesis, which is certainly debatable, is supported by Emil Nasritdinov, a Kyrgyz researcher who has long frequented the movement and worked on its activities.[75] He stresses that Tablighi Jamaat has developed a mode of communication and *da'wah* that privileges the oral mode, allocating only a small role to written texts. In fact, they only use one textbook, the famous *Fazail-e-Amaal*,[76] because proselytizing by roaming and orality take precedence—a certain *orature*, as suggested by Rémi Dor.[77] And among the Kyrgyz, oral traditions are very powerful and highly prized. The Manas epic, one of the longest in the world, occupies a central place in the Kyrgyz people's culture and identity.[78] This shared inclination for the oral tradition is said to have contributed to Tablighi success among the Kyrgyz, facilitating its establishment in the country. Moreover, the nomadic tradition, which is still very significant among the Kyrgyz,[79] at least symbolically, was conducive to the favourable reception of Tablighi preachers, whose basic preaching principle consists in motion—peregrination in space, roaming around and meetings. Thanks to it, hundreds or even thousands of Kyrgyz live a spiritual connection with a religious school that was originally completely alien to them, as it derived from the Indian subcontinent—a first in the history of Kyrgyz Islam. How, and to what extent, has this connection been established?

The first Tablighi to arrive in Kyrgyzstan were foreigners. Since its implantation, however, the movement has trained local followers, and the Kyrgyz branch of Tablighi Jamaat is led, inspired and developed by Kyrgyz. The members travel a good deal, as far as the three countries that may be regarded as the movement's original home: India, Pakistan and Bangladesh. Initial contacts were rather strong with Pakistan, where Kyrgyz travelled regularly, especially to attend the great annual meeting in the city of Raiwind, which gathers together more of the faithful than the pilgrimage to Mecca. In the early years of independence, some arrived by car or bus, making difficult journeys and running considerable risks. Then, from 2001 onwards and the events of 11 September, travel to Pakistan became more difficult. This orientated Tablighi more towards India or Bangladesh. In truth, the selection of India, Pakistan or Bangladesh was made mainly in accordance with the modalities for obtaining a visa. But travelling to India was particularly prized, because candidates appreciated visiting Nizamuddin Markaz, the global centre of Tablighi Jamaat on the outskirts of New Delhi. The movement's historical headquarters attracted people from throughout the world, who came for advice and new directives on perfecting *da'wah*. In this five-storey building, headquarters of the movement's supreme authorities, visitors spend three days before being sent on *da'wah* to other Indian towns and cities to meet Tablighi from all over. *Beyan*, speeches given by major authorities, are translated into several languages, depending on the groups of Tablighi in attendance. I was able to observe *in situ* how, on the occasion of these speeches, origins in the ex-USSR and the Russian language united Muslims from across the old Soviet Union. Gathered together in a reserved space on the fourth floor, Russian-speaking Tablighi, whether Kyrgyz, Kazakhs, Tajiks, Tatars or Russians, listened to sermons by the great local Tablighi figures, courtesy of translation from Urdu into Russian by a student who had been at Markaz for several years.

Obviously, the intensity of the interaction between Kyrgyzstan's Tablighi and those of the Indian subcontinent should not be exaggerated. The standard of living in Kyrgyzstan remains low and few have the resources to travel to Delhi, Dhaka, Lahore or Raiwind. But however relative, interaction exists and galvanizes the Islamic revival in Kyrgyzstan. It helps open up the country, for, though few in number, Tablighi roam, make contacts and exchange with the Muslims of the subcontinent—but not only them. They are open to Tablighi across the world: Europe, Africa, the Middle East. And, as in antiquity, the exchange of ideas is conducive to the exchange of goods, trade and investment. Thus, the Tablighi pilgrimage also facilitates commercial links between Kyrgyzstan and the three countries of the Indian subcontinent. The volume of trade is doubtless not large, but given the economic situation in Kyrgyzstan every new opening is to be seized on and is not insignificant, even if it only involves religious objects, prayer mats, Islamic costumes, literature and knick-knacks of every sort. Thus, although the procession of Kyrgyz Tablighi to the Indian subcontinent remains modest when compared with others, such as Turkey, it boasts a community of several thousand faithful, including the country's mufti. This places official Islam's whole hierarchy under its influence, at the expense of Turkey's *Diyanet*, which has two theology faculties on the ground and maintains a policy of training new Islamic elites in Kyrgyzstan as well as Turkey.

But is the Tablighi Jamaat's record in Kyrgyzstan sufficient to characterize the Indian subcontinent's influence on Central Asian Islam as significant? This is far from clear, for the following reasons. Firstly, for all its activism, Tablighi Jamaat does not represent the totality of the subcontinent's Islam, which is also inspired by other currents, notably brotherhoods, but also by more political ones such as Jamiat-e-Islami. Moreover, Tablighi Jamaat's activism, impressive as it is in Central Asia, is mainly confined to Kyrgyzstan, which is not the most populous country in Central Asia. In Uzbekistan, which has 27 million inhabitants, and Kazakhstan, which has 17 million, its roots are weak. Finally, in Kyrgyzstan, where it is highly influential, including at the summit of the religious hierarchy, the brotherhood is subject to such surveillance that its ability to develop links with South Asia is limited. Thus, candidates for journeying to various cities in India or Pakistan regularly face problems over visas, which the authorities there issue sparingly.[80]

Conclusion: South Asian Islam's Impact on Central Asia

The end of the USSR and the opening up of the Central Asia republics made it possible to restore links with South Asia, which previously had no real borders with Central Asia. Like other regions in the Muslim sphere, the Indian subcontinent is thus once again connected to Central

Asia. Yet it cannot be said that the parenthesis opened by Russian and Soviet domination has been completely closed as a result. In fact, as natural inheritors and products of the ex-USSR, the Central Asian countries continue to harbour a certain distrust of, even hostility towards, a number of intellectual currents, particularly religious ones, from the south. In the mind of the ruling elites, they are associated with Islamic fundamentalism, the Afghan threat, the Taliban and a variety of forms of trafficking.

Formerly multifaceted and varied, intellectual cooperation extended to music, architecture, philosophy and religion. And it operated in both directions. Today, the exchanges are one-way, from the south to the north, from South Asia to Central Asia, and are limited to the religious domain, which is itself restricted and limited to one current—Tablighi Jamaat. Furthermore, Tablighi influence predominantly concerns Kyrgyzstan and involves popular strata. Very few elites, still less scholarly elites, are subject to it.

Thus, Tablighi Jamaat's regional development remains inferior to what this missionary group—the most transnational Islamic movement—might achieve. Greater religious freedom in the countries where it is illegal—particularly Uzbekistan—would allow it to become more firmly established, and might ultimately support more economic cooperation between Central Asia and South Asia. At present, few Central Asian countries accept greater openness to the south—but nothing is immutable, especially when dealing with the circulation of religious ideas.

6

THE ADMINISTRATION OF RELIGION IN THE NEWLY INDEPENDENT REPUBLICS

Introduction: Abandonment of the Collective Administration of Religion

Contrary to a number of theories predicting the break-up of the Soviet Union through the implosion of its periphery and, in particular, its Muslim republics,[1] it was the latter that were most disconcerted by the system's disappearance. Far from seeking independence, the political elites in Central Asia and Azerbaijan, who made the most of their room for manoeuvre as local minor potentates, were ultimately supporters of the status quo and not supporters of independence. Even the oppositional currents that flourished in the wake of *perestroika* did not think to demand it. As for the opposition's Muslim component—the Party of Islamic Renaissance—it did not demand the end of the Union, but advocated its preservation in the name of Muslim unity. Evidence of this is the fact that during the referendum on the status of the USSR, organized in March 1991, all the republics expressed a very clear desire to remain in the Union. Thus, the Turkmens voted almost 98 per cent for maintaining the Union and the Kazakhs 94 per cent, whereas Ukraine and Russia, by contrast, only registered 70 per cent in favour of its preservation.[2]

The independence imposed on the Central Asian republics represented a turning point, a milestone in their history and that of their populations. Each of them initially sought to root the nation in an ancient, glorious history that legitimated its existence. The end of the USSR in the early 1990s marked the beginning of a new national narrative, which was to determine the new relations between state, nation, religion and society, as well as the country's role in the concert of nations. In the new policy of consolidation of a country inherited from the Soviet era, but whose unique identity and ideological singularity had to be constructed, religion, formerly banished from public discourse and confined to private conscience or forced underground, was going to be *de-privatized* (to quote José Casanova),[3] and fully associated with the new identity policy.

The *de facto* dismantlement of the Spiritual Administration of the Muslims of Central Asia (SADUM in the Russian acronym that entered all the local languages), following the declarations of independence, marked the start of this alteration. Based in Tashkent, this directorate was responsible for the Muslims of Central Asia's five republics. It appointed official servants and administered places of worship which, though far from numerous, required some supervision. With their declarations of independence, each republic created its own Directorate of Spiritual Affairs and, with rare exceptions, the political authorities had no difficulty imposing control over religion. In the Caucasus, the Spiritual Directorate, based in Baku, likewise recovered a national dimension; its regional remit was limited to Azerbaijan and then the small Muslim Azeri minority in Georgia, following an accord between Tbilisi and Baku.[4] Thus with independence, a process of national administration of Islam was put in place, which gradually differentiated Central Asian Islam, creating a specific Islam in each country that bore the stamp of the new authorities' political and cultural options. Thus, while it was perfectly apt during the Soviet period to refer to a Central Asian Islam and a Caucasian Islam, such general terms became less and less pertinent because, now enclosed within national frontiers, Islam developed differentially.

In all these countries, religion is nevertheless administered in the same ways. To varying degrees, religion is incorporated into the new identity or ideological policy, in which the state is highly interventionist, to the point of implementing a policy on religious education. Similarly, mechanisms and tools for administering religion, which combine co-option and repression, have been put in place by the new states, which thus ultimately continue the Soviet policy of monitoring and controlling religion. These national religious policies were implemented very gradually and in accordance with social developments and the changing regional geopolitical context. Religious policy is sometimes proactive, based on criteria that include the significance of the country's Islamic heritage or the strength or weakness of political Islam, but also and above all considerations of security and geostrategic order regionally. Thus, the nomadic past of the Kyrgyz, whose Islamization was belated and superficial, does not lead to the same grip on religious affairs as in Uzbekistan, where Islam is deeply rooted in the history and memory of a people that has been sedentary for several centuries.

A Vigilant Benevolence towards Islam

In general, even prior to the end of the USSR, all the leaders in post adopted a new attitude towards religious phenomena and symbols. This was not confined to countries with a majority Muslim population, but extended to the whole former Soviet bloc and even beyond. In the ex-socialist countries, there was a noticeable revival of interest in both Islam and Christianity. However, among the leaders of the Muslim countries, the new national ideology made official recognition of Islam a key factor in the country's identity and cultural heritage. Even so, in line with the Soviet era, the reflex of control and repression persisted whenever actors in civil society sought to elude the official framework of the 'good' Islam. Ultimately, compared with the Soviet period, the religious policies in force today throughout Central Asia and the Caucasus betray a much more marked intrusion of the political into the religious sphere, to repress as well as promote.

The most notable change compared with the Soviet era is that in every country, albeit to varying degrees, Islam is fully associated with the new national ideology or, at any rate, called upon to play a role in creating the new identity. This is especially true of Uzbekistan, which contains the region's largest Muslim community. The Islamic heritage there is strongly rooted in its past and is active in everyday, traditional practice. In Uzbekistan more than elsewhere, the political authorities face the unprecedented challenge of getting the people to adhere to the new values and ideals of a nation redefined in its independent statehood. From the outset, to guarantee the regime's stability, indoctrination was favoured over the creation of a democratic pact between people and leaders. In all the region's countries, rulers banked exclusively on national ideology to unify and cement individuals around the new identity policy and thereby ensure a level of political and social stability.[5] The construction of the new ideology takes the form of an idealized view of the people's past. Once again, the phenomenon is particularly marked in Uzbekistan where, since independence, the country has appropriated the heritage of Tamerlane and his descendants, glorifying their past as empire-builders and conquerors. But this take on the past in order to consolidate the present compels orientation towards Islam, which for several centuries, with the exception of the Soviet parenthesis, has been an integral part of these peoples' identity.

Consequently, in integrating Islam into their past, post-Soviet leaders, like other leaders of Muslim countries in the Middle and Near East, encountered the same dilemma as their predecessors in Central Asia. It consists in valuing religion without allowing it the political power to which Islam actually aspires, to administer polity and community. Similarly, as a result of the identitarian and Islamic revival underway, various local religious figures emerged and acquired greater notoriety and a prestige that the political authorities have, where necessary, to control and regulate.

The parry conceived and executed, especially in Uzbekistan, was the creation from scratch of a composite ideology composed of nationalism and Islam. President Islam Karimov was the first to develop it with the outset of independence, referring systematically to 'our Islam', endowing it with a particular connotation and content which he ensured remained under his control. It involves the instrumentalization of Islam as a tool of propaganda and vehicle for strict control of religious dissidence. At the same time, care was taken that the Islamic elites did not become unduly influential, especially given that some of them possessed great charisma—for example, the former mufti of Uzbekistan, Muhammad Yusuf Muhammad Sodiq—and were highly regarded by the population. In virtually all the region's countries, from their 'arrival' in power—i.e. from their conversion from Soviet socialism to dyed-in-the-wool nationalism—the leaders opted to embody the new Islam by taking the pledge with their hand on the constitution and Koran, by making the pilgrimage to Mecca, and by participating in prayers and other ceremonies to show their respect for Islam and to boost their personal image with a religious gloss. In their words, deeds and gestures, replete with positive references to the Muslim religion, the region's Karimovs and Nazarbayevs displayed their benevolence. These public displays sufficed to engage the whole state in a relationship to religion that was at once benevolent and vigilant, echoing the situation in the Middle East.

The media, TV and official newspapers acted as relays promoting this official Islam. In Uzbekistan more than in the other countries, the idea was to diffuse the 'good' Islam—positive for society and innocuous for the regime—via official channels. At the same time, it was a question of combatting the 'bad' Islam, which advocated social disorder, even violence, encouraged intolerance and threatened the powers that be. In this campaign, it was not unusual to see the head of state enter the fray and to find in the mouth of President Karimov slogans such as '*Uz dinimizi himoya qilamiz*' (let's defend our own religion), or '*Bizim Muqaddas dinimizni hic kimga bermaylik*' (let's not abandon our sacred religion to anyone). This promotion was sometimes accompanied by lectures on the morality and social conduct compatible with the national ideology and even the economy. Thus, for example, traditional parties for birth, marriage and circumcision, which might occasion excessive, ostentatious expenditure, were denounced. Along with the media, local state structures played their part in reinforcing the new norms of religiously inspired morality. In Uzbekistan, this was true of the *mahallas*, the smallest local administrative structure, in principle set up by the neighbourhood's inhabitants and outside state control, which increasingly supervised it.[6]

The reconciliation of Islam and nationalism, Islamic heritage and new national identity, also took the form of rehabilitating major intellectual, religious or national figures from the past and consequently restoring the sites or cities associated with them. In Kazakhstan, along with the major historical figures discredited during the Soviet period but rehabilitated after independence, such as Ablai Khan[7] or Abul Khair,[8] we find religious figures like Ahmad Yassawi in the new national pantheon. A mystical figure and founder of the brotherhood that bears his name, Ahmad Yassawi, who was absent from official Soviet discourse, has enjoyed a veritable cult since 1991.[9] The Kazakh state elevated him into a major mystical and intellectual figure by printing and distributing his literary output in abundance. His mausoleum, to be found in the city of Turkestan, was restored in the framework of a programme of cooperation with Turkey. This included the construction of an Ahmad Yassawi University a few hundred metres from his mausoleum. Today, this enormous complex contains eleven faculties and is home to thousands of students. In Kyrgyzstan, a country of nomadic traditions whose population was belatedly Islamized, it is the mythical, legendary figure of Manas who serves the state's nationalist needs. In addition to the epic and legend, Manas can sometimes be depicted as a religious figure peculiar to the Kyrgyz.[10] More recently, another legendary figure in Kyrgyz history, Kurmanjan Datka (1811–1907), has become the object of a national cult for her part in defending the Kyrgyz homeland during the Russian conquest of Central Asia. In Turkmenistan, it is the mystical figure of Najmuddin Kubra (born in 1145) who is glorified by the regime. Founder of the eponymous Sufi brotherhood of the Kubraviyah, he has gone down in history for his valour in the struggle against the Mongol hordes when they descended upon Central Asia. His mausoleum, located in the city of Konye-Urgench,[11] was restored by the Turkmen state and opened to the public, which has always attributed great significance to visiting holy places. Azerbaijan boasts fewer mystical figures than the rest of Central Asia. The *imamzade* are celebrated above all others there as national heroes. In the Shia tradition, which has been majoritarian in Azerbaijan since the sixteenth century, the *imamzade* are the religious authorities descending from Imam Ali. Azerbaijani territory is thus home to several mausoleums dedicated to his descendants. The mausoleum of Bibi-Heybat, containing the tomb of the daughter of the seventh imam Musa al-Kazim, who was particularly neglected during the Soviet period, was restored under the presidency of Heydar Aliyev, concerned to break with his image as a KGB man and gain the people's confidence by respecting and promoting the Islamic heritage.

But it is unquestionably in Uzbekistan that this rehabilitation of Islamic figures from the past has been most pronounced, but also, in some instances, most problematic. The regime has utilized it to such an extent that an exhaustive enumeration of the ancestral religious figures brought back into fashion would be long and pointless. But let us note at least two cases, one crowned by success, the other by persistent ambiguity. Bahauddin Naqshband (1318–89) was one of two founders of the eponymous brotherhood of the Naqshbandi, which to this day remains the most widespread brotherhood in the whole Muslim world. On account of its global dimensions and recognition, the regime has understandably made him—a native of Bukhara—into a national hero. Because he advocated a moderate, wise and mystical Islam, the new Uzbek national ideology exploits his discourse in its entirety. An international jubilee was devoted to him in 1999; an abundant literature on his *oeuvre* and legacy is widely disseminated; his mausoleum, situated on the outskirts of Bukhara, has been generously restored and opened to the public, pilgrims and foreign tourists. Islam Karimov occasionally acted as a spokesman for the ideas of Bahauddin Naqshband, whose legacy he was even tempted to make use of in foreign policy, in order to consolidate links with Muslim countries.

Conversely, Uzbekistan affords a textbook example of 'aborted' rehabilitation. In the Naqshbandi, Khwaja Ubaydullah Ahrar (1404–90)[12] emerges as a central mystical figure. Recognized and highly regarded throughout the Muslim world, in his turn he elicited interest from the Uzbek authorities, anxious to demonstrate that their country was the cradle of numerous intellectual figures instrumental in the blossoming of Islamic and world civilization. Thus, a presidential decree ordered the organization of his jubilee in 2004. Serious preparatory work by historians, charged with rendering his legacy intelligible and presentable to the maximum number of people, indicated that in addition to his contributions to Sufi doctrine there was a political dimension to Ahrar, who had advocated moral control of politics by religion. There was no question of the regime allowing such ideas to leak out, since they were liable to dent the inflexibility of Karimov's authoritarian regime. The incompatibility between mystical heritage and political subversion forced the regime to reduce the scope of a process of rehabilitation that had gone too far to be peremptorily cancelled: the international conference and popularization of his ideas disappeared from the agenda. Similarly, Dukchi Ishan, a warlord who struggled against colonial domination by attacking a Russian garrison in Andijan in 1898, might have served as a legitimating figure for the Uzbek regime. But it was not to be, because in-depth research disclosed links with the Naqshbandi and a degree of political and social influence throughout the Fergana Valley—something obviously incompatible with the country's new ideology, wherein religion is expected not to get mixed up in politics.

As is readily apparent, nothing is left to chance in the national policy of the new Central Asian states. Reconciliation with history and its political, religious and intellectual figures can only occur if the latter are completely bland and innocuous. Thus, all these improvised public policies correspond to strictly supervised ideological options. The authorities only rehabilitate the least political figures, especially those who help justify the political and ideological choices made after the end of the Soviet Union. As regards Islam, and the selection of Islamic figures to be included in the national pantheon, the regime's highest priority takes precedence over national policy. Only the least politicized figures, those least influential in running the polity and in the court of previous sovereigns, are admitted. However, if a controversial or ambiguous, but nevertheless unavoidable, hero or heritage is of interest to the political authorities, then a selective reading and sterilized, apolitical interpretation is proffered. Thus, the political and social dimension of the so-called Jadid reformist intellectual current, so important in the intellectual history of all the peoples of Central Asia, but especially Uzbekistan and Tajikistan, is frowned upon. Tashkent has no hesitation in erasing it, conserving and glorifying only the intellectual struggle against Russian domination or modernization by means of schooling.

More generally, this politics of memory is part and parcel of the regimes' desire to distinguish 'good' Islam—'our Islam', the local, tolerant, progressive traditional Islam, Sufi and mystical, which is constitutive of identity—from all other, 'bad' Islams—political, subversive, foreign—which are to be rejected. Thus, the practice of popular, apolitical Islam, such as pilgrimages to holy sites and mausoleums, is encouraged. The policy of fostering popular religiosity sometimes approximates to folklore, where observance boils down to symbolic gestures. At the same time, the 'museification'[13] of religious establishments—rehabilitated old mosques and other religious buildings, as well as new institutions—crystallizes Islam in defined settings, rather than being conducive to its practice flourishing. Even less do these Islamic establishments serve as sites for intellectual and religious debate, as might have been the case previously and as is the case in other Muslim countries, where mosques are also a religious school and open forum. The policy of controlling Islam and even inflecting piety, which was initiated when the states became independent, has accelerated with the emergence of a fundamentalist Islam, sometimes politically extremist and/or terrorist, in several countries. To confront the fundamentalist phenomenon, whose origins are in fact local and date back to the Soviet era, but which has been amplified by foreign currents, states have implemented policies to control religion through strict legislative measures, but also educational ones.

The Development of an Oppositional Islam in Reaction against the Official 'Good' Islam

The sham 'good' Islam promoted by officials should not lead us to forget the whole range of currents operating in the post-Soviet sphere. The religious policy of the states of Central Asia and the Caucasus cannot be understood without casting an analytical eye on oppositional Islam, which the authorities denigrate and indiscriminately characterize as Wahhabism, extremism, fundamentalism or Salafism. These deliberate amalgams between different forms of oppositional Islam and the anti-Islamist propaganda are so pervasive that they obscure a clear view of what is really happening on the ground.[14] Islamism is, in the first instance, the Western term for an awakening of Islam at the time of Western modernity. In this sense, it is a socio-political ideology born in the nineteenth century on a religious basis. In the post-Soviet sphere, whose elites are still very much marked by the USSR's anti-clerical heritage, as in other regions where modernity has been identified as a Western value, Islamism is frequently counterposed to progress. Yet this ideology, at least when founded in the nineteenth century, especially in the Jadid form specific to the region, was not in the least opposed to modernity. On the contrary, the founding fathers of Islamism advocated a re-establishment of Islam in Muslim societies that was perfectly compatible with modern values. In many respects,

Islamism counts among the major ideologies that marked the nineteenth century, like socialism, liberalism and Marxism. At its inception, the Muslim Brotherhood is a good example of political Islam seeking to Islamize state and society, in order to govern them with laws founded on or inspired by Islam. In Central Asia, political Islam was above all embodied in the Party of Islamic Renaissance (PIR), active in Tajikistan until September 2015, when it was declared illegal by the government, whereas it was never recognized by the regimes in the other republics.

On the other hand, radical Islamism or violent Islamism, also called jihadism, is one of the extreme forms that Islamism can take. It may be illustrated by the case of the Taliban in Afghanistan or the international al-Qaeda movement and its various offshoots. In Central Asia, the Islamic Movement of Uzbekistan (IMU), which we shall discuss later, is an emanation of this radical jihadist Islam.

But Islamism can also be embodied in peaceful proselytizing movements that reject violence. Such is the philosophy of Tablighi Jamaat, founded in British India in the 1920s, which is the most transnational of Islamic movements. This Islam can also be related to Salafism, which, as its name indicates (*salaf* means 'ancestor' in Arabic), advocates Islam as practised at the time of the first Muslims, without concerning itself with the political character of state and government.

In Central Asia, the political authorities make no distinction between these different forms of Islam, all of which are officially rejected as fuelling oppositional Islam, and therefore sometimes forced to go underground. Erected into a sword of Damocles, the latter has played a significant role in the development of official religious policy. In return, the authorities' reaction to its expansion and handling of the religious question have played a decisive role in the scale and nature of the Islamic opposition. It is difficult to know who is primarily responsible for the stand-off, but there is no doubt that it exists and has proved extremely tense. As we have seen, the region's states administer and control official Islam and this variegated oppositional Islam differently. In fact, the latter is far from forming a monolithic bloc, as is often mistakenly believed. And it is a commonplace error to condemn uniformly all Islamic currents that express their dissatisfaction with the way in which the state runs religious affairs and interferes in them.

THE ADMINISTRATION OF RELIGION

In Central Asia, the initial seeds of oppositional Islam were sown in the 1970s, but this only involved a handful of followers trained by Domullah Hindustani, whose role in preserving the Islamic heritage in Central Asia we have already underscored. Bahtiyor Babadzhanov's profound work on the subject refers to a schism in characterizing the subsequent rupture between Hindustani and his followers. The latter,[15] having drunk at the source of the master's ideas, ended up deeming them too weak and indulgent towards the Soviet system and too lax towards 'straying' from Islam, which in their view had been perverted by illicit practices, particularly pilgrimages to holy places—and especially the mausoleums of mystical figures. A controversy also erupted over the conduct of daily prayers. The rebellious disciples, organized into an informal group called *Mujaddidiyya* (Arabic for 'renovation'), advocated the Hanbali method, which is very widespread in Saudi Arabia and regarded as optimal because it is practised in the birthplace of Islam and its prophet, Muhammad. This dissident group was labelled Wahhabi by Domullah Hindustani, referring to the philosophy of Muhammad Abud Wahhab, initiator of the Islamic ideology espoused by the Saudi kingdom founded by Ibn al Sa'ud.[16] The term, which (it is often forgotten) was first used by Hindustani to denigrate his disciples, enjoyed great success.

For now any Islamic movement in conflict with the authorities, directly or indirectly, was pejoratively characterized as 'Wahhabi' throughout the Soviet sphere. Notwithstanding its verbal violence, this debate over 'genuine' Islam and 'perverted' Islam remained confined to, and focused within, the group. It was exclusive to the elites of Soviet Islam, without any real impact on the wider population. Independence having altered the political and religious context, and allowed for a wider debate on Islam, the issue of Wahhabism aroused greater curiosity, including among ordinary believers. Predominantly used pejoratively by the authorities to denigrate all Islamic organizations that reject the state's monopoly on religious affairs, the term was adopted by the official media and is bandied about to refer to a multiplicity of realities. It is applied to the fundamentalists of Islam—that is, those who advocate practising Islam as it was practised at the time of the Prophet. The term also refers to Salafists, another form of fundamentalist Islam obsessed with a return to the origins of Islam. Widely used and abused, it also designates the political Islam whose foundations were laid during the Soviet era.

Authentically political Islam in Central Asia emerged with the foundation of the Party of Islamic Renaissance. It was set up by several Muslim intellectuals from throughout the Soviet Union in the city of Astrakhan in the Volga delta in 1990. Dominated in the main by Tatar and Caucasian Islamic leaders, the party established branches in Central Asia, particularly Tajikistan, where it was nurtured by Sayid Abdullah Nuri. It is currently led by Muhiddin Kabiri, who has lived in exile since September 2015, when the party was outlawed. Attempts to maintain a branch in Uzbekistan ended in failure, because the Uzbek authorities constantly put spokes in the wheels, preventing meetings from being held and pursuing and proscribing the least of its activities.[17] Although identifying with political Islam, the party is not comparable to those we observe in the Middle and Near East. While its original programme demanded the creation of an Islamic state, this is a long-term or even very long-term objective, for from the outset its leaders were conscious of the fact that it was first necessary to foster a spiritual revival and reconvert Central Asian Muslims, who had been secularized or, at any rate, profoundly marked by the Soviet anti-clerical heritage. A major political actor in the united Tajik opposition, the PIR, like all the country's other political formations, was drawn into the civil war that tore Tajikistan apart between 1992 and 1997. Its active involvement in the civil war sometimes served as a pretext for neighbouring countries—especially Uzbekistan—to conflate instability and political Islam. Yet while not exempt from responsibility for the violence and the death of several thousand people, which seriously affected its popularity, the PIR was actually among the most moderate forces in the conflict. Included in the political process during national reconciliation in 1997, it became the sole legalized Islamic party in Central Asia. But although associated with power, it has been consistently marginalized by the Tajik government, which misses no opportunity to criticize it for its indulgence towards, or even complicity with, the radical Islam that sometimes strikes at the country. On the pretext of collaborating with radical Islam, the party was banned in September 2015.

Oppositional Islam in Central Asia also comprises a radical, jihadist variant which, though marginal, should not be underestimated. It is above all embodied in the Islamic Movement of Uzbekistan (IMU), built on the ruins of several Islamic revivalist organizations active in the Fergana Valley after the end of the Soviet Union. One of them—*Adolat* (justice)—had two key figures in Uzbek jihadism, Juma Namangani and Tohir Yoldashev, as its founding leaders. The most famous episode in its history was the direct confrontation in 1990 between these two men and Islam Karimov, at the time general secretary of the Uzbek Communist Party. On a trip to Namangan, where there had been several incidents between the security forces and opposition groups, including religious organizations such as *Adolat*, Namangani and Yoldashev felt encouraged by the crowd following them and violently tackled Karimov to demand the restoration of an Islamic order in the country. Utterly symptomatic, the episode has entered posterity thanks to a video immortalizing it which still circulates widely on the internet.[18] Repressed by Karimov's regime, which constantly reinforced control over the religious groups challenging it, *Adolat* and its leaders were driven into exile in neighbouring Tajikistan, where, amid the disorder of the civil war, these Uzbek Islamists joined the ranks of the opposition to the neo-communists supported by Tashkent and Moscow.

An Islamist organization on its arrival in Tajikistan, *Adolat* was gradually transformed into a political movement and party, renaming itself *O'zbekistan Islami Harakati*, Islamic Movement of Uzbekistan. This veritable metamorphosis into an Islamic political structure occurred after 1997 when, with the end of the Tajik civil war, the Uzbek Islamists were forced into more remote exile and found refuge in Afghanistan, where the pervasive instability was conducive to their subversive activities against the Karimov regime. The latter had no respect for his opponents, whom he hunted relentlessly. The Islamic Movement of Uzbekistan proved to be not so much a formation with a veritable Islamist ideology, structured and cohesive, as a radical jihadist movement intent above all on putting an end to the Karimov regime by any means, including utilizing religious rhetoric for the purposes of mobilization. That said, in reality the IMU possesses meagre resources for achieving its ends.[19] In February 1999, Tashkent awoke to several simultaneous explosions targeted at institutions related to the security forces. Not claimed by anyone, the attacks were attributed to the IMU, though it is not certain that it was the perpetrator. At the same time, however, various guerrilla actions against the Uzbek and Kyrgyz security forces in different parts of the Fergana Valley were carried out by its men. Similarly, several terrorist acts were perpetrated by IMU militants in the region in 2004. However, following the IMU's settlement among its Taliban hosts in Afghanistan, it has gradually distanced itself from its original home and been absorbed by the international jihadist spiral. In fact, its links with the Taliban and al-Qaeda led it to join terrorist camps on the border between Afghanistan and Pakistan, where it is involved in opposing Pakistan and Afghan security forces. Decapitated by the elimination of Namangani and Yoldashev in US drone attacks in 2001 and 2009, the IMU has been weakened but continues to act in concert with Pakistani and Afghan jihadists.

More political, Hizb ut-Tahrir (Arabic for 'Party of Liberation') is the Central Asian Islamic movement by far the most monitored and combatted by the existing regimes, especially in Uzbekistan. The most surprising thing in Hizb ut-Tahrir's relative local success is that it is a formation which, historically, has no roots in Central Asia. Founded in Jordan by the Palestinian Taqiuddin al-Nabhani, this Islamist organization penetrated the region in the early 2000s. Ultra-secret and ferociously combatted by all regimes, it eludes observation and analysis. The main activity of its members, who are organized into small cells of three to five people, consists in disseminating literature and ideas that denounce the existing regimes' corruption.[20] Its obsessional watchword is reversion to the Caliphate, whose establishment on a global scale it advocates as the only true solution to all the ills of Muslims, whatever and wherever they are. Having rubbed shoulders with some of its members in Kyrgyzstan, I can say that this Islamist formation offers a glimpse of a completely dogmatic political organization, closer in some respects to a Marxist–Leninist approach than a classical Islamist movement. Its discourse is focused on restoring the Caliphate, but is virtually silent on everyday individual or collective religious practice. Its denunciation of corruption and poverty in Central Asia largely accounts for its apparent popularity. In fact, this is difficult to measure and confirm, inasmuch as the organization remains underground and the regimes, to justify repression of it but also to legitimate strict social and police control, tend to overestimate its strength, in order to postpone reform and attract the attention of international powers.[21]

THE ADMINISTRATION OF RELIGION

Oppositional Islam in Azerbaijan presents a similar picture of diversity, reinforced by the deep rift between Shia and Sunnis in the country. Inherited from history, this division has tended to become more marked since the end of the Soviet era. As in Central Asia, the origins of political Islam go back to the time of the USSR. Two formations—one an association, the other more structured as a political movement—have stood out in public. The first, the *Tövbe* or 'repentance' foundation, was created in the Baku region around the figure of Haji Ebdul, the mullah of a mosque in a popular quarter of the Azerbaijani capital. As its name indicates, the foundation calls upon Muslims to repent their sins and return to 'the right path, that of Islam'. Before 1991, *Tövbe* prioritized the fight against alcoholism, one of the worst social scourges afflicting post-Soviet societies. With the approach of independence, it became more politicized and Haji Ebdul was elected to the Azerbaijani parliament.[22] In conflict with the country's political and official religious authorities, the *Tövbe* foundation lost much of its aura. With independence, other movements emerged, thanks in particular to the formation of new elites abroad, in Iran, the Arab countries and Turkey.

In a similar context and affiliated to Shiism, though he does not highlight his confessional orientation, Haji Ilgar Ibrahimoglu personifies another Islamist oppositional tendency. Hailing from a family that was religious during the Soviet era, and having had the opportunity to pursue Islamic studies in Iran, for several years Ilgar Ibrahimoglu was the imam of the old city's Friday Mosque, one of the oldest in Baku. There was nothing personal about his rebellion against the official Islam embodied by the Directorate of Spiritual Affairs and its president, Allah Shukur Pashazadeh. He criticized the state for endeavouring to dominate people's consciences and denounced the *de facto* monopoly exercised by the government over what was said to be official Islam. He revolted against the state's wish to impose a single Islamic norm as regards worship, the running of mosques and the organization of Islamic education. This was an Islam in opposition, but not a radical one, in the sense that it did not advocate any resort to force.[23] It was also a politicized Islam in the sense that its leader, Haji Ilgar Ibrahimoglu, had no hesitation in publicly extending his support, and that of his community, to opposition parties, particularly *Musavat* ('Equality') and its leader, Isa Gamber.

ISLAM IN CENTRAL ASIA AND THE CAUCASUS

On the Sunni spectrum of oppositional Islam, we find the so-called Salafist community of the imam Gamet Suleimanov. Trained in several Arab countries, particularly the University of Medina, he has gathered around him a community of young Muslims with a strict, fundamentalist view of Islam, but one which is not jihadist.[24] Their main demand is to live their religion in freedom, without fear of repression or supervision in accordance with imposed norms that they do not recognize. Originally structured around the Abu Bakr mosque, the community has been deprived of this meeting place: the mosque was closed on government orders, on the pretext that it was liable to serve as a rallying point for radical jihadists of North Caucasian inspiration, Chechen and Daghestani in particular.[25] Gamet Souleimanov has distanced himself from the most Salafist and radical of the *Khawarij* ('expelled') group and clarified his positions. But the Azerbaijani state prefers to define all currents as 'Salafist' and repress them indiscriminately, at the risk of alienating malcontents even further and swelling the opposition's ranks.

In Azerbaijan, the most notable organization espousing political Islam is the *Azerbaycan Islam Partiyasi*, the Islamic Party of Azerbaijan. Its history is closely bound up with the city of Nardaran, whose religious character—it contains the tomb of Rahim Hanim, daughter of the seventh imam Musa al-Kazim—had already led to it resembling a sort of Islamic enclave during the Soviet era in a country subject to an anticlerical order. The party was founded by cadres and activists from the city at the end of the Soviet period. It was recognized and accredited by the authorities at independence, but a few years later returned underground, when a distrustful state refused renewal of its accreditation—that is, official registration with the Justice Ministry, allowing it to operate legally. Its first chairman, Alikram Aliev, was arrested and imprisoned with other cadres, officially for spying for Iran. The charge was probably unfounded, but the party and its cadres do have close links with Iran, which are natural and inevitable for a Shia organization.[26] The party programme opens by advocating the creation of an Islamic republic in Azerbaijan. But as the state has imposed its control over the whole country, and tightened its grip on the most radical opposition organizations, the party has downgraded its ambitions, prioritizing re-Islamization of the population and putting its strictly political ambitions second. Officially proscribed, it is nevertheless tolerated and continues to exist, regularly organizing meetings and publishing its official journal *Islam Sesi* ('The Voice of Islam'). During legislative or presidential elections, it usually supports the political party closest to its Islamist aspirations.

The Issue of Islamic Education and Instruments for Regulating Islam

The utilization of Islam in constructing the new identity of state and nation, which we have seen everywhere but to different degrees, was insufficiently convincing to secure unanimous popular support. Accordingly, the promotion of 'good Islam', as defined and desired by the authorities, required proactive measures to encourage its development and establishment, particularly among youth. Islamic education therefore became a priority. Educating future generations of good Muslims, faithful and loyal to their country, took the form of both educational and security measures.

The issue of education did not arise immediately after independence, but gradually imposed itself in response to part of the population, in its search for identity, expressing the need for their children to receive a genuinely religious education. Thus, the state invested in the educational issue as a way of promoting good Islam and ensuring the maintenance of a secular state.

During the Soviet period, Islamic education was entrusted to a severely restricted number of establishments, which trained the religious elites for the whole Soviet Union under the surveillance of official power.[27] In reality, a mere two institutions provided for the training of religious cadres: the Mir-i Arab madrasa in Bukhara and, to a lesser extent, the Bukhari Institute in Tashkent. Soviet Muslims from the Caucasus, Central Asia and Russia, from Tatarstan to Bashkortostan, attended these establishments and received the knowledge required to perform official Islamic duties. However, operating in parallel, more or less clandestinely, in several cities, in particular around places of pilgrimage and some traditional quarters, were *hujras*—informal cells where a certain Islamic instruction was disseminated. This generally involved someone with sufficient knowledge, inherited from parents, passing it on by giving private lessons to a small number of children in his locality. In the opinion of experts, it was thanks to the close-knit, relatively invisible character of these cells that Islam was well-preserved in these countries.[28] In Azerbaijan, for example, on the outskirts of the city of Sheki, I had the opportunity to observe how religious figures had devised textbooks for reading the Koran based on the model of an old Ottoman—hence pre-Soviet—textbook, without any authorization from the official Muslim leadership in the Caucasus. During my investigations in various parts of the region at different times, a number of these old local religious authorities testified to their involvement in the development and maintenance of such informal cells of Islamic teaching.

With independence, the demand for religious education coincided with the quest for identity and the construction of the state, thus becoming a crucial issue. But in all these countries the authorities were faced with a serious lack of instructors and educators to satisfy demand. So they cobbled things together, with the meagre resources at their disposal, and created various religious establishments, ranging from simple secondary schools (madrasas) to Islamic universities. Since its inception, this Islamic education has been a source of controversy and division among the official political and religious elites, who had divergent views on the place of religion in society and hence on the way to educate future generations. In spring 2016, intense debates occurred in Kyrgyzstan over the implementation of a new religious education policy, whose objective was to promote dissemination of a moderate Hanafi Sunni Islam derived from the teaching of the theologian Abu Mansur al-Maturidi, a native of Central Asia.[29] In Kyrgyzstan as in the other republics, the general tendency is to promote the legacy of this scholar of medieval Islam, which is thought the best solution to the spiritual needs of the new societies.

Things have been most difficult in Uzbekistan. Within the religious elites, among the cast of religious professionals, a climate of suspicion of tendencies charged with Wahhabism and Salafism has persisted. The threat of fundamentalist Islam and fears of Salafist infection of the regime and its secular cadres loomed large when an official programme of Islamic instruction was being established. It was not unusual for experts and government advisers on religious affairs to accuse one another of Salafism and Wahhabism. How often did eminent experts, well-known and influential in Islamic affairs in Uzbekistan, like

THE ADMINISTRATION OF RELIGION

Bahtiyor Babajanov, complain of the presence of Salafists on the team advising the president on religious matters? Similarly, Bahtiyor Babajanov reckoned that Salafist literature circulated quite legally in all religious establishments approved by the state, evading control and prohibition because of ignorance of radical doctrines on the part of the officials responsible for religious instruction.[30] Another colleague, Achirbek Muminov, likewise highly respected for his research on Islam in Central Asia, deplored a similar state of affairs in Kazakhstan, where President Nazarbayev unwittingly had himself advised by experts trained in various Arab countries under the influence of Salafism or the thinking of the Muslim Brotherhood.[31]

For this reason, and to avert the development of an oppositional Islam, the training of religious cadres who respect the state's secular principles is closely supervised. Some specific examples of educational establishments warrant a mention. In Tashkent, in April 1999, three months after the alleged Islamist explosions in the city, a presidential decree made the creation of the country's first Islamic university official. Being both a madrasa and a university, it had to reconcile, and even fuse, religious teaching and a secular mindset. The president's religious affairs advisers soon realized that the establishment was utterly failing in this objective and was instead contributing to the Islamization of youth. Attracting children from the most religious strata of society, it offered students a specialization that was not necessarily compatible with the secular, lay spirit desired and defended by the regime. Registering this drift, the Uzbek government proceeded to a total reorganization of the university in May 2006, appointing as its head Shuhrat Yovqochev, who had held the post of presidential adviser on religious affairs since October 2005. The changes introduced by the new rector transformed the Islamic university into a theology faculty where Islam was taught in a purely secular context. The restructuring followed the model of Washington University in Seattle in the USA, which the rector, along with other Uzbek academics, had visited in the context of a programme of cooperation between the Uzbek and American governments. During the regular interviews he granted us between September 2006 and June 2008, the rector constantly stressed his plan to train secular cadres who could provide an account of Islam that was depoliticized and compatible with modern times, where observance of Islamic precepts was a matter of personal choice rather than an obligation imposed by a group.[32]

The other countries of Central Asia, particularly Kazakhstan and Kyrgyzstan, were subject to the same constraints. However, unlike Uzbekistan, which has always been reluctant to cooperate with Muslim countries to train its religious cadres, the Kyrgyz, Kazakh and even Turkmen and Tajik authorities appealed widely to foreign partners to set up their religious education. In 2001, Kazakhstan founded the Nur-Mubarak University in the framework of cooperation with Hosni Mubarak's Egypt. Similarly, Turkey was a privileged partner for these countries in religious education. In Shymkent in southern Kazakhstan and Och in the south of Kyrgyzstan, Turkey participated in creating theology faculties as well as financing study in Turkish cities and universities through a residence and grants programme. In Turkmenistan, President Turkmenbashi's cult of personality was almost elevated to the rank of an official religion rivalling Islam, in particular through the inclusion of his *summa*, the *Ruhnama*,[33] on all the country's educational programmes. A single educational establishment saw the light there, once again on Turkish initiative. Open since independence, this theology faculty closed its doors in 2008, having supposedly accomplished its mission and trained the number of religious cadres strictly necessary for the country.[34]

By contrast, no religious education, even of an optional or discretionary character, has been introduced into primary and secondary schools in any of the region's countries. Courses approximating to moral indoctrination have been made compulsory in primary and secondary education, particularly in Uzbekistan. Called *marifat ve manaviyat*, enlightenment and spirituality, they prescribe the correct moral and ethical conduct for children to adopt in everyday life. To a certain extent, these courses replace the courses in 'scientific atheism' of the Soviet period and are like a form of religious instruction where the only thing retained is the moral substance directly involved in the functioning of society.[35]

When it comes to Islamic education, the case of Azerbaijan is somewhat apart, once again on account of its simultaneously Shia and Sunni character. During the Soviet period, because no such religious structure existed in Azerbaijan, all religious cadres, whether Shia or Sunni,

THE ADMINISTRATION OF RELIGION

were trained in Uzbekistan. The current supreme official religious authority, Allah Shukur Pashazadeh, was himself trained in Bukhara. Like the other countries, Azerbaijan sought its population's support for the new national ideology and used tools supplied in the context of organizing religious education to achieve its ends. Thus, several small madrasas were set up throughout the country, but above all two higher education establishments were created. An Islamic institute created in 1991 was transformed into an Islamic university in 1995 and entrusted to Haji Sabir. Although not formally mentioned in the establishment's official programme, teaching is more orientated towards Shiism and most of the students are Shia. On the other hand, the theology faculty founded by Turkey and affiliated to the state university of Baku is openly Sunni and follows the programme of Turkey's theology faculties. Both Islamic establishments have branches in several provincial cities, particularly in Lenkeran in the south and Sheki and Zakatala in the north and west of the country. In every instance, the curriculum is subject to strict control by the government, which, through its Higher Education Minister and Directorate of Spiritual Affairs, monitors the compliance of its programmes and teaching with respect for the state's secular character.

The difficulty involved in establishing an Islamic education in these countries extends to the Islamic literature required for teaching. The choice of textbooks, their conception and content, has never been unanimous among the religious professionals. Once again the sensitive issue of the distribution of literature, and all it entails in terms of the dissemination of ideas and indoctrination, illustrates and reveals a certain schizophrenia about religion among the post-Soviet elites. They combine a desire to meet popular demand for religious education and a strong attachment to secular values, inherited from the Soviet past. In the collective unconscious, however, those values are associated with colonization and the imposition of norms which are regarded as alien to the people, their culture and traditions, and are therefore potentially destabilizing.

With official propaganda, presidential speeches and educational and religious policies having proved inadequate to control religion, and for fear of seeing the country lapse into instability and chaos, all the post-Soviet regimes have developed policies for regulating religion. To this end, states have equipped themselves with suitable tools in the shape of powerful bodies and legislative measures, which have certainly made it possible to control religion, but often at the expense of religious freedom—dented or even flouted, and in some cases repressed by the elimination of discordant voices.

With the state's consolidation in a novel form or one inherited from the Soviet past, the authorities have put in place different instruments for controlling or regulating Islam from country to country. A legal arsenal of control measures has been devised and implemented, along with polices to integrate Islam into the new state and national ideology and identity. In general, each country has created a special ministry for religious affairs, called the State Committee for Religious Affairs (Uzbekistan), the Council of Religious Affairs (Tajikistan) and the State Committee for Working with Religious Bodies (Azerbaijan). In Uzbekistan, the State Committee operates directly under the authority of the presidential apparatus, within which the Presidential Adviser for Religious Affairs and Inter-Ethnic Relations decides the basic principles of religious policy with the president. The State Committee is composed not of religious figures, but of technocrats loyal to the system and political regime. A comparable structure exists in Azerbaijan and functions in almost the same way. In other words, it takes its orders directly from the presidential apparatus and is accountable to it, which demonstrates the importance of the religious issue for the political authorities.

The second tool for administering and controlling Islam is an institution composed of strictly religious figures, who possess higher education in Islamic studies and have at some stage of their career performed the role of imam, akhund or mullah, depending on the country and local terminology. In Uzbekistan, this is the Directorate of Spiritual Affairs, which exists in different forms in the other countries, where it is called kaziate or muftiate. With the disappearance of the Soviet Union, the Spiritual Administration of the Muslims of Central Asia (SADUM) disintegrated and each country created its own directorate out of its ashes.

Relations between the two structures—State Committee and Spiritual Directorate—are sometimes tense, for their respective spheres of competence are not always clearly demarcated. In Uzbekistan, things are simpler because the State Committee has absolute control over the Spiritual Directorate. But in Azerbaijan, relations between the two apparatuses are more ambiguous and it is not uncommon to see the chairman of the State Committee and the spiritual head of the country publicly arguing about political or religious issues. Elsewhere—in Turkmenistan, Kazakhstan, Kyrgyzstan and Tajikistan—the political imposes its views on the religious with less difficulty.

What does the work of the State Committee and Spiritual Directorate consist of? How are they distinguished from one another? And how are they complementary? What are their shortcomings? In fact, the two of them, sometimes with the support of the Justice Ministry, are responsible for all needs and for answering all questions concerning Islam. Firstly, they give their approval to the registration of any new mosque or religious association or organism. The rules are strict throughout Central Asia, and ultra-strict in Uzbekistan and Turkmenistan, where the procedures are extremely exacting. To obtain legal status, a religious association must collect between 200 and 500 signatures depending on the country, deposit a complete administrative file, and overcome various obstacles, particularly those erected by the security forces, police and intelligence agencies. Similarly, mosques must be registered with the State Committee for Religious Affairs, which gives its authorization in dribs and drabs. Such obstacles are a major problem, especially for small religious communities like the Baha'is, followers of Ahmadiyya, or small Christian communities like Baptists, Pentecostalists or Jehovah's Witnesses. Moreover, the government frowns on the proliferation of mosques, which then become more difficult to control. In any event, in Uzbekistan and increasingly in Tajikistan, as well as in the region's other countries to a lesser extent, Friday prayers are permitted in a limited number of mosques, for the authorities would appear to lack the resources to control the content, audience and impact of every *khutbah*. The topic of Friday's preaching is up to the imam, but it can be imposed by the government via the Spiritual Directorate. This is sometimes the case in Uzbekistan, where Tashkent orders its imams to deal with issues of national interest like eulogizing the nation, the constitution and sometimes even the president, projected as protector and benefactor of Islam. Similarly, it is for the Spiritual Administration, in agreement with the State Committee, to appoint and, if needs be, revoke the imams who officiate in the country's mosques. They are selected in accordance with criteria of loyalty to the regime and fidelity to the values of national, traditional, official Islam, as promoted by the government. In Azerbaijan, imams are appointed according to the same rules, but respecting the Shia-Sunni dichotomy. Moreover—and this has been the case since the Soviet period—the number two in the Spiritual Directorate is always a Sunni, while its chairman is always a Shia. Despite this control over associations, mosques and imams, some establishments operate without a legal basis. The government tolerates them when they are small, isolated mosques, attended by the elderly, which are so haphazard that they lack sufficient resources for official registration and present no threat to government. By contrast, religious figures who are refractory to state control are systemically harassed and expelled from their mosque. Some, like Haji Ilgar and Gamet Suleimanov in Azerbaijan, continue to defy the authorities, appearing in the media and in public to point up their popularity and make themselves untouchable by the government. By refusing them a legal existence and recognized meeting place, the government simply makes them even more popular. Thus, they put the political authorities, forced to recognize their weakness, in a difficult position.

The control of Islamic education, publishing and literature is among the prerogatives of the organs that control religion—the State Committee and Spiritual Directorate. They decide on importing certain works, like translations of the Koran in various local languages and dialects. Religious education in the mosques is well-nigh systematically banned and confined to public establishments registered and controlled by the state. However, such are the restrictions in religious affairs that, as in the days of the Soviet Union, there is a growth in clandestine *hujras*—informal cells of religious teaching by some local authority. These represent an internal threat for the government and could be a cause for concern.

The official instruments of control are not in fact sufficient. The political authorities also resort to repression of any form of Islam regarded as incompatible with official norms and dangerous for internal stability. Thus, reports by a number of human rights organizations, such as Human Rights Watch, Forum 18, or the United States

Commission on International Religious Freedom,[36] frequently denounce flagrant violations of freedom of conscience and condemn campaigns of violent repression perpetrated in the name of security. In all reports on the state of religious freedom in these countries, frequent reference is made to the arbitrary role of the law, which criminalizes any activity that is not officially registered and even any non-conformist dress code. In Uzbekistan, the anti-terrorist law passed in 2000 in itself represents a flagrant violation of the individual rights guaranteed in principle by the Uzbek constitution, as by the international accords to which the country is a signatory. It facilitates and legitimates all forms of repression. The phobia about extremist Islam, the obsession with completely eliminating Hizb ut-Tahrir from the country and, generally, a fear of any dissident Islam have resulted in the arbitrary, unjustified arrest of hundreds of people who are either innocent or guilty merely of having distributed tracts or religious literature, not necessarily of an Islamist character, but unwelcome to the government. Moreover, it is not unusual for religious policy, on account of its incoherence, to contradict itself completely. Thus in Uzbekistan, for example, as we saw in the chapter devoted to Turkish influence in Central Asia, students who attended Turkish schools when they operated perfectly legally on Uzbek territory have been prosecuted for adhering to the 'seditious' ideas of Fethullah Gülen, the inspiration behind those Turkish schools.

Conclusion: The Primacy of a Security Approach in Administering Religion

The climate of political and social effervescence created by *perestroika* and the early years of independence brought relative religious freedom to every country in Central Asia and the Caucasus. These initial surges of religiosity and religious curiosity made it possible for various currents of thinking to emerge and express themselves without being unduly bothered by the state apparatuses. We can therefore say that the relations between state and religion experienced a certain discontinuity, in the sense that the public sphere was now shared by state and society, whereas previously it was wholly monopolized by official institutions. The break with the past was not total, however, and the state's attitude to religion was also continuous with the Soviet era. Thus, benevolence towards Islam betokened neither complete freedom for religious actors, nor an absence of surveillance and control. In the event, the spirit of openness towards Islam was relative and selective. Rather than a separation between state and Islam, rather than a neutral and open secularism, state supremacy in religious affairs—a kind of militant, liberticidal secularism—actually prevailed.

Despite surveillance intended to ensure the security of young states that had just achieved independence, a certain oppositional Islam developed. In many respects, it might even be said that this religious dissidence was fuelled and reinforced by states' surveillance policies. Thus, the birth of an oppositional, radical Islam was at once cause and consequence of state policies for administering religion. More than a domestic opposition, what states principally feared and sought to fend off was foreign Islamic currents and traditions. Despite all the measures of surveillance and deterrence, however, notwithstanding all the efforts to ban or, alternatively, supervise any encounter between their Islam and foreign, globalized Islam, that encounter did occur. In fact, despite all precautions on the part of states, Central Asian Islam naturally and inevitably reconnected with currents and ideas from regions with which, prior to the establishment of the Russian and Soviet order, it had had strong ties. Thus, in spite of all the measures taken, influences from Turkey, Iran, the Arabian Peninsula and the Indian subcontinent arrived, as we have seen, to impact on Islam and the societies of Central Asia and the Caucasus.

CONCLUSION

THE END OF ISLAM IN THE SINGULAR

Approximately one generation after the implosion of the USSR, the post-Soviet zone had fragmented into fifteen new states, which inherited borders and populations that they had not chosen, let alone forged into a nation in the course of history. The search for identity, common to a disorientated population deprived of the USSR as a source of pride and a state lacking geographical and historical legitimacy, generated formidable cultural impetus in these countries in the early 1990s. However, nation-building rapidly assumed the form of negative self-differentiation, falling back on what each country was not, compared with its neighbour, as opposed to what it intrinsically was. These processes intensified the individuation of each of the zone's countries, which thereafter evolved differently. Among the profound cultural upheavals, multiform changes in Islam are specific to each society. They are all the more interesting to observe and study because they have resulted in a marked religious revival in less than twenty-five years, characterized by diversity in its forms and its openness to foreign influences, the strongest of which did not necessarily hail from where they were expected.

In fact, since the emergence of newly independent republics, states and societies have followed different paths, which have impacted differently on the development of Islam and fostered diversification in beliefs and practices. The Spiritual Administration that managed all of Central Asian Islam from Tashkent in the Soviet era no longer exists. Nor does the one based in Baku that administered Caucasian Islam. With independence, each country equipped itself with a national mufti who administered religious affairs on behalf of the state, in accordance with political imperatives and interests peculiar to each country. In fact, the administration of worship, the administration and organization of religious spaces but also of education, and the relations established with the Islam of other countries—these were determined by procedures that had been approved by the government or even imposed by it on the religious community and authorities. Different national contexts skew generalization to such an extent that it is hard for cross-sectional studies to refer to 'Central Asian Islam'. We must therefore analyse the development of local Islam at country level, paying particular attention to the links between Islam, politics, state and society. However, diversification in the administration of Islam does not necessarily entail diversification in the way that Islam is given expression in each country. The paradox is as follows. With the opening of borders, relative religious freedom allowed for a liberation of religious needs and forms of expression, fostering a proliferation of religious actors and movements. But ultimately, such is the formatting of religion by state control that it results in a certain homogenization of national Islam. In fact, while open borders provide new opportunities for forms of religious inspiration, and are likely to render Islam in each country plural, policies for constructing state, nation, and ethnic and religious identity tend to foster a homogenous national Islam more amenable to facilitating the political authorities' control over society and country.

Thus, during the early years of independence, the new states permitted religious freedom that allowed Islam to flourish in diversity and open itself up to multiple outside influences. Gradually, however, as threats of political destabilization loomed and forms of authoritarianism were reinforced, the states imposed a controlled form of national, uniform, official Islam to various degrees. Thus, each endowed itself with a 'good' Islam, a *preconceived Islam*, supposed to be the respectable guarantor of national traditions when it was in fact merely an instrument of social control serving political purposes. The desire to control Islam in order to channel the construction of the nation-state more effectively compelled political interference in religion, despite the secular framework of the state inherited from the Soviet era to which

CONCLUSION

the new elites pledged allegiance. They justify this paradox by their wish to protect society from bad external Islamic influences, which might prevent modern, secular republics from taking their place on the international stage. For this reason, they favour not a 'genuine' secularism, but a form of official religion in the shape of a Sunni Islam loyal to the teachings of traditional Sunnism represented by Abu Hanifah and al-Maturidi. This is particularly true of Uzbekistan and Tajikistan, the countries where the Islamic legacy is strongest. There, as in the rest of the region but even more so, the state is not a neutral secular actor that leaves it to society and its members to organize Islam, but a highly interventionist force, which imposes its view of religion and religious practice, defining its precise, acceptable forms. Thus, ostensibly in the name of social peace and domestic stability, the state decides who is authorized to engage in religious activity and within what framework, even if it means expelling and banning from the public sphere all competing forms of Islam, foreign influences deemed undesirable, and any opposition movement on the grounds of fallacious proselytizing. Thus, not only are the most openly extremist Islamic tendencies marginalized—which is understandable—but so are moderate tendencies unlikely to follow the official line. This is notably the case with Sufism and the Islam of the brotherhoods, traditionally highly influential in Central Asia. In fact, though we have not discussed it at length in this book, in a country like Uzbekistan, where the Naqshbandi was born, Sufi Islam is not allowed to develop autonomously by the official authorities. In the name of an official policy of promoting scholarly, wise and peaceful Islam, Sufi Islam has been recuperated by the government, which has transformed its institutions—convents, mazars and mausoleums—into sites for expressing undying loyalty and fidelity to the state. Thus, paradoxically, states have permitted an openness to religious globalization, resulting in Islam's enrichment and diversification, but at the same time stifled unduly pluralistic expressions of it, as potentially subversive and threatening to its own survival, in favour of a single, strict definition of acceptable religion. In this, the post-Soviet states have not made a clean break with the Soviet ideology and practice of controlling religion. On the contrary, there is a certain continuity between past and present.

Another striking fact in Islam's development in the ex-USSR since 1991 is that the break with the past and inclusion in globalization entail cooperation, voluntary or forced, with various foreign Islamic influences. Their geographical origin is varied, to say the least, and the way they operate locally is surprising. Contrary to all expectations, it is not the champions of Islam, who present themselves as such or whose objective is the defence or dissemination of Islam, who have most marked the post-Soviet sphere. Contradicting initial Western fears, neither Iran nor Saudi Arabia, for all their considerable presence in the Caucasus and Central Asia, has evinced any real desire or capacity to impose itself in these territories, which have been left spiritually and ideologically fallow by the collapse of the communist system. In fact, it is republican, secular Turkey that has been most instrumental in fashioning Islam in these countries. The Turks have invested massive financial and human resources in the whole region to develop the religious education system and train new elites. Paradoxically, once again, we see the extent to which the secular Turkish republic conducts itself as an Islamic actor when it comes to defending its national interests, promoting its image abroad and expanding its zone of influence to satisfy its aspirations to regional leadership. Conversely, the Islamic Republic of Iran has not engaged to the same extent in Shia proselytism, although it features among its supreme national interests. These two leading countries in the Muslim world are therefore not lacking in pragmatic contradictions and internal paradoxes, depending on international circumstances. Turkey's influence over the region is so profound that it informs the official national Islam promoted by the new states. Although they do not admit it, they organize and administer Hanafi Sunni Islam as if making it an official religion, relegating the Sufi heritage and local particularisms, and affirming loud and clear loyalty to the principles of secularism, inherited from Kemalism and the Soviet model respectively.

The ongoing development of Iran and Turkey will doubtless clarify the situation in this regard. Erdoğan's Turkey is increasingly heading towards a manifestly Islamic role and model. Turkey's growing Islamization is beginning to cause concern and suspicion in the post-Soviet republics, which never look favourably on close cooperation with a power that is ideologically or religiously too committed. Cooperating with Teheran might rapidly alter the regional situation and create interest and goodwill in a number of countries, which are now

CONCLUSION

turning away from Turkey. The exchange of roles between Turkey and Iran in the jockeying for influence in the region is to be monitored closely, including in its religious dimension and in view of the past influence noted above. Will this geopolitical reversal be sufficient to bring about a reversal in the religious situation?

For now, analysis indicates that every Muslim country in the post-Soviet sphere is absorbing a certain dose of Turkish, Arab, Iranian or Indo-Pakistani influence, which it assimilates more or less successfully depending on the strength of popular spiritual demand and the resources invested in official control of religion. The model is constructed in line with the previous history of the country and its population and with the geostrategic situation, but also depending on the economic resources that do or do not enable it to open up to a particular external influence. Thus, two countries that are comparable in terms of population, but which do not have the same resources or the same past—Turkmenistan and Kyrgyzstan—have diametrically opposite ways of managing the relations between politics and religion. The same might be said of Uzbekistan and Kyrgyzstan, which have different perceptions of Islam and consequently developed different strategies for dealing with religious phenomena. Whatever the preferred mode of regulation, the six post-Soviet republics of Central Asia and Azerbaijan, whether they like it or not, are subject to external influence because of their involvement in the globalization of religion, which at the same time ensures their inclusion in the international community.

To be convinced of this, it is enough to observe how these countries have recently responded to the 'crusades' against jihadism launched by the international community. Neighbours of Afghanistan, having become a battlefield in the struggle against Islamist radicalism, the Central Asian republics have all participated in the international community's struggle against the Taliban and their protégés, whether from Central Asia or elsewhere. In addition to legitimate security concerns, on account of Afghanistan's proximity and the presence of Central Asian and Caucasian jihadists in the Afghan–Pakistani zone, all the countries have cooperated with the international coalition with a view to improving their position internationally. By offering their services to countries important to them, such as the USA, the European Union and Russia, they have acquired a real relevance to the national and supra-national interests of the powerful. Thus, for these six post-Soviet countries with a Muslim culture, the fight against terrorism has been, and remains, a way of playing an international role. Today, the international community is focused on a different jihadist terrain. The Middle East is in the process of supplanting the Afghan theatre, and the fight against the 'Islamic State' organization has become the Western powers' absolute priority. Like others, the countries of the Caucasus and Central Asia have nationals who have left to join jihad in Syria and Iraq. The very presence of these fighters on foreign territory, after so many decades of Soviet isolation and Tsarist isolation prior to that, is symptomatic of post-Soviet Islam's integration into the rest of the Muslim world. Unfortunately, it is not a positive signal. Varieties of extremism are succeeding in recruiting nihilistic, suicidal, berserk individuals among those left behind by today's world. Cooperation with the international community in the fight against jihadist terrorism is conducive to the international integration of the post-Soviet states. At the same time, domestically, the scarecrow of the extremist threat, embodied *inter alia* by 'Islamic State', is subject to facile political exploitation, justifying repressive religious policies in most countries of Central Asia and the Caucasus—and this with the tacit assent of Western partners petrified by the global expansion of jihadism. At all events, with the exception of a handful of paid-up jihadist nihilists, the forms of Islam germinating in Central Asia and the Caucasus distance themselves from all forms of extremism, which they condemn, advocating apolitical moderation and pacifism.

After three generations of political, human, cultural and religious isolation, the Muslim peoples of Central Asia and the Caucasus are recreating and rediscovering their place in the great global Islamic community—the *ummah*—closing the Russo-Soviet parenthesis. But the reunion is not palpable. It has not yet given rise to the creation of close links, because everything is to be reconstructed—popular religiosity as well as the means of enriching it by contact with the other. For in the interim, during the Russian and Soviet experience, the Russian Empire's Muslims and their descendants have changed. The Turkish, Arab, Iranian and Indo-Pakistani brothers in religion who are their neighbours, and sometimes their cousins, have themselves developed considerably during the twentieth century and at the start of the twenty-first. In addi-

CONCLUSION

tion, the peoples of Central Asia and the Caucasus are recreating their relationship with the Muslim religion and world, not from where they had got to, but in practice starting from scratch. The bases have been eroded after three generations of ideological atheism and religious control, even repression. Consequently, differentiated national Islamic identities are in the process of being constructed throughout Central Asia and the Caucasus on the basis of new interpretations of past legacies, and new perceptions of foreign religious phenomena, under the watchful, guiding eye of the governing elites. The future will tell if they are going to reinforce the great global Islamic surge or to undermine it from within, by dividing it more than it is today.

NOTES

PREFACE

1. Translation by Jonathan Laurence, Boston College.

INTRODUCTION: THE END OF THE USSR AND A NEW PERCEPTION OF RELIGION

1. Olivier Roy, 'Islam et politique en Asie centrale', *Archives de sciences sociales des religions*, no. 115, 2001, pp. 49–61.
2. Shoshana Keller, *To Moscow, Not Mecca: The Soviet Campaign against Islam in Central Asia 1917–1941*, Praeger: Westport, CT, 2001.
3. Yaacov Ro'i, *Islam in the Soviet Union: From the Second World War to Perestroika*, Columbia University Press: New York, 2000.
4. On this issue in particular, see Stephane A. Dudoignon, and Christian Noack, *Allah's Kolkhozes: Migration, De-Stalinisation, Privatisation and the New Muslim Congregations in the Soviet Realm (1950s-2000s)*, Klaus Schwarz Verlag: Berlin, 2014.
5. Adeeb Khalid, *The Politics of Muslim Cultural Reform: Jadidism in Central Asia*, University of California Press: Oakland, CA, 2007.
6. Bakhtiyar Babadjanov, and Muzaffar Kamilov, 'Muhammadjan Hindustani (1892–1989) and the Beginning of the "Great Schism" among Muslims in Uzbekistan', in Stephane A. Dudoignon, and Hisao Komatsu, *Islam and Politics in Russia and Central Asia (Early Eighteenth to Late Twentieth Centuries)*, Routledge: Abingdon, 2001.
7. Michael Kemper, Raoul Motika and Stefan Reichmuth, *Islamic Education in the Soviet Union and its Successor States*, Routledge: Abingdon, 2000.

1. INHERITED ISLAM: AN ISLAM MARKED BY RUSSIAN AND SOVIET DOMINATION

1. Lucien Kehren, *Tamerlan: l'empire du seigneur de fer*, La Braconnière: Neuchâtel, 1978.
2. Frederick Starr, *Lost Enlightenment: Central Asia's Golden Age from the Arab Conquest to Tamerlane*, Princeton University Press: Princeton, NJ, 2013, pp. 492–500.
3. Edward Allworth, *The Modern Uzbeks from the Fourteenth Century to the Present: A Cultural History*, Hoover Institution Press: Stanford, CA, 1990, p. 229.
4. The Shaybanids were a Mongol dynasty descending from Shiban, one of the sons of Jochi, himself the eldest son of Genghis Khan. Their people adopted the name of Uzbeks with reference to Uzbeg, a relative who was khan of the Golden Horde.
5. Pierre Chuvin, René Létolle and Sébastien Peyrouse, *Histoire de l'Asie centrale contemporaine*, Fayard: Paris, 2008, pp. 87–103.
6. David Christian, 'Silk Road or Steppe Roads? The Silk Roads in World History', *Journal of World History*, vol. 11, no. 1, 2000, pp. 1–26.
7. Adeeb Khalid, *Islam after Communism*, University of California Press: Oakland, CA, 2014, pp. 29–31.
8. On the mirrors and Islam, see Jocelyne Dakhlia, 'Les miroirs des princes islamiques: une modernité sourde?', *Annales. Histoire, Sciences Sociales*, vol. 57, no. 5, 2002, pp. 1191–1206.
9. Khalid, *Islam after Communism*.
10. Tadeusz Swietochowski, *Russian Azerbaijan, 1905–1920: The Shaping of a National Identity in a Muslim Community*, Cambridge University Press: Cambridge, 1985, pp. 1–37.
11. Andreas Kappeler, Gerhard Simon and Georg Brunner, *Muslim Communities Reemerge: Historical Perspectives on Nationality, Politics, and Opposition in the Former Soviet Union and Yugoslavia*, Duke University Press: Durham, NC, 1994, p. 147.
12. Khalid, *Islam after Communism*, p. 29.
13. Komatsu Hisao, 'The Andijan Uprising Reconsidered', in Sato Tsugitaka, *Muslim Societies: Historical and Comparative Perspectives*, Routledge: Abingdon, 2004, pp. 29–61.
14. Keller, *To Moscow, Not Mecca*, pp. 5–29.
15. Hakan Kirimli, *National Movements and National Identity among the Crimean Tatars (1905–1916)*, Brill: Leiden, 1996, pp. 32–55.
16. Audrey Alstadt, *The Azerbaijani Turks: Power and Identity under Russian Rule*, Hoover Institute Press: Stanford, CA, 1992, pp. 50–73.
17. Ibid., pp. 89–107.
18. Khalid, *The Politics of Muslim Cultural Reform*, pp. 245–78.

19. Ludmila Polonskaya, and Alexei Malashenko, *Islam in Central Asia*, Ithaca Press: Reading, 1994, pp. 89–90.
20. Ro'i, *Islam in the Soviet Union*, pp. 550–89.
21. Khalid, *Islam after Communism*, p. 70.
22. Chantal Lemercier-Quelquejay, 'Islam and Identity in Azerbaijan', *Central Asian Survey*, vol. 3, no. 2, 1984, pp. 29–55.
23. Keller, *To Moscow, Not Mecca*, pp. 141–55.
24. Stephane A. Dudoignon, 'Islam et nationalisme en Asie centrale au début de la période soviétique (1924–1937). L'exemple de l'Ouzbékistan, à travers quelques sources littéraires', *Revue des mondes musulmans et de la Méditerranée*, 2002, pp. 95–8, http://remmm.revues.org/230
25. Allworth, *The Modern Uzbeks*, pp. 3–79.
26. Olivier Roy, 'Ethnies et politique en Asia centrale', *Revue du monde musulman et de la Méditerranée*, nos. 59/60, 1992, pp. 17–37, http://remmm.revues.org/persee-178997
27. Olivier Roy, *La nouvelle Asie centrale ou la fabrication des nations*, Seuil: Paris, 1997.
28. Laura Adams, 'Public and Private Celebrations: Uzbekistan's National Holidays', in Jeff Sahadeo and Russell Zanca, *Everyday Life in Central Asia, Past and Present*, Indiana University Press: Bloomington, IN, 2007, pp. 198–213.
29. Ariane Zevaco, 'From Old to New Matcha: Mass Resettlement and the New Redefinition of Islamic Practice between Tajikistan's Upper Valleys and Cotton Lowlands', in Dudoignon, *Allah's Kolkhozes*, pp. 148–201.
30. Dudoignon, *Allah's Kolkhozes*, pp. 9–46.
31. Olivier Roy, 'En Asie centrale: kolkhozien et entreprenants', in Jean-François Bayart, *La Réinvention du capitalisme*, Karthala: Paris, 1994, pp. 73–86.
32. Khalid, *Islam after Communism*, p. 105.
33. Catherine Poujol, *L'Islam en Asie centrale: vers la nouvelle donne*, Ellipse: Paris, 2001.
34. Silvia Serrano, 'L'Eglise orthodoxe géorgienne, un référent identitaire ambigu', in Bayram Balci and Raoul Motika, *Religion et politique dans le Caucase post soviétique*, Maisonneuve et Larose: Paris, 2007, pp. 251–76.
35. Babadjanov and Kamilov, 'Muhammadjan Hindustani', pp. 195–219.
36. Dudoignon, *Allah's Kolkhozes*, pp. 9–46.
37. Timothy Edmunds, 'The Environmental Movement in Kazakhstan: Ecology, Democracy and Nationalism', in Stephen Hussey and Paul Thompson, *The Roots of Environmental Consciousness*, Routledge: New York, 2000, pp. 139–59.
38. Dilip Hiro, *Inside Central Asia: A Political and Cultural History of*

Uzbekistan, Turkmenistan, Kazakhstan, Kyrgyzstan, Tajikistan, Turkey and Iran, Overlook Press: New York, 2009, pp. 244–5.
39. Ibid., pp. 125–91.
40. Bayram Balci, 'Le renouveau islamique en Azerbaïdjan entre dynamiques internes et influences extérieures', *Études du CERI*, no. 138, 2007, http://www.sciencespo.fr/ceri/sites/sciencespo.fr.ceri/files/etude138.pdf
41. Krisztina Kehl-Bodrogi, *'Religion is not so strong here': Muslim Religious Life in Khorezm after Socialism*, Halle Studies in the Anthropology of Eurasia, no. 18, Lit Verlag: Berlin, 2008.
42. Starr, *Lost Enlightenment*, pp. 1–28.
43. Robert Saunders, 'A Forgotten Core? Mapping the Globality of Central Asia', *Globality Studies Journal*, 2010, http://www.oalib.com/paper/2178855#.U81fl1d5Bqw
44. Patrick Domborwsky, 'L'Asie centrale face à la mondialisation', *La Pensée*, no. 338, 2004, pp. 37–45.

2. TURKEY AS AN ISLAMIC ACTOR IN CENTRAL ASIA AND THE CAUCASUS

1. Lowell Bezanis, 'Soviet Muslim Émigrés in the Republic of Turkey', *Central Asian Survey*, vol. 13, no. 1, 1994, pp. 59–180.
2. Ibid.
3. Mustafa Aydin, 'Foucault's Pendulum: Turkey in Central Asia and the Caucasus', *Turkish Studies*, vol. 5, no. 2, 2004, pp. 1–22.
4. Ibid.
5. Carlo Frappi, *Central Asia's Place in Turkey's Foreign Policy*, Instituto per Gli Studi di Politica Internazionale (ISP), no. 225, 2013, http://www.ispionline.it/sites/default/files/pubblicazioni/analysis_225_2013.pdf
6. Bertrand Buchwalter, 'Les sommets de la Turcophonie', in Bayram Balci and Bertrand Buchwalter, *La Turquie en Asie centrale: La conversion au réalisme 1991–2000*, Institut Français d'Études Anatoliennes (IFEA): Istanbul, http://www.ifea-istanbul.net/dossiers_ifea/Bulten_05.pdf
7. Idris Bal, 'The Turkish Model and the Turkic Republics', in Vedat Yücel and Salomon Ruysdael, *New Trends in Turkish Foreign Affairs*, Writers Club Press: New York, 2002, pp. 211–34.
8. Gareth Winrow, *Turkey's Energy Aspirations: Pipe Dream or Real Projects?*, Brookings Institute Policy Paper no. 4, April 2014, http://www.brookings.edu/~/media/research/files/papers/2014/04/realization%20turkeys%20energy%20aspirations%20winrow/turkeys%20energy%20aspirations.pdf

9. Lerna Yanik, 'The Politics of Education Exchange: Turkish Education in Eurasia', *Europe-Asia Studies*, vol. 56, no. 2, 2004, pp. 293–307.
10. Bayram Balci, 'Hoca Ahmet Yesevi: le mausolée et l'université', *Cahiers d'Études sur la Méditerranée Orientale et le monde Turco-Iranien*, no. 27, 1999, http://cemoti.revues.org/67, accessed 24 April 2016.
11. Jacob Landau, and Barbara Kellner-Heinkele, *Language Politics in Contemporary Central Asia: National and Ethnic Identity and the Soviet Legacy*, I. B. Tauris: London, 2012.
12. Zafer Yorük, and Pantelis Vatikiotis, 'Izmir University of Economics: Soft Power or Illusion of Hegemony', *International Journal of Communication*, vol. 7, 2013, pp. 2361–85.
13. Kanykei Tursunbaeva, 'Central Asia's Rulers View Turkish "Soap Power" with Suspicion', *Global Voices*, 7 August 2014, http://globalvoicesonline.org/2014/08/07/central-asias-rulers-view-turkish-soap-power-with-suspicion
14. Firat Purtas, 'Kültürel Diplomasi ve TÜRKSOY', http://mekam.org/mekam/kulturel-diplomasi-ve-turksoy
15. Berg Fragner, 'Soviet Nationalism: An Ideological Legacy to the Independent Republics of Central Asia', in Willem van Schendel and Erik J. Zürcher, *Identity Politics in Central Asia and the Muslim World*, I. B. Tauris: London, 2001, pp. 13–34.
16. Forced into exile, the Uzbek nationalist opposition, represented by the *Birlik* (Unity) Party led by Abdurrahman Polatov and *Erk* (Liberty) Party headed by Muhammad Salih, settled in Turkey from 1993. Embarrassed by the affair, Ankara, which could not agree to President Karimov's demand for the extradition of his opponents to Uzbekistan, did everything it could to prevent deterioration in its relations with Tashkent. Its support for the opposition was very limited and predominantly the work of private foundations that did not represent Turkey's official position. But the very fact of refusing to return them to Tashkent significantly worsened relations between Turkey and Uzbekistan, which are still in a parlous state.
17. Ertan Efegil, 'Turkish AK Party's Central Asia and Caucasus Policies: Critiques and Suggestions', *Caucasian Review of International Affairs*, vol. 2, no. 3, 2008, pp. 166–72, http://www.cria-online.org4_6.html
18. Ibid.
19. Bayram Balci, and Stéphane de Tapia, 'Mouvements migratoires entre la Turquie et les Républiques turcophones du Caucase et d'Asie centrale: les impacts religieux', *Revue européenne des migrations internationales*, vol. 26, no. 3, 2010, http://remi.revues.org/5225.
20. On the foundations and operation of *Diyanet*, see Istar Gozaydin, *Diyanet, Türkiye Cumhuriyetinde Dinin Tanzimi*, Iletisim Yayinlari: Istanbul,

2009. See also Istar Gozaydin, '*Diyanet* and Politics', *Muslim World*, vol. 98, nos. 2–3, pp. 216–27, April 2008, http://onlinelibrary.wiley.com/doi/10.1111/j.1478-1913.2008.00220.x/abstract

21. Elise Massicard, 'L'organisation des rapports entre État et religion en Turquie', *CRDF*, no. 4, 2005, pp. 119–28, http://www.unicaen.fr/puc/ecrire/revues/crdf/crdf4/crdf0411breuillard.pdf

22. On *Diyanet*'s services in Europe, see Benjamin Bruce, 'Gérer l'Islam à l'étranger; entre service public et outil de la politique étrangère turque', *Revue Anatoli*, no. 3, 2012, pp. 131–47.

23. Baskýn Oran, 'Occidentalisation, nationalisme et "synthèse turco-islamique"', *Cahiers d'Études sur la Méditerranée Orientale et le monde Turco-Iranien*, no. 10, 1990, http://cemoti.revues.org/417; placed online 30 March 2004 and accessed 1 June 2016.

24. Sedat Laçiner, 'Turgut Özal Period in Turkish Foreign Policy: Özalism', *Journal of Turkish Weekly*, 9 March 2009, http://www.turkishweekly.net/print.asp?type=2&id=333

25. Mehmet Özkan, 'Turkey's Religious and Socio-Political Depth in Africa', *London School of Economics*, http://www.lse.ac.uk/IDEAS/publications/reports/pdf/SR016/SR-016-Ozkan.pdf

26. On the activities of the Eurasian Islamic Council, see the *Diyanet* site: URL: http://www.avrasya-is.org/eski/index.php?Zm9ua3NpeW9uX2FkaT1hbmFzYXlmYV9pY2VyaWdp

27. Şenol Korkut, 'The Diyanet of Turkey and its Activities in Eurasia after the Cold War', *Acta Slavica Iaponica*, vol. 28, pp. 117–39, http://src-hokudai-ac.jp/publictn/acta/28/06Korkut.pdf

28. Iren Özgür, *Islamic Schools in Modern Turkey: Faith, Politics and Education*, Cambridge University Press: Cambridge, 2012.

29. There is an abundant literature in Turkish and English on Said Nursi and his thought. See in particular Mardin, Serif, *Religion and Social Change in Modern Turkey: The Case of Bediuzzaman Said Nursi*, State University of New York Press: New York, 1989. Readers might also refer to a site in French that presents Said Nursi's thinking pedagogically: http://www.hayratvakfi.org/fr

30. Louis-Marie Bureau, *La Pensée de Fethullah Gülen*, L'Harmattan: Paris, 2013.

31. Joshua Hendrick, *Gülen: The Ambiguous Politics of Market Islam in Turkey and the World*, New York University Press: New York, 2013.

32. From its website: http://www.zaman.com.tr/mainAction.action; and the international version in English: http://www.todayszaman.com/mainAction.action. (The websites are no longer accessible.)

33. The editorial line of these two dailies has changed radically since they

were put under administrative supervision by the Turkish state, which made them tools of official propaganda from March 2016 onwards.
34. In Turkey, the foundation that organizes intra- and inter-faith debates and meetings is *Turkiye Gazeteciler ve Yazarlar Vafki* (Turkish Writers and Journalists Association): http://www.gyv.org.tr. Hundreds of other similar structures have been launched in the world: for example, La plate-forme de Paris in Paris (http://www.plateformedeparis.fr) or the Rumi Forum in Washington (http://www.rumiform.org/).
35. Bayram Balci, *Missionnaires de l'Islam en Asie centrale, the écoles turques de Fethullah Gülen*, Maisonneuve et Larose and Institut français d'études anatoliennes: Paris, 2003.
36. For a brief presentation of this NGO, see http://www.ngo-monitor.org/article/world_vision_international
37. David Tittensor, *The House of Service: The Gülen Movement and Islam's Third Way*, Oxford University Press: Oxford, 2014.
38. Gabriel Compayré, 'Grandeur et limite de l'enseignement jésuite', *Encyclopédie de l'Agora*, http://agora.qc.ca/documents/jesuites—grandeur_et_limites de lenseignement _ jesuite_par Gabriel compayre
39. See the site of the Katev Society, which runs the Turkish schools in Kazakhstan: http://www.katev.kz/
40. On the Turkish schools in Tajikistan, see the site of the association that runs them, *Shelale*: http://www.shelale.org/tj/
41. Farhad Aliyev, 'The Gulen Movement in Azerbaijan', *Current Trends in Islamist Ideology*, no. 5, 2012, http://www.currenttrends.org/docLib/20130124_CT14Aliev.pdf
42. Fethullah Gülen, *Terror and Suicide Attacks: An Islamic Perspective*, The Light: New Jersey, 2004.
43. Nadir Devlet, 'Taking Stock: Turkey and the Turkic World 20 Years Later', *The German Marshall Fund of United States*, 10 November 2011, http://www.gmfus.org/wp-content/blogs.dir/1/files_mf/1321555956_magicfields_attachment_1_1.pdf
44. Bayram Balci, 'Les écoles néo-nurcu de Fethullah Gülen en Asie centrale: implantation, fonctionnement et nature du message véhiculé par le biais de la coopération éducative', *Revue des mondes musulmans et de la Méditerranée*, nos. 101–2, 2003, http://remmm.revues.org/54
45. Bayram Balci, 'Fethullah Gülen's Missionary Schools in Central Asia and their Role in the Spreading of Turkism and Islam', *Religion, State and Society*, vol. 31, no. 2, 2003, pp. 151–77.
46. Aliyev, 'The Gulen Movement in Azerbaijan'.
47. The Ergenekon affair (a mythical name referring to a region of Siberia from which the Turks originate) refers to a failed plot, uncovered in 2007, involving hundreds of military figures, but also civilians, who

sought by various means (assassinations, agitation, attacks) to cause instability in Turkey in order to legitimate military intervention and overthrow the Islamic-conservative civilian government of Recep Tayyip Erdoğan. Uncovered and foiled, these attempts to mount a *coup d'état* gave rise to historical trials, including that of September 2012, which saw hundreds of officers and some generals condemned to long prison sentences. Seen as evidence of democratic progress by some, and as a political settling of accounts by others, the trials signalled the end of the omnipotence of the army, which was now subject to civil power. The Gülen movement was criticized for exploiting the trials, thanks to its networks of influence in the judicial apparatus, to settle its accounts with the army and the Kemalist circles by which it believes it has long been targeted. As a consequence of the break between Erdoğan and the Gülen camp in 2013, the trials in connection with the affair were reopened in April 2016 and the Turkish Supreme Court decided to acquit most of the individuals who had been condemned for attempting a *coup*. This demonstrates nothing less than a reversal of alliances—that is, the effective end of the alliance between Erdoğan and Gülen and a reconciliation between the Turkish army, which had been severely mauled in the trials, and President Erdoğan.

48. Bayram Balci, 'Turkey's Political Crisis Undermining Democracy', *Carnegie Endowment for International Peace*, 21 March 2014, http://carnegieendowment.org/2014/03/21/turkey-s-plitical-crisis-undermining-democracy/h54e
49. Michael A. Reynolds, 'Damaging Democracy: The U.S., Fethullah Gülen, and Turkey's Upheaval', *Foreign Policy Research Institute*, September 2016, http://www.fpri.org/article/2016/09/damaging-democracy-u-s-fethullah-gulen-turkeys-upheaval/
50. Catherine Putz, 'Turkish Targeting of Gülen Movement Reaches into Central Asia', *The Diplomat*, 25 July 2016, http://thediplomat.com/2016/07/turkish-targeting-of-gulen-movement-reaches-into-central-asia/

3. IRAN: A MINOR RELIGIOUS ACTOR IN CENTRAL ASIA AND THE CAUCASUS

1. Mohammad Reza-Djalili, 'L'Iran face aux développements en Transcaucasie et en Asie Centrale', *Cahiers d'Etudes sur la Méditerranée Orientale et le monde Turco-Iranien*, no. 16, 1993, http://cemoti.revues.org/313
2. Ali A. Jalali, 'Iran–Central Asia: Reminiscing the Past and Looking to

the Future', *Journal of Iranian Research and Analysis*, vol. 16, no. 2, 2000, pp. 72–8.
3. Mohammad Ahrari, *The New Great Game in Muslim Central Asia*, National Defense University: Washington, DC, 1996, pp. 49–71.
4. K.L. Adrasiabi, *After Khomeini: New Directions in Iran's Foreign Policy*, Westview Press: Boulder, CO, San Francisco, CA and Oxford, 1994.
5. John Esposito, *The Iranian Revolution: Its Global Impact*, University of Florida: Gainesville, FL, 1990.
6. Bahram Alavi, 'Ayatollah's Death Brings Rafsanjani Closer to Both Power and Problems', *Washington Report on Middle East Affairs*, August 1989, pp. 7–37.
7. Shireen Hunter, *Iran's Foreign Policy in the Post-Soviet Era: Resisting the New International Order*, ABC-CLIO/Greenwood: Westport, CT, 2010, pp. 169–85.
8. Thomas De Waal, *Black Garden: Armenia and Azerbaijan through Peace and War*, New York University Press: New York, 2003.
9. Svante Cornell, *Small Nations and Great Powers: A Study of Ethnopolitical Conflict in the Caucasus*, Routledge-Curzon: London and New York, 2001.
10. Shireen Hunter, 'Security and Environment in the Caspian Sea', in William Ascher and Natalia Mirovitskaya, *The Caspian Sea: A Quest for Environmental Security*, Kluwer Academic Publishers: Dordrecht, 2000, pp. 117–24.
11. Manochehr Dorraj, and Nader Entessar, *Iran's Northern Exposure: Foreign Policy Challenges in Eurasia*, Center for International and Regional Studies, Georgetown University School of Foreign Service in Qatar, 2013, Occasional Paper no. 13, https://repository.library.georgetown.edu/bitstream/handle/10822/708817/CIRSOoccasionalPaper13DorrajEntessar2013.pdf?sequence =5
12. Shireen Hunter, *Iran's Foreign Policy in the Post-Soviet Era: Resisting the New International Order*, ABC-CLIO/Greenwood: Westport, CT, 2010, pp. 169–85.
13. Robert L. Canfield, *Turko-Persia in Historical Perspective*, Cambridge University Press: Cambridge, 2002.
14. Jalali, 'Iran—Central Asia: Reminiscing the Past and Looking to the Future', pp. 72–8.
15. Garnik Asatrian, and Habib Borjian, 'Talish and the Talishis: The State of Research', *Iran and the Caucasus*, vol. 9, no. 1, 2005, pp. 43–72.
16. Edmund Herzig, *Iran and the Former Soviet South*, Royal Institute of International Affairs: London, 1995.
17. Mohammad Reza Djalili, 'L'Iran et la Turquie face à l'Asie centrale', *Journal for International and Strategic Studies*, no. 1, 2008, pp. 13–19.

18. Mohammad Reza Djalili, 'Iran and the Caucasus: Maintaining Some Pragmatism', *Quarterly Journal*, no. 3, September 2002, pp. 49–57.
19. Tadeusz Swietochowski, *Russia and Azerbaijan: A Borderland in Transition*, Columbia University Press: New York, 1995.
20. Shireen Hunter, 'Greater Azerbaijan: Myth or Reality', in Mohammad Reza-Djalili, *Le Caucase post-soviétique. La transition dans le conflit*, Bruylant: Brussels, 1995, pp. 115–42.
21. Sherri Liberman, *A Historical Atlas of Azerbaijan*, Rosen Publishing Group: New York, 2004.
22. Fernande Raine, 'Stalin and the Creation of the Azerbaijan Democratic Party in Iran, 1945', *Cold War History*, vol. 2, no. 1, 2001, pp. 1–38.
23. Audrey Alstadt, *The Azerbaijani Turks: Power and Identity under Russian Rule*, Hoover Institute Press: Stanford, CA, 1992.
24. Mohammad Reza Djalili, 'Iran and the Caucasus: Maintaining Some Pragmatism', *Quarterly Journal*, no. 3, September 2002, pp. 49–57.
25. Kaweh Sadegh-Zadeh, 'Iran's Strategy in the South Caucasus', *Caucasian Review of International Affairs*, vol. 2, no. 1, Winter 2008, pp. 1–7.
26. Shireen Hunter, 'Iran and the Transcaucasus in the Post-Soviet Era', in David Menashri, *Central Asia Meets the Middle East*, Frank Cass: London, 1998, pp. 98–125.
27. Hunter, 'Iran and the Transcaucasus in the Post-Soviet Era', pp. 98–125.
28. Alla Mirzoyan, *Armenia, the Regional Powers, and the West: Between History and Geopolitics*, Palgrave Macmillan: Basingstoke, 2010.
29. Kornely K. Kakachia, 'Iran and Georgia: Genuine Partnership or Marriage of Convenience?', *PONARIS*, Eurasia Policy Memo, no. 186, September 2011, http://www.gwu.edu/~ieresgwu/assets/docs/ponars/pepm_186.pdf
30. Nika Chitadze, 'Geopolitical Interests of Iran in South Caucasus and Georgian–Iranian Relations', *Journal of Social Sciences*, vol. 1, no. 2, 2012, pp. 5–12.
31. Brenton Clark, 'Persian Games: Iran's Strategic Foothold in Tajikistan', *Open Democracy*, April 2012, https://www.opendemocracy.net/od-russia/brenton-clark/persian-games-iran%E2%80%99s-strategic-foothold-in-tajikistan
32. William Beeman, 'The Struggle for Identity in Post-Soviet Tajikistan', *Middle East Review of International Affairs*, vol. 3, no. 4, 1999.
33. Jamshid Gaziyev, *Ethnonationalism in Central Asia: Inter-Ethnic Conflicts and Institutional Ethnicity in the Land of Eternal Friendship and Brotherly Nations*, LAP LAMBERT Academic Publishing: Sarrbrücken, 2010.
34. Mohammad Reza Djalili, and Thierry Kellner, *Géopolitique de la nouvelle Asie centrale, de la fin de l'URSS à l'après-11 septembre*, Graduate Institute Publications: Geneva, 2001, ch. 5, pp. 185–278.

35. Sébastian Peyrouse, 'Iran's Growing Role in Central Asia? Geopolitical, Economic and Political Profit and Loss Account', *Al Jazeera*, 2014, http://studies.aljazeera.net/en/dossiers/2014/04/2014416940377354.html
36. Robert M. Shelala II, Nori Kasting and Anthony H. Cordesman, 'US and Iranian Strategic Competition: Afghanistan, Pakistan, India, and Central Asia', *Center for Strategic and International Studies*: Washington, DC, 2013, http://csis.org/files/publication/130626_AfPak_Asia.pdf
37. In May 2005, an uprising broke out in the city of Andijan, initially religious in character and motivated by the desire of various individuals to obtain the liberation of friends and relatives who had been imprisoned by the government on the grounds that they formed a radical Islamist group. The uprising rapidly turned into a general protest movement against arbitrary rule and economic conditions. The response of the forces of law and order was of the utmost brutality, since the army fired indiscriminately into the crowd, killing 187 people according to official figures, but more than 1,000 according to some human rights organizations. See Martha Brill Olcott, and Marina Barnett, *The Andijan Uprising, Akramiya and Akram Yuldashev*, Carnegie, June 2006, http://carnegie.ru/publications/?fa=18453. In foreign policy, the Andijan tragedy resulted in a close rapprochement between Uzbekistan, Russia and China, at the expense of its relations with the West, particularly the USA, because the Karimov government was convinced that the uprising was an attempted revolution, resembling others in the post-Soviet zone, instigated by the USA via various Western NGOs.
38. Alexander Cooley, *Great Games, Local Rules: The New Great Power Contest in Central Asia*, Oxford University Press: Oxford, 2012.
39. Atai, Farhad, and Hamidreza Azizi, 'The Energy Factor in Iran—Turkmenistan Relations', *Iranian Studies*, vol. 5, no. 6, 2012, pp. 745–58.
40. Shireen Hunter, *Iran's Foreign Policy in the Post-Soviet Era: Resisting the New International Order*, ABC-CLIO/Greenwood: Westport, CT, 2010, pp. 169–85.
41. Ibid.
42. Ibid., p. 182.
43. Karl DeRouen, *Civil Wars of the World: Major Conflicts since World War II*, ABC-CLIO/Greenwood: Westport, CT, vol. 1, 2007, pp. 753–71.
44. Edward Wastnidge, 'Pragmatic Politics: Iran, Central Asia and the Cultural Foreign Policy', *Central Asia and the Caucasus*, vol. 15, no. 4, 2014, http://www.ca-c.org/online/2014/journal_eng/cac-04/11.shtml

45. Behrooz Moazami, *State, Religion, and Revolution in Iran, 1796 to the Present*, Palgrave Macmillan: Basingstoke, 2013, pp. 93–117.
46. A tribally based dynasty founded by Aga Mohammad Khan Qajar, which ruled Iran between 1794 and 1924, when it ceded its role to the Pahlavi dynasty, itself terminated by the advent of the Islamic Republic in 1979. See Jean Calmard, 'Qâdjâr, 1794–1925', *Encyclopédie Universalis*, http://www.universalis.fr/encyclopedie/les-qadjar
47. An Iranian dynasty founded by Shah Ismail which ruled Iran between 1501 and 1722; 1722–36 was an intermediate period when various Safavid princes sought to seize back power; 1736–47 was when Nader Shah reconstructed the empire. Next came the short period of the Sand and then that of the Qajar. The Safavid dynasty has gone down in history for having been the first to establish Twelver Shia Islam as the official religion. See Jean Calmard, 'Safavides, or Séfévides or Safawides', *Encyclopédie Universalis* online, http://www.universalis.fr/encyclopedie/safavides-sefevides-safawides
48. A.H. Morton, 'The Early Years of Shah Ismail in the Afzal al tavarikh and Elsewhere', in Charles Melville, *Safavid Persia: The History and Politics of an Islamic Society*, I. B. Tauris: London, 1999.
49. Caroline Finkel, *Osman's Dream: The Story of the Ottoman Empire 1300–1923*, John Murray: London, 2006.
50. Sabrina Mervin, *Les Mondes chiites et l'Iran*, Karthala/IFPO: Paris and Beirut, 2007, pp. 9–28.
51. Kayhan Barzegar, 'Foreign Policy Department/Middle East and Persian Gulf Studies Group', *Center for Strategic Research*, 2008, http://www.csr.ir/departments.aspx?lng=en&abtid=07&&depid=74&semid=1421
52. Rodger Shanahan, 'Iranian Foreign Policy under Rouhani', Lowy Institute for International Policy: Sydney, February 2015.
53. The term Jafarism refers to Jafar al-Sadiq, who was principally responsible for defining Twelver Shia doctrine. It is in fact synonymous with Twelver Shia Islam.
54. Boris Petric, 'Les Ironis en Ouzbékistan post-soviétique ou les vertus de la dissimulation mentale (taqiyya) dans un contexte de sunnitisation de la société', in Mervin, *Les mondes chiites et l'Iran*, pp. 189–210.
55. 'Samarkand Resident Sentenced for Propagating Sh'ite Islam', Radio Free Europe, Radio Liberty, November 2013, http://www.referl.org/content/uzbek-propagating-islam/25175284.html
56. A theological school known for its moderation, which owes its name to its founder, Abu Mansur Al Maturidi, a native of the Samarkand region. See W. Madelung, *Māturīdiyya. Encyclopédie de l'Islam*, Brill Online, 2015, http://referenceworks.brillonline.com/entries/encyclopedie-de-l-islam/ma-turi-diyya-SIM_5046
57. Igor Rotar, 'Uzbekistan: Tight Restrictions on Shia Muslim Minority',

Forum 18, April 2004, http://www.forum18.org/archive.php?article_id=307&pdf=Y
58. Adeeb Khalid, 'Ulama and the State in Uzbekistan', *Asian Journal of Social Science*, vol. 42, no. 5, 2014, pp. 517–35.
59. The term *Hussainiya* refers to Hussain and, without being a mosque, serves as a meeting-place where the faithful gather to pray and remember the martyrdom and passion of Hussain, killed in Karbala in 680.
60. Otambek Mastibekov, *Leadership and Authority in Central Asia: The Ismaili Community in Tajikistan*, Routledge: New York, 2014, pp. 83–112, 127–48.
61. Farhad Daftary, *The Isma'ilis: Their History and Doctrines*, Cambridge University Press: Cambridge, 1992, pp. 91–143.
62. Sarfaroz Niyozov, 'Evolution of the Shi'a Ismaili Tradition in Central Asia', Institute of Ismaili Studies, *The Ismaili UK*, March 2002, http://www.iis.ac.uk/SiteAssets/pdf/evolution_central_asia.pdf
63. Bruno De Cordier, 'Islamic Faith-Based Development Organizations in Former Soviet Muslim Environments: the Mountain Societies Development Support Programme in the Rasht Valley, Tajikistan', *Central Asian Survey*, vol. 27, no. 2, 2008, pp. 169–84.
64. Sébastien Peyrouse, and Sadykzhan Ibraimov, 'Iran's Central Asia Temptations', *Current Trends in Islamist Ideology*, vol. 10, 2010, pp. 87–101.
65. Edward Wastnidge, 'Pragmatic Politics: Iran, Central Asia and the Cultural Foreign Policy', *Central Asia and the Caucasus*, vol. 15, no. 4, 2014, http://www.ca-c.org/online/2014/journal_eng/cac-04/11.shtml
66. http://www.tehrantimes.com/arts-and-culture/99372-persian-teaching-center-opens-in-bishkek
67. Peyrouse and Ibraimov, 'Iran's Central Asia Temptations'.
68. Ibid.
69. Neil J. Melvin, *Uzbekistan: Transition to Authoritarianism on the Silk Road*, Taylor and Francis Library, 2005, p. 42.
70. Rollie Lal, *Central Asia and its Asian Neighbors: Security and Commerce at the Crossroads*, Rand Corporation, 2006, p. 11.
71. Tatevik Mkrtchyan, 'Shi'a Politics, "Strategic Culture" and Iran's Relations with the South Caucasus', in Alexander Agadjanian, Ansgar Jödicke and Evert van der Zweerde (eds), *Religion, Nation and Democracy in the South Caucasus*, Brill: Leiden 2014, pp. 221–37.
72. Volker Adam, 'Why Do They Cry? Criticism of Muharram Celebration in Tsarist and Socialist Azerbaijan', in Rainer Brunner and Ender Verner (eds), *The Twelver Shia in Modern Times: Religious Culture and Political History*, Brill: Leiden, 2000, pp. 114–34.

73. Mehrangiz Najafizadeh, 'Gender and Ideology: Social Change and Islam in Post-Soviet Azerbaijan', *Journal of Third World Studies*, vol. 29, no. 1, 2012, pp. 81–107.
74. Raoul Motika, 'Islam in Post-Soviet Azerbaijan', *Archives de sciences sociales des religions*, no. 115, July–September 2001, http://assr.revues.org/18423; DOI: 10.4000/assr.18423; placed online 19 August 2009 and accessed 1 March 2015.
75. Laurence Louër, 'Déconstruire le croissant chiite', *Revue internationale et stratégique*, no. 76, 2009, pp. 45–54.
76. Svante Cornell, *Azerbaijan since Independence*, M. E. Sharpe: New York, 2011.
77. Mkrtchyan, 'Shi'a Politics, "Strategic Culture" and Iran's Relations with the South Caucasus'.
78. Bayram Balci, 'Between Sunnism and Shiism: Islam in Post-Soviet Azerbaijan', *Central Asian Survey*, vol. 23, no. 2, 2004, pp. 205–17.
79. Regular interviews with Rafik Aliyev, Baku, between 2003 and 2006.
80. Rufat Sattarov, 'Islamic Revival and Islamic Activism in Post-Soviet Azerbaijan', in Galina Yemelianova (ed.), *Islamic Radicalism in the Former Soviet Union*, Routledge: New York, 2011, pp. 146–211.
81. Cornell, *Azerbaijan since Independence*, pp. 60–80.
82. Shahin Abbasov, 'Azerbaijan: Iran Taking a Beating in Baku Press', *Eurasianet*, 14 February 2011, http://www.eurasianet.org/node/62889
83. Sofi Bedford, *Islamic Activism in Azerbaijan: Repression and Mobilization in a Post-Soviet Context*, Stockholm Studies in Politics, no. 129, 2009, pp. 137–49.
84. Sabrina Mervin, *Histoire de l'Islam, fondements et doctrines*, Flammarion: Paris 2000.
85. Sabrina Mervin, 'Les autorités religieuses dans le chiisme duodécimain contemporain', *Archives de sciences sociales des religions*, no. 125, January–March 2004, http://assr.revues.org/index1033.html; placed online 22 February 2007.
86. Momen Moojan, *An Introduction to Shi'i Islam: The History and Doctrines of Twelver Shiism*, Yale University Press: New Haven, CT, 1985.
87. Mervin, 'Les autorités religieuses dans le chiisme duodécimain contemporain'.
88. Ibid.
89. Mehdi Khalaji, 'The Last Marja: Sistani and the End of Traditional Religious Authority in Shiism', *Washington Institute for Near Eastern Policy*, September 2006, http://www.washingtoninstitute.org/uploads/Documents/pubs/PolicyFocus59final.pdf
90. 'Georgia's Armenian and Azeri Minorities', International Crisis Group, Europe Report no. 178, 2006, https://www.files.ethz.ch/isn/26285/178_georgias_armenian_and_azeri_minorities.pdf

91. Swietochowski, *Russia and Azerbaijan*, pp. 27–8.
92. On this magazine, see Elizabeth Minkel, 'The magazine that almost changed the world', *New Yorker*, 26 May 2011; URL: http://www.newyorker.com/books/page-turner/the-magazine-that-almost-changed-the-world
93. Bayram Balci, and Raoul Motika, 'Islam in Post-Soviet Georgia', *Central Asian Survey*, vol. 26, no. 3, 2007, pp. 335–53.
94. Conor Prasad, *Georgia's Muslim Community: A Self-Fulfilling Prophecy?*, European Center for Minority Issues, Working Paper no. 58, 2012, http://www.ecmi.de/uploads/tx_Ifpubdb/Working_Paper_58_En.pdf
95. Ibid.
96. Adeline Braux, 'Azerbaijanis in Russia: An "Imagined" Diaspora?', in Marlène Laruelle (ed.), *Migration and Social Upheaval as the Face of Globalization in Central Asia*, Brill: Leiden, 2012, pp. 167–86.
97. Dina Lisnyyansky, 'Tashaya (Conversion to Shiism) in Central Asia and Russia', *Current Trends in Islamist Ideology*, vol. 8, 2009, pp. 108–17.
98. Adeline Braux, *Moscou—Caucase: Migrations et diasporas dans l'espace post-soviétique*, Editions Pétra/IFEAC, Central Asia Collection, 2014.

4. INFLUENCES FROM THE ARABIAN PENINSULA ON THE REVIVAL OF ISLAM IN CENTRAL ASIA AND THE CAUCASUS

1. Sir Hamilton Alexander Rosskeen Gibb, *The Arab Conquests in Central Asia*, Royal Asiatic Society, London, 1923, https://archive.org/details/arabconquestssince00gibbuoft
2. Vincent Fourniau, 'Les Arabes d'Asie central soviétique: maintenance et mutation de l'identité ethnique', *Revue du monde musulman et de la Méditerranée*, nos. 59–60, 1991, pp. 83–100, http://www.persee.fr/web/revues/home/prescript/article/remmm_0997-1327_1991_num_59_1_1493
3. Robert D. McChesney, 'Central Asia's Place in the Middle East—Some Historical Considerations', in David Menashri, *Central Asia Meets the Middle East*, Frank Cass: London, 1998, pp. 25–51.
4. Khalid, *The Politics of Muslim Cultural Reform*, pp. 80–113.
5. Altstadt, *The Azerbaijani Turks*, pp. 50–73.
6. Aryeh Y. Yodfat, *The Soviet Union and the Arabian Peninsula: Soviet Policy towards the Persian Gulf and Arabia*, Routledge: New York, 1983, pp. 1–32.
7. O. Igho Natufe, *Soviet Policy in Africa from Lenin to Brezhnev*, Bloomington University Press: Bloomington, MD, 2011.
8. Yodfat, *The Soviet Union and the Arabian Peninsula*.
9. Ibid.

10. David Commins, *The Wahhabi Mission and Saudi Arabia*, I. B. Tauris: London, 2006.
11. Yodfat, *The Soviet Union and the Arabian Peninsula*.
12. Golan Galia, *Soviet Policies in the Middle East*, Cambridge University Press: Cambridge, 1990.
13. Hélène Carrère d'Encausse, *La Politique soviétique au Moyen-Orient, 1955–1975*, Presses des Sciences Po: Paris, 1975.
14. Rami Ginat, *The Soviet Union and Egypt, 1945–1958*, Frank Cass: London, 1993.
15. Alima Bissenova, 'Central Asian Encounters in the Middle East: Nationalism, Islam and Postcoloniality in Al-Azhar', *Religion, State and Society*, vol. 33, no. 3, September 2005, pp. 254–64. See also Abramson, David, *Foreign Religious Education and the Central Asian Islamic Revival: Impact and Prospects for Stability*, Central Asia-Caucasus Institute and Silk Road Studies Program—A Joint Transatlantic Research and Policy Center: Washington, DC, 2010, http://www.isdp.eu/images/stories/isdp-main-pdf/2010_abramson_foreign-religious-education.pdf
16. Galina Yemelianova, 'Islam, National Identity and Politics in Contemporary Kazakhstan', *Asian Ethnicity*, vol. 15, no. 3, 2014, pp. 286–301, http://pureoai.bham.ac.uk/ws/files/17507783/Yemelianova_Islam_national_identity_politics_contemporary_Kazakhstan_Asian_Ethnicity_2014.pdf
17. On ISESCO and its activity in the Muslim world, see its website: http://www.isesco.org.ma/index.php
18. On IRCICA and its activity in the Muslim world, see its website: http://www.ircica.org
19. Suraiya Faroqhi, *Pilgrims and Sultans: The Hajj under the Ottomans*, I. B. Tauris: London, 2014.
20. Audrey Burton, 'Relations between the Khanate of Bukhara and Ottoman Turkey (1558–1702)', *International Journal of Turkish Studies*, vol. 5, 1990–91, pp. 83–103.
21. Madawi Al-Rasheed, *History of Saudi Arabia*, Cambridge University Press: Cambridge, 2010.
22. Thierry Zarcone, 'Réseaux confrériques et guides charismatiques dans les relations turco-arabes (héritage de l'histoire et situation actuelle)', *Anatolia Moderna*, IV (IFEA): Istanbul, 1992.
23. On the links between the Mughal princes and the pilgrimage to Mecca, see M.N. Pearson, 'Mughals and the Hajj', *Journal of Oriental Society of Australia*, vols. 18–19, 1986–7, pp. 164–79.
24. Roger Savory, *Iran under the Safavids*, Cambridge University Press: Cambridge, 1980.
25. Ignace Leverrier, 'L'Arabie saoudite, le pèlerinage et l'Iran', *Cahiers*

d'Études sur la Méditerranée Orientale et le monde Turco-Iranien, no. 22, 1996, http://cemoti.revues.org/137; placed online 4 March 2005 and accessed 4 September 2015.

26. Sylvia Chiffoleau, 'Le pèlerinage à la Mecque: une industrie sous contrôle', *La vie des idées*, April 2014, http://www.laviedesidees.fr/le-pelerinage-a-La-Mecque-une.html
27. Sylvia Chiffoleau, *Le Voyage à La Mecque. Un pèlerinage mondial en terre d'islam*, Belin: Paris, 2015.
28. Daniel Brower, 'Russian Roads to Mecca: Religious Tolerance and Muslim Pilgrimage in the Russian Empire', *Slavic Review*, vol. 55, no. 3, 1996, pp. 567–84.
29. Eileen Kane, *Odessa as a Hajj Hub: 1880s to 1910s*, National Council for Eurasian and East European Research, March 2011.
30. Eileen Kane, *Russian Hajj: Empire and Pilgrimage to Mecca*, Cornell University Press: Ithaca, NY, 2015.
31. Eric Togliacozzo, *The Longest Journey: Southeast Asians and the Pilgrimage to Mecca*, Oxford University Press: Oxford, 2013, pp. 157–77.
32. Kane, *Russian Hajj: Empire and Pilgrimage to Mecca*.
33. Michael Christopher Low, *Empire of the Hajj: Pilgrims, Plagues, and Pan Islam under British Surveillance, 1865–1926*, History thesis, University of Georgia: Athens, OH, 2007, http://scholarworks.gsu.edu/cgi/viewcontent.cgi?article=1021&context=history_theses
34. Kane, *Russian Hajj: Empire and Pilgrimage to Mecca*, pp. 86–119.
35. Slimane Zeghidour, *La Vie quotidienne à La Mecque, de Mahomet à nos jours*, Hachette: Paris, 1989.
36. On the various sites of substitute pilgrimages throughout Central Asia in the broad sense (i.e. post-Soviet and Xinjiang), see Thierry Zarcone, 'Pilgrimage to the "Second Mecca" and Ka'bas's of Central Asia', in Alexandre Papas, Thomas Welsford and Thierry Zarcone, *Hajj Routes and Pious Visits between Central Asia and the Hijaz*, Islamkundliche Untersuchungen Band 308, Klaus Schwarz Verlag: Berlin, 2011, pp. 251–77.
37. For an overview of the principal sites of substitute pilgrimages in the Muslim world, see Zarcone, 'Pilgrimage to the "Second Mecca" and Ka'bas's of Central Asia'.
38. Ro'i, *Islam in the Soviet Union*, p. 173.
39. Email interview with Bakhtiyar Babadjanov, researcher at the Academy of Sciences, Republic of Uzbekistan, June 2015.
40. See the site of the Uzbek committee of religious affairs in the cabinet of ministers, which supplied the figure for the applicants for the lesser pilgrimage for 2015: http://religions.uz/eng
41. Email interview with Kenan Rovsanoglu, independent researcher in Azerbaijan, September 2015.

42. Interview with Ravshan Eratov, Directorate of Religious Affairs, Bishkek, March 2015.
43. Robert R. Bianchi, *Guests of God: Pilgrimage and Politics in the Islamic World*, Oxford University Press: Oxford, 2004.
44. Jacqueline Hagan, and Helen Rose-Ebaugh, 'Calling upon the Sacred: Migrants' Use of Religion in the Migration Process', *International Migration Review*, vol. 37, no. 4, 2003, pp. 1145–62.
45. Bayram Balci, 'Central Asian Refugees in Saudi Arabia: Religious Evolution and Contribution to the Reislamization of their Motherland', *Refugee Survey Quarterly*, vol. 26, no. 2, 2007, pp. 12–21.
46. Tim Niblock, *Saudi Arabia: Power, Legitimacy and Survival*, Routledge: New York, 2006.
47. Hege Ishakova, and Khadia Akhmedova, 'Les migrations des Ouïgours vers l'Asie centrale ex-soviétique', *Cahiers d'Études sur la Méditerranée Orientale et le monde Turco-Iranien*, no. 25, 1998, http://cemoti.revues.org/59
48. Bayram Balci, 'La communauté ouzbèke d'Arabie saoudite: entre assimilation et renouveau identitaire', *Revue européenne des migrations internationales*, vol. 19, no. 3, 2003, http://remi.revues.org/2684: placed online 9 June 2006 and accessed 31 May 2016.
49. The *Basmachi* (from the Turkish *basmak*, to rebel, to carry out a raid) were a spontaneous, unorganized insurrectionary movement started by indigenous groups in Central Asia in revolt against the Soviet government. The movement began in 1917 and was gradually extinguished in the late 1920s, when the Bolsheviks established control over the whole of Russian Turkestan. Pejorative and synonymous with bandit and criminal for the Soviets, the movement was credited with a certain nobility among a number of Turco-Muslim intellectuals opposed to Bolshevism, which for them was merely a new form of Russian colonialism. See Marie Broxup, 'The Basmachis', *Central Asian Survey*, vol. 2, no. 1, 1987, pp. 57–81.
50. On migratory flows between the Soviet Union and Afghanistan and, more particularly, on the Uzbeks of the Soviet Union and those of Afghanistan, see Audrey Shalinski, 'Islam and Ethnicity: The Northern Afghan Perspective', *Central Asian Survey*, vol. 1, nos. 2–3, 1982, pp. 71–84. See also Delia Rahmonova-Schwarz, 'Migrations during the Soviet Period and in the Early Years of the USSR's Dissolution: A Focus on Central Asia', *Revue européenne des migrations internationales* [online], vol. 26, no. 3, 2010, http://remi.revues.org/5196; placed online 1 December 2013 and accessed 4 September 2015. Readers are also referred to Eden Naby, 'The Uzbeks of Afghanistan', *Central Asian Survey*, vol. 3, no. 1, 1984, pp. 1–21.
51. Bayram Balci, 'Les Ouzbeks d'Arabie saoudite entre intégration et

renouveau identitaire via le pèlerinage', *Central Asian Survey*, vol. 22, no. 1, 2003, pp. 23–44.
52. Chiffoleau, 'Le pèlerinage à La Mecque: une industrie sous contrôle'.
53. Hailil Açikgöz, *Türkistan İstiklâl Yolunda Hicret Yllari, Zuhriddin Mirza Abid Türkistanî*, Doğu Kütüphanesi: Istanbul, 2013. See also Ahat Andican, *Osmanli'dan Günümüze Türkiye ve Orta Asya*, Dogan Kitap: Istanbul, 2009, pp. 421–68.
54. Stuart Hall, 'Cultural Identity and Diaspora', in Jonathan Rutherford (ed.), *Identity: Community, Culture, Difference*, Lawrence and Wishart, London, 1990, pp. 222–37.
55. Thierry Zarcone, 'Une route de sainteté islamique entre l'Asie centrale et l'Inde: la voie Ush-Kashghar-Srinagar', *Cahiers d'Asie centrale*, nos. 1–2, 1996, pp. 227–54.
56. Altay Goyushov, and Elçin Eskerov, 'Islam and Islamic Education in Soviet and Independent Azerbaijan', in Kemper, *Islamic Education in the Soviet Union and its Successor States*, pp. 168–222.
57. Samir Amghar, 'La Ligue islamique mondiale en Europe: un instrument de défense des intérêts stratégiques saoudiens', *Critique Internationale*, no. 51, 2011, pp. 113–27, http://www.cairn.info/revue-critique-internationale-2011-2-page-113.htm
58. Peter Chalk, *Encyclopedia of Terrorism*, ABC-CLIO: Santa Barbara, CA, 2012.
59. Bayram Balci, 'Politique identitaire et construction diasporique en Azerbaïdjan post-Soviétique', *Cahiers d'Asie centrale*, nos. 19–20, 2011, pp. 261–76.
60. Oka Natsuko, 'A Note on Ethnic Migration Policy in Kazakhstan: Changing Priority and a Growing Dilemma', Institute of Developing Economies: Tokyo, March 2013, https://ir.ide.go.jp/dspace/bitstream/2344/1218/1/ARRIDE_Discussion_No._394_oka.pdf
61. Matteo Fumagalli, 'Ethnicity, State Formation and Foreign Policy: Uzbekistan and "Uzbeks Abroad"', *Central Asian Survey*, vol. 26, no. 1, 2007, pp. 105–22.
62. Matteo Fumagalli, 'Framing Ethnic Minority Mobilisation in Central Asia: The Case of Uzbeks in Kyrgyzstan and Tajikistan', *Europe–Asia Studies*, vol. 59, no. 4, 2007, pp. 567–90.
63. Bayram Balci, 'Identité nationale et gestion du fait minoritaire en Asie centrale: analyse des affrontements interethniques d'Och en juin 2010', *Cahiers d'Asie centrale*, nos. 19–20, 2011, pp. 470–84.
64. Allen Charles, 'The Hidden Roots of Wahhabism in British India', *World Policy Journal*, Summer 2005, pp. 87–93.
65. Bianchi, *Guests of God*.
66. Christiaan Snouck Hurgronje, 'Notes sur le mouvement du pèlerinage

de la Mecque aux Indes Néerlandaises', *Revue du Monde Musulman*, no. 15, 1911, pp. 397–413.

5. SOUTH ASIA'S INFLUENCE ON THE REVIVAL OF ISLAM IN CENTRAL ASIA

1. Edvard Rtveladze, 'The Great Indian Road: India–Central Asia–Transcaucasia', in Anita Sengupta and Mirzhoid Rakhimov (eds), *Insight and Communities: South and Central and South*, KW Publishers: New Delhi, 2015, pp. 59–74.
2. Mansura Haidar, *Central Asia in the Sixteenth Century*, Manohar, 2002.
3. Introduction to Scott Levi, and Muzaffar Alam, *India and Central Asia: Commerce and Culture, 1500–1800*, Oxford University Press: New Delhi, 2007, pp. 1–37.
4. K. Warikoo, 'Trade Relations between Central Asia and Kashmir Himalayas during the Dogra Period (1846–1947)', *Cahiers d'Asie Centrale*, nos. 1–2, 1996, pp. 113–24.
5. Levi and Alam, *India and Central Asia*, pp. 93–126.
6. Scott Levi, *Indian Merchants on the Silk Road*, Penguin/Allen Lane: London, 2015.
7. Razia Mukminova, 'Les routes caravanières entre villes de l'Inde et de l'Asie centrale: déplacements des artisans et circulation des articles artisanaux', *Cahiers d'Asie centrale*, nos. 1–2, 1996, pp. 85–90.
8. Marc Le Berre, and Gérard Fussman, 'Monuments bouddhiques de la region de Caboul, 1, Le monastère de Gul Dara', *Mémoires de la Délégation Archéologique Française en Afghanistan*, Vol. XXII, Diffusion de Boccard: Paris, 1976.
9. Lena Jonson, *Tajikistan in the New Central Asia: Geopolitics, Great Power Rivalry and Radical Islam*, I. B. Tauris: London, 2006, p. 25.
10. Margarita Filanovic, and Zamira Usmanova, 'Les frontières occidentales de la diffusion du bouddhisme en Asie centrale', *Cahiers d'Asie centrale*, nos. 1–2, 1996, pp. 185–201.
11. Laurent Gayer, 'From the Oxus to the Indus: Looking Back at India—Central Asia Connections in the Early Modern Age', in Marlène Laruelle, Sébastien Peyrouse, Jean-François Huchet and Bayram Balci, *China and India in Central Asia. A New "Great Game"?*, Palgrave Macmillian: New York, 2010.
12. Levi and Alam, *India and Central Asia*, p. 159.
13. Richard Foltz, 'Cultural Contacts between Central Asia and Mughal India', *Central Asiatic Journal*, vol. 42, no. 1, 1998, pp. 44–65.
14. Aftandil Erkinov, 'Manuscripts of the Works by Classical Persian Authors (Hafiz, Jami, Bidil): Quantitative Analysis of 17th-19th c.

Central Asian Copies', in *Iran: Questions et connaissances. Actes du IVe Congrès Européen des études iraniennes organisés par la Societas Iranologica Europeana, Paris, 6–10 September 1999*, Vol. II, *Périodes médiévale et moderne*. [Cahiers de Studia Iranica 26], M. Szuppe, Association pour l'avancement des études iraniennes, Peeters Press: Paris and Leiden, 2002, pp. 213–28.
15. Vladimir Lukonin, and Anatoli Ivanov, *Central Asian Arts*, Parkstone International: London, 2012.
16. Monique Kervran, 'Entre l'Inde et l'Asie centrale: les mausolées islamiques du Sind et du sud Penjab', *Cahiers d'Asie centrale*, nos. 1–2, 1996, pp. 133–71.
17. W.M. Thackston, Jr, *The Baburnama: Memoirs of Babur, Prince and Emperor*, Modern Library: New York, 2002.
18. Peter Jackson, *The Delhi Sultanate: A Political and Military History*, Cambridge University Press: Cambridge 1999.
19. Foltz, 'Cultural Contacts between Central Asia and Mughal India'.
20. Stephen Frederic Dale, 'The Legacy of the Timurids', *Journal of the Royal Asiatic Society*, 3rd series, vol. 8, no. 1, 1998, pp. 43–58.
21. Jo-Ann Gross, 'The Naqshibandiyya Connection from Central Asia to India and Back (16th-19th centuries)', in Scott Levi, *India and Central Asia: Commerce and Culture, 1500–1800*, Oxford University Press: New Delhi, 2007, pp. 233–59.
22. Itzchak Weismann, *The Naqshbandiyya: Orthodoxy and Activism in a Worldwide Sufi Tradition*, Routledge: New York, 2007.
23. Arthur Buehler, *Revealed Grace: The Juristic Sufism of Ahmad Sirhindi (1564–1624)*, Fons Vitae: Louisville, KY, 2011.
24. Yohannan Friedmann, *Shaikh Ahmad Sirhindi: An Outline of his Thought and a Study of his Image in the Eyes of Posterity*, Oxford University Press: New Delhi, 2000.
25. Bakhtiyar Babadjanov, 'On the History of the Naqsbandiya-Mugaddidiya in the Central Ma'wara'an-nahr in the Late 18th and Early 19th Centuries', in Michael Kemper, Anke von Kügelgen and Dmitruy Yermankov, *Muslim Culture in Russia and Central Asia from the 18th to the Early 20th Century*, vol. 1, Berlin, 1999, pp. 385–413.
26. Zarcone, 'Une route de sainteté', pp. 227–54.
27. Robert Horn, *Soviet–Indian Relations: Issues and Influences*, Praeger: New York, 1982.
28. Michael Kemper, Raoul Motika and Stefan Reichmuth, *Islamic Education in the Soviet Union and its Successor States*, Routledge: Abingdon, 2000, pp. 1–21.
29. Gerdien Jonker, *The Ahmadiyya Quest for Religious Progress: Missionizing Europe 1900–1965*, Brill: Leiden 2009.

30. Nathalie Clayer, 'La *Ahmadiyya lahori* et la réforme de l'islam albanais dans l'entre-deux-guerres', in Véronique Bouillier and Catherine Servan-Schreiber, *De l'Arabie à l'Himalaya. Chemins croisés en hommage à Marc Gaborieau*, Maisonneuve et Larose: Paris, 2004, pp. 211–28.
31. Martha Brill Olcott, *Sufism in Central Asia: A Force of Moderation or a Cause of Politicization?*, Carnegie Papers no. 84: Washington, DC, 2007.
32. Emily O'Dell, 'The Teaching, Practice and Political Role of Sufism in Dushanbe', NCEEER Working Paper, 2011, https://www.ucis.pitt.edu/nceeer/2011_825-01h_O'Dell.pdf
33. Barbara Metcalf, *Islamic Revival in British India: Deoband, 1860–1900*, Princeton University Press: Princeton, NJ, 2005.
34. Olivier Roy, *L'Islam mondialisé*, Seuil: Paris, 2002.
35. Christophe Jaffrelot, 'Le syncrétisme stratégique et la construction de l'identité nationaliste hindoue', *Revue française de science politique*, vol. 42, no. 4, 1992, pp. 594–617.
36. Christophe Jaffrelot, *The Hindu Nationalist Movement and Indian Politics, 1925 to the 1990s*, Hurst: London, 1996.
37. Jan Ali, 'Tabligh Jama'at: A Transnational Movement of Islamic Faith Regeneration', *European Journal of Economic and Political Studies*, vol. 3, 2010, pp. 110–13, http://ejeps.faith.edu.tr/docs/articles/67.pdf
38. Marc Gaborieau, 'The Transformation of Tablighi Jama'at into a Transnational Movement', in Muhammad Khalid Masud, *Travellers in Faith: Studies of the Tablighi Jama'at as a Transnational Movement for Faith Renewal*, Brill: Leiden, 2010, pp. 121–38.
39. Zakarias Pieri, *Tablighi Jamaat and the Quest for the London Mega Mosque: Continuity and Change*, Palgrave: Basingstoke, 2015.
40. Marloes Janson, 'Roaming about for God's Sake: The Upsurge of the Tabligh Jama'at in Gambia', *Journal of Religions in Africa*, vol. 35, no. 4, 2005, pp. 450–81.
41. Mohamed Tozy, 'Sequences of a Quest: Tablighi Jama'at in Morocco', in Masud, *Travelers in Faith*, pp. 161–73.
42. Aminah Muhammad Arif, *Salaam America: South Asian Muslims in New York*, Anthem Press: London, 2002.
43. Gilles Kepel, '*Foi et pratique*: Tablighi Jama'at in France', in Masud, *Travelers in Faith*, pp. 188–205.
44. Carl Ernst, and Bruce Lawrence, *Sufi Martyrs of Love: The Chisti Order in South Asia and Beyond*, Palgrave Macmillan: New York, 2002, pp. 65–83.
45. Christian Troll, 'Two Conceptions of Da'wa in India: Jama'at-i Islami and Tablighi Jama'at', *Archives de sciences sociales des religions*, no. 87, July–September 1994, pp. 115–33.
46. Metcalf, *Islamic Revival in British India*.
47. A Sufi brotherhood founded in the late twelfth century by Moinuddin

Chisti, it is distinguished from other brotherhoods in particular by the fact that its followers draw inspiration from music and singing. See Claire Devos, *Qawwali, la musique des maîtres du soufisme*, Editions du Makar: Paris, 1995.

48. Anna Suvorova, *Muslim Saints of South Asia: The Eleventh to Fifteenth Centuries*, Routledge: London, 2004, pp. 59–80.
49. Alix Philippon, *Soufisme et politique au Pakistan. Le mouvement barelwi à l'heure de la 'guerre contre terrorisme'*, Khartala: Paris, 2011.
50. Marc Gaborieau, 'What is Left of Sufism in Tablighi Jama'at?', *Archives de sciences sociales des religions*, no. 135, 2006, pp. 53–72.
51. Arthur Buehler, *Sufi Heirs of the Prophet: The Indian Naqshbandiyya and the Rise of the Mediating Sufi Shaykh*, University of South Carolina Press: Columbia, SC, 1992, p. 22.
52. Thierry Zarcone, *Le Soufisme. Voie mystique de l'islam*, Gallimard: Paris, 2009.
53. Alex Alexiev, 'Tablighi Jamaat: Jihad's Stealthy Legions', *Middle East Quarterly*, Winter 2005, pp. 3–11.
54. Ziya Ul-Hasan Faruqi, 'The Tablighi Jama'at', in S. T. Likandwala (ed.), *Islam and Contemporary India*, Indian Institute of Advanced Study: Simla, 1971, p. 60.
55. Yahya Sadowsky, 'For the Tablighi Islam is not Totalitarian', *Brookings Review*, vol. 14, no. 3, Summer 1996, p. 3.
56. Yoginder Sikand, 'The Tabligh Jama'at and Politics: A Critical Re-Appraisal', *Muslim World*, vol. 96, no. 1, pp. 175–95, January 2006.
57. Ibid.
58. Kathryn Haahr, 'Spanish Police Arrest Jamaat al-Tabligh Members in Bomb Threat', Jamestown, February 2008, http://www.jamestown.org/single/?tx_ttnews%5Btt_news%5D=4722&no_cache=1#.VrbrbljhDIU
59. Yoginder Sikand, 'Plane "Plot": Media Targets Tablighi Jamaat', *Milli Gazette Online*, 19 August 2006, http://www.milligazette.com/daily-update/2006/20060819_Tablighi-Jamaat_terrorism.htm
60. Bakhtiyar Babadjanov, 'Islam et activisme politique. Le cas Ouzbek', *Annales. Histoire, Sciences Sociales*, 2004/2005, pp. 1139–56.
61. Sébastien Peyrouse, *Turkménistan. Un destin au carrefour des empires*, Belin: Paris, 2007.
62. See http://almanac.afpc.org/Turkmenistan
63. Jean-Baptiste Jeangène, *Turkménistan*, CNRS Éditions: Paris, 2010.
64. 'One three-year jail term, 5 or 25 more to follow', European Country of Origin Information Network, https://www.ecoi.net/en/document/1109714.html
65. 'Kazakhstan: Wave of Prosecutions Against "Extremist" Muslims',

Eurasia Review, http://www.eurasiareview.com/09102015-kazakhstan-wave-of-prosecutions-against-extremist-muslims

66. 'Tajikistan: Why are around 93 Muslims being detained?', Forum 18, http:www.forum18.org/archive.php?article_id=1297
67. John Heathershaw, and David W. Montgomery, *The Myth of Post-Soviet Muslim Radicalization in the Central Asian Republics*, Royal Institute of International Affairs: Chatham House, London, November 2015, https://www.chathamhouse.org/sites/files/chathamhouse/field/field_document/20141111PostSovietRadicalizationHeathershawMontgomery.pdf
68. Ibid.
69. Eugene Huskey, 'National Identity from Scratch: Defining Kyrgyzstan's Role in World Affairs', *Journal of Communist Studies and Transition Politics*, vol. 19, no. 3, 2003, pp. 111–38.
70. Mukaram Toktogulova, 'The Localization of the Transnational Tablighi Jama'at in Kyrgyzstan: Structures, Concepts, Practices and Metaphors', *Crossroads Asia: Conflict, Migration, Development*, Bonn, March 2014.
71. Ibid.
72. Example of the *elechek*: https://fr.pinterest.com/pin/318911217334833416
73. Eric Enno Tamm, *The Horse That Leaps through Clouds: A Tale of Espionage, the Silk Road and the Rise of Modern China*, Douglas & McIntyre: Vancouver, 2010.
74. John Anderson, *Kyrgyzstan: Central Asia's Island of Democracy?*, Routledge: New York, 1999.
75. Aksana Ismailbekova, and Emil Nasritdinov, 'Transnational Social Networks in Central Asia: Structure, Travel, and Culture of Krygyz Tablighi Jama'at', *Transnational Social Review*, vol. 2, no. 2, 2012, pp. 177–95.
76. Muhammad Khalid Masud, 'Ideology and Legitimacy', in Masud, *Travellers in Faith*, pp. 3–44.
77. Rémy Dor, *Chants du Toit du monde. Textes d'orature kirghize*, Maisonneuve et Larose: Paris, 1982.
78. Nienke van der Heide, *The Manas Epic and Society in Kyrgyzstan*, Rozenberg Publishers: Amsterdam, 2008.
79. Ismailbekova and Nasritdinov, 'Transnational Social Networks in Central Asia'.
80. Interview with Emil Nasritdinov, researcher at the American University of Bishkek and an intellectual close to the Tabligh movement, Bishkek, March 2016.

6. THE ADMINISTRATION OF RELIGION IN THE NEWLY INDEPENDENT REPUBLICS

1. Hélène Carrère d'Encausse, *L'Empire éclaté: la révolte des nations en URSS*, Flammarion: Paris, 1978.
2. Khalid, *Islam after Communism*, p. 93.
3. José Casanova, *Public Religions in the Modern World*, University of Chicago Press: Chicago, IL, 2004.
4. Balci and Motika, 'Islam in Post-Soviet Georgia', pp. 335–53.
5. Martha Brill Olcott, *In the Whirlwind of Jihad*, Carnegie Endowment for International Peace: Washington, DC, 2012, p. 221.
6. Johan Rasanayagam, 'Morality, Self and Power: The Idea of Mahalla in Uzbekistan', in Monica Heintz, *The Anthropology of Moralities*, Berghahn Books: Oxford, 2009, pp. 102–17.
7. Shirin Akiner, *The Formation of Kazakh Identity: From Tribe to Nation-State*, Royal Institute of International Affairs, 1995.
8. On Abul Khayr Khan, see Y. Bregel, 'Abu'l-Kayr Khan', *Encyclopaedia Iranica*, 1/3, pp. 331–2, http://www.iranicaonline.org/articles/abul-kayr-khan-oglan; accessed on 31 January 2014.
9. Thierry Zarcone, 'Ahmad Yasavï héros des nouvelles républiques centrasiatiques', *Revues des mondes musulmans et de la Méditerranée*, nos. 89–90, July 2000, http://remmm.revues.org/284
10. Mathijs Pelkmans, 'Realigning Religion and Power in Central Asia: Islam, Nation-State and (Post)socialism', *Europe–Asia Studies*, vol. 61, no. 9, 2009, pp. 1517–41.
11. On Najmuddin Kubra, see Spencer Trimingham, *The Sufi Orders in Islam*, Oxford University Press: Oxford, 1971, pp. 55–8. See also Devin De Weese, 'The Eclipse of the Kubraviyah in Central Asia', *Iranian Studies*, vol. 21, no. 1–2, 1988, pp. 45–83.
12. Denis Gril, 'De l'usage sanctifiant des biens en islam', *Revue de l'histoire des religions*, vol. 215, no. 1, 1998, pp. 59–89.
13. Maria Elisabeth Louw, *Everyday Islam in Post-Soviet Central Asia*, Routledge: New York, 2007, pp. 52–4.
14. Olivier Roy, *Généalogie de l'islamisme*, Pluriel: Paris, 2002.
15. Bakhtiyar Babadjanov, 'Islam in Uzbekistan: From the Struggle for "Religious Purity" to Political Activism', in Boris Rumer, *Central Asia: A Gathering Storm?*, M. E. Sharpe: New York, 2005, pp. 299–330.
16. Hamit Algar, *Wahhabism: A Critical Essay*, Islamic Publications International, 2002.
17. Polonskaya and Malashenko, *Islam in Central Asia*, pp. 121–41.
18. See the Uzbek video on the encounter: https://www.youtube.com/watch?v-xwVS8CQg2s4

19. Vitaly V. Naumkin, 'Militant Islam in Central Asia: The Case of the Islamic Movement of Uzbekistan', Berkeley Program in Soviet and Post-Soviet Studies, Working Papers Series, Spring 2003, pp. 44–8, http://iseees.berkeley.edu/bps/publications/2003_06-naum.pdf
20. Emmanuel Karagiannis, *Political Islam in Central Asia: The Challenge of Hizb ut-Tahrir*, Routledge: New York, 2011.
21. Bayram Balci, and Didier Chaudet, 'Jihadism in Central Asia: A Credible Threat after the Western Withdrawal from Afghanistan?', *Carnegie Endowment for International Peace*, August 2014, http://carnegieendowment.org/2014/08/13/jihadism-in-central-asia-credible-threat-after-western-withdrawal-from-afghanistan/hkro
22. Sattarov, 'Islamic Revival and Islamic Activism in Post-Soviet Azerbaijan'.
23. Altay Goyushov, 'Islamic Revival in Azerbaijan', *Current Trends in Islamic Ideology*, vol. 7, November 2008, pp. 66–81.
24. American Foreign Policy Council, *World Almanac of Islamism*, chapter on Azerbaijan, http://almanac.afpc.org/Azerbaijan
25. Emil Souleimanov, and Maya Ehremann, 'The Rise of Militant Salafism in Azerbaijan and its Regional Implications', *Middle East Policy Council*, vol. 20, no. 3, 2013, http://www.readcube.com/articles/10.1111/mepo.12037
26. Sattarov, 'Islamic Revival and Islamic Activism in Post-Soviet Azerbaijan'.
27. Kemper, *Islamic Education in the Soviet Union and its Successor States*.
28. Achirbek Muminov, Uygun Gafurov and Rinat Shigabidinov, 'Islamic Education in Soviet and Post-Soviet Uzbekistan', in Kemper, *Islamic Education in the Soviet Union and its Successor States*, pp. 223–80.
29. On the thought of Abu Mansur al-Maturidi, see Rudolph Ulrich, *Al-Maturidi and the Development of Sunni Theology in Samarquand*, Brill: Leiden, 2014.
30. Brill Olcott, *In the Whirlwind of Jihad*, pp. 208–9.
31. Interview with Ashirbek Muminov, researcher at the Academy of Sciences of the Republic of Kazakhstan, Almaty, May 2010 and December 2014.
32. Interviews with Shuhrat Yovqochev, Tashkent, May 2007 and May 2008.
33. The *Ruhnama*, Turco-Persian for 'The Book of the Soul', is a treatise of moral precepts, philosophical reflections, legends and historical references, written by the first president of Turkmenistan, Saparmurat Niyazov, called *Turkmenbashi*, Head of the Turkmen. Imposed throughout the country's education system, the treatise also had a religious function and reading of it, alongside the Koran, was encouraged in all the country's mosques.
34. Interview with the head of the theology faculty, Ashkhabad, September 2008.

35. Brill Olcott, *In the Whirlwind of Jihad*, p. 207.
36. '2014 Annual report', United States Commission on International Religious Freedom, http://www.uscirf.gov/reports-briefs/annual-report/2014-annual-report

BIBLIOGRAPHY

Abbasov, Shahin, 'Azerbaijan: Iran Taking a Beating in Baku Press', *Eurasianet*, 14 February 2011, http://www.eurasianet.org/node/62889

Abramson, David, *Foreign Religious Education and the Central Asian Islamic Revival: Impact and Prospects for Stability*, Central Asia-Caucasus Institute and Silk Road Studies Program—A Joint Transatlantic Research and Policy Center: Washington, DC, 2010, http://www.isdp.eu/images/stories/isdp-main-pdf/2010_abramson_foreign-religious-education.pdf

Açikgöz, Hailil, *Türkistan İstiklâl Yolunda Hicret Yllari, Zuhriddin Mirza Abid Türkistanî*, Doğu Kütüphanesi: Istanbul, 2013.

Adam, Volker, 'Why Do They Cry? Criticism of Muharram Celebration in Tsarist and Socialist Azerbaijan', in Rainer Brunner and Ender Verner (eds), *The Twelver Shia in Modern Times: Religious Culture and Political History*, Brill: Leiden, 2000, pp. 114–34.

Adams, Laura, 'Public and Private Celebrations: Uzbekistan's National Holidays', in Jeff Sahadeo and Russell Zanca, *Everyday Life in Central Asia, Past and Present*, Indiana University Press: Bloomington, IN, 2007, pp. 198–213.

Afrasiabi, K. L., *After Khomeini: New Directions in Iran's Foreign Policy*, Westview Press: Boulder, CO, San Francisco, CA and Oxford, 1994.

Ahrari, Mohammad, *The New Great Game in Muslim Central Asia*, National Defense University: Washington, DC, 1996.

Akiner, Shirin, *The Formation of Kazakh Identity: From Tribe to Nation-State*, Royal Institute of International Affairs, 1995.

Alavi, Bahram, 'Ayatollah's Death Brings Rafsanjani Closer to Both Power and Problems', *Washington Report on Middle East Affairs*, August 1989, pp. 7–37.

Alexiev, Alex, 'Tablighi Jamaat: Jihad's Stealthy Legions', *Middle East Quarterly*, Winter 2005, pp. 3–11.

Algar, Hamit, *Wahhabism: A Critical Essay*, Islamic Publications International, 2002.

BIBLIOGRAPHY

Ali, Jan, 'Tabligh Jama'at: A Transnational Movement of Islamic Faith Regeneration', *European Journal of Economic and Political Studies*, vol. 3, 2010, pp. 110–13, http://ejeps.faith.edu.tr/docs/articles/67.pdf

Aliyev, Farhad, 'The Gulen Movement in Azerbaijan', *Current Trends in Islamist Ideology*, no. 5, 2012, http://www.currenttrends.org/docLib/20130124_CT14Aliev.pdf

Allen, Charles, 'The Hidden Roots of Wahhabism in British India', *World Policy Journal*, Summer 2005, pp. 87–93.

Allworth, Edward, *The Modern Uzbeks from the Fourteenth Century to the Present: A Cultural History*, Hoover Institution Press: Stanford, CA, 1990.

Al Rasheed, Madawi, *History of Saudi Arabia*, Cambridge University Press: Cambridge, 2010.

Alstadt, Audrey, *The Azerbaijani Turks: Power and Identity under Russian Rule*, Hoover Institute Press: Stanford, CA, 1992.

Amghar, Samir, 'La Ligue islamique mondiale en Europe: un instrument de défense des intérêts stratégiques saoudiens', *Critique Internationale*, no. 51, 2011, pp. 113–27, http://www.cairn.info/revue-critique-internationale-2011-2-page-113.htm

Anderson, John, *Kyrgyzstan: Central Asia's Island of Democracy?*, Routledge: New York, 1999.

Andican, Ahat, *Osmanli'dan Günümüze Türkiye ve Orta Asya*, Dogan Kitap: Istanbul, 2009, pp. 421–68.

Arif, Aminah Muhammad, *Salaam America: South Asian Muslims in New York*, Anthem Press: London, 2002.

Asatrian, Garnik, and Habib Borjian, 'Talish and the Talishis: The State of Research', *Iran and the Caucasus*, vol. 9, no. 1, 2005, pp. 43–72.

Atai, Farhad, and Hamidreza Azizi, 'The Energy Factor in Iran–Turkmenistan Relations', *Iranian Studies*, vol. 5, no. 6, 2012, pp. 745–58.

Aydin, Mustafa, 'Foucault's Pendulum: Turkey in Central Asia and the Caucasus', *Turkish Studies*, vol. 5, no. 2, 2004, pp. 1–22.

Babadjanov, Bakhtiyar, 'Islam in Uzbekistan: From the Struggle for "Religious Purity" to Political Activism', in Rumer Boris, *Central Asia: A Gathering Storm?*, M. E. Sharpe: New York, 2005, pp. 299–330.

———, 'Islam et activisme politique. Le cas Ouzbek', *Annales. Histoire, Sciences Sociales*, 2004/2005, pp. 1139–56.

Babadjanov, Bakhtiyar, and Muzaffar Kamilov, 'Muhammadjan Hindustani (1892–1989) and the Beginning of the "Great Schism" among Muslims in Uzbekistan', in Stéphane A. Dudoignon and Hisao Komatsu, *Islam and Politics in Russia and Central Asia (Early Eighteenth to Late Twentieth Centuries)*, Routledge: Abingdon, 2001.

Babadjanov, Bakhtiyar, 'On the History of the Naqsbandiya-Mugaddidiya in the Central Ma'wara'an-nahr in the Late 18th and Early 19th Centuries', in

BIBLIOGRAPHY

Michael Kemper, Anke von Kügelgen and Dmitruy Yermankov, *Muslim Culture in Russia and Central Asia from the 18th to the Early 20th Century*, vol. 1, Berlin, 1999, pp. 385–413.

Bal, Idris, 'The Turkish Model and the Turkic Republics', in Vedat Yücel and Salomon Ruysdael, *New Trends in Turkish Foreign Affairs*, Writers Club Press: New York, 2002, pp. 211–34.

Balci, Bayram, and Didier Chaudet, 'Jihadism in Central Asia: A Credible Threat after the Western Withdrawal from Afghanistan?', *Carnegie Endowment for International Peace*, August 2014, http://carnegieendowment.org/2014/08/13/jihadism-in-central-asia-credible-threat-after-western-withdrawal-from-afghanistan/hkro

———, 'Turkey's Political Crisis Undermining Democracy', *Carnegie Endowment for International Peace*, 21 March 2014, http://carnegieendowment.org/2014/03/21/turkey-s-plitical-crisis-undermining-democracy/h54e

———, 'Identité nationale et gestion du fait minoritaire en Asie centrale: analyse des affrontements interethniques d'Och en juin 2010', *Cahiers d'Asie centrale*, nos. 19–20, 2011, pp. 470–84.

———, 'Politique identitaire et construction diasporique en Azerbaïdjan post-Soviétique', *Cahiers d'Asie centrale*, nos. 19–20, 2011, pp. 261–76.

———, and Stéphane de Tapia, 'Mouvements migratoires entre la Turquie et les Républiques turcophones du Caucase et d'Asie centrale: les impacts religieux', *Revue européenne des migrations internationales*, vol. 26, no. 3, 2010, http://remi.revues.org/5225

———, 'Le renouveau islamique en Azerbaïdjan entre dynamiques internes et influences extérieures', *Études du CERI*, no. 138, 2007, http://www.sciencespo.fr/ceri/sites/sciencespo.fr.ceri/files/etude138.pdf

———, and Raoul Motika, 'Islam in Post-Soviet Georgia', *Central Asian Survey*, vol. 26, no. 3, 2007, pp. 335–53.

———, 'Central Asian Refugees in Saudi Arabia: Religious Evolution and Contribution to the Reislamization of their Motherland', *Refugee Survey Quarterly*, vol. 26, no. 2, 2007, pp. 12–21.

———, 'Between Sunnism and Shiism: Islam in Post-Soviet Azerbaijan', *Central Asian Survey*, vol. 23, no. 2, 2004, pp. 205–17.

———, 'La communauté ouzbèke d'Arabie saoudite: entre assimilation et renouveau identitaire', *Revue européenne des migrations internationales*, vol. 19, no. 3, 2003, http://remi.revues.org/2684

———, 'Les Ouzbeks d'Arabie saoudite entre intégration et renouveau identitaire via le pèlerinage', *Central Asian Survey*, vol. 22, no. 1, 2003, pp. 23–44.

———, 'Fethullah Gülen's Missionary Schools in Central Asia and their Role in the Spreading of Turkism and Islam', *Religion, State and Society*, vol. 31, no. 2, 2003, pp. 151–77.

BIBLIOGRAPHY

———, *Missionnaires de l'Islam en Asie centrale, the écoles turques de Fethullah Gülen*, Maisonneuve et Larose and Institut français d'études anatoliennes: Paris, 2003.

———, 'Les écoles néo-nurcu de Fethullah Gülen en Asie centrale: implantation, fonctionnement et nature du message véhiculé par le biais de la coopération éducative', *Revue des mondes musulmans et de la Méditerranée*, nos. 101–2, 2003, http://remmm.revues.org/54

———, 'Hoca Ahmet Yesevi: le mausolée et l'université', *Cahiers d'Études sur la Méditerranée Orientale et le monde Turco-Iranien*, no. 27, 1999, http://cemoti.revues.org/67

Barzegar, Kayhan, 'Foreign Policy Department/Middle East and Persian Gulf Studies Group', *Center for Strategic Research*, 2008, http://www.csr.ir/departments.aspx?Ing=en&abtid=07&&depid=74&semid=1421

Bedford, Sofi, *Islamic Activism in Azerbaijan: Repression and Mobilization in a Post-Soviet Context*, Stockholm Studies in Politics, no. 129, 2009, pp. 137–49.

Beeman, Milliam, 'The Struggle for Identity in Post-Soviet Tajikistan', *Middle East Review of International Affairs*, vol. 3, no. 4, 1999.

Bezanis, Lowell, 'Soviet Muslim Émigrés in the Republic of Turkey', *Central Asian Survey*, vol. 13, no. 1, 1994, pp. 59–180.

Bianchi, Robert R., *Guests of God: Pilgrimage and Politics in the Islamic World*, Oxford University Press: Oxford, 2004.

Bissenova, Alima, 'Central Asian Encounters in the Middle East: Nationalism, Islam and Postcoloniality in Al-Azhar', *Religion, State and Society*, vol. 33, no. 3, September 2005, pp. 254–64.

Braux, Adeline, *Moscou-Caucase: Migrations et diasporas dans l'espace post-soviétique*, Editions Pétra/IFEAC, Central Asia Collection, 2014.

Braux, Adeline, 'Azerbaijanis in Russia: An "Imagined" Diaspora?', in Marlène Laruelle (ed.), *Migration and Social Upheaval as the Face of Globalization in Central Asia*, Brill: Leiden, 2012, pp. 167–86.

Bregel, Y., 'Abu'l-Kayr Khan', *Encyclopaedia Iranica*, 1/3, pp. 331–2, http://www.iranicaonline.org/articles/abul-kayr-khan-oglan

Brill Olcott, Martha, *In the Whirlwind of Jihad*, Carnegie Endowment for International Peace: Washington, DC, 2012.

———, *Sufism in Central Asia: A Force of Moderation or a Cause of Politicization?*, Carnegie Papers: Washington, DC, no. 84, 2007.

Brill Olcott, Martha, and Marina Barnett, *The Andijan Uprising, Akramiya and Akram Yuldashev*, Carnegie, June 2006, http://carnegie.ru/publications/?fa=18453

Brower, Daniel, 'Russian Roads to Mecca: Religious Tolerance and Muslim Pilgrimage in the Russian Empire', *Slavic Review*, vol. 55, no. 3, 1996, pp. 567–84.

Broxup, Marie, 'The Basmachis', *Central Asian Survey*, vol. 2, no. 1, 1987, pp. 57–81, Washington, DC, 2012.

BIBLIOGRAPHY

Bruce, Benjamin, 'Gérer l'Islam à l'étranger; entre service public et outil de la politique étrangère turque', *Revue Anatoli*, no. 3, 2012, pp. 131–47.

Buchwalter, Bertrand, 'Les sommets de la Turcophonie', in Bayram Balci and Bertrand Buchwalter, *La Turquie en Asie centrale: La conversion au réalisme 1991–2000*, Institut Français d'Études Anatoliennes (IFEA): Istanbul, http://www.ifea-istanbul.net/dossiers_ifea/Bulten_05.pdf

Buehler, Arthur, *Revealed Grace: The Juristic Sufism of Ahmad Sirhindi (1564–1624)*, Fons Vitae: Louisville, KY, 2011.

———, *Sufi Heirs of the Prophet: The Indian Naqshbandiyya and the Rise of the Mediating Sufi Shaykh*, University of South Carolina Press: Columbia, SC, 1992, p. 22.

Bureau, Louis-Marie, *La Pensée de Fethullah Gülen*, L'Harmattan: Paris, 2013.

Burton, Audrey, 'Relations between the Khanate of Bukhara and Ottoman Turkey (1558–1702)', *International Journal of Turkish Studies*, vol. 5, 1990–91, pp. 83–103.

Calmard, Jean, 'Qâdjâr, 1794–1925', *Encyclopédie Universalis*, http://www.universalis.fr/encyclopedie/les-qadjar

Canfield, Robert L., *Turko-Persia in Historical Perspective*, Cambridge University Press: Cambridge, 2002.

Carrère d'Encausse, Hélène, *L'Empire éclaté: la révolte des nations en URSS*, Flammarion: Paris, 1978.

———, *La Politique soviétique au Moyen-Orient, 1955–1975*, Presses des Sciences Po: Paris, 1975.

Casanova, José, *Public Religions in the Modern World*, University of Chicago Press: Chicago, IL, 2004.

Chalk, Peter, *Encyclopedia of Terrorism*, ABC-CLIO: Santa Barbara, CA, 2012.

Chiffoleau, Sylvia, *Le Voyage à La Mecque. Un pèlerinage mondial en terre d'islam*, Belin: Paris, 2015.

———, 'Le pèlerinage à la Mecque: une industrie sous contrôle', *La vie des idées*, April 2014, http://www.laviedesidees.fr/le-pelerinage-a-La-Mecque-une.html

Chitadze, Nika, 'Geopolitical Interests of Iran in South Caucasus and Georgian–Iranian Relations', *Journal of Social Sciences*, vol. 1, no. 2, 2012, pp. 5–12.

Christian, David, 'Silk Road or Steppe Roads? The Silk Roads in World History', *Journal of World History*, vol. 11, no. 1, 2000, pp. 1–26.

Chuvin, Pierre, René Létolle and Sébastien Peyrouse, *Histoire de l'Asie centrale contemporaine*, Fayard: Paris, 2008.

Clark, Brenton, 'Persian Games: Iran's Strategic Foothold in Tajikistan', *Open Democracy*, April 2012, https://www.opendemocracy.net/od-russia/brenton-clark/persian-games-iran%E2%80%99s-strategic-foothold-in-tajikistan

BIBLIOGRAPHY

Clayer, Nathalie, 'La *Ahmadiyya lahori* et la réforme de l'islam albanais dans l'entre-deux-guerres', in Véronique Bouillier and Catherine Servan-Schreiber, *De l'Arabie à l'Himalaya. Chemins croisés en hommage à Marc Gaborieau*, Maisonneuve et Larose: Paris, 2004, pp. 211–28.

Commins, David, *The Wahhabi Mission and Saudi Arabia*, I. B. Tauris: London, 2006.

Compayré, Gabriel, 'Grandeur et limite de l'enseignement jésuite', *Encyclopédie de l'Agora*, http://agora.qc.ca/documents/jesuites—grandeur_et_limites de lenseignement _ jesuite_par Gabriel compayre

Cooley, Alexander, *Great Games, Local Rules: The New Great Power Contest in Central Asia*, Oxford University Press: Oxford, 2012.

Cornell, Svante, *Azerbaijan since Independence*, M. E. Sharpe: New York, 2011.

———, *Small Nations and Great Powers: A Study of Ethnopolitical Conflict in the Caucasus*, Routledge-Curzon: London and New York, 2001.

Daftary, Farhad, *The Isma'ilis: Their History and Doctrines*, Cambridge University Press: Cambridge, 1992, pp. 91–143.

Dakhlia, Jocelyne, 'Les miroirs des princes islamiques: une modernité sourde?', *Annales. Histoires, Sciences Sociales*, vol. 57, no. 5, 2002, pp. 1191–1206.

Dale, Stephen Frederic, 'The Legacy of the Timurids', *Journal of the Royal Asiatic Society*, 3rd series, vol. 8, no. 1, 1998, pp. 43–58.

Devlet, Nadir, 'Taking Stock: Turkey and the Turkic World 20 Years Later', *The German Marshall Fund of United States*, 10 November 2011, http://www.gmfus.org/wp-content/blogs.dir/1/files_mf/1321555956_magicfields_attachment_1_1.pdf

Devos, Claire, *Qawwali, la musique des maîtres du soufisme*, Editions du Makar: Paris, 1995.

De Cordier, Bruno, 'Islamic Faith-Based Development Organizations in Former Soviet Muslim Environments: the Mountain Societies Development Support Programme in the Rasht Valley, Tajikistan', *Central Asian Survey*, vol. 27, no. 2, 2008, pp. 169–84.

DeRouen, Karl, *Civil Wars of the World: Major Conflicts since World War II*, ABC-CLIO/ Greenwood: Westport, CT, vol. 1, 2007, pp. 753–71.

De Waal, Thomas, *Black Garden: Armenia and Azerbaijan through Peace and War*, New York University Press, 2003.

De Weese, Devin, 'The Eclipse of the Kubraviyah in Central Asia', *Iranian Studies*, vol. 21, no. 1–2, 1988, pp. 45–83.

Domborwsky, Patrick, 'L'Asie centrale face à la mondialisation', *La Pensée*, no. 338, 2004, pp. 37–45.

Dor, Rémy, *Chants du Toit du monde. Textes d'orature kirghize*, Maisonneuve et Larose: Paris, 1982.

Dorraj, Manochehr, and Nader Entessar, *Iran's Northern Exposure: Foreign Policy*

BIBLIOGRAPHY

Challenges in Eurasia, Center for International and Regional Studies, Georgetown University School of Foreign Service in Qatar, 2013, Occasional Paper no. 13, https://repository.library.georgetown.edu/bitstream/handle/10822/708817/CIRSOccasionalPaper13Dorraj Entessar2013.pdf?sequence=5

Dudoignon, Stéphane A., and Christian Noack, *Allah's Kolkhozes: Migration, De-Stalinisation, Privatisation and the New Muslim Congregations in the Soviet Realm (1950s-2000s)*, Klaus Schwarz Verlag: Berlin, 2014.

Dudoignon, Stéphane A., 'Islam et nationalisme en Asie centrale au début de la période soviétique (1924–1937). L'exemple de l'Ouzbékistan, à travers quelques sources littéraires', *Revue des mondes musulmans et de la Méditerranée*, 2002, pp. 95–8, http://remmm.revues.org/230

Edmunds, Timothy, 'The Environmental Movement in Kazakhstan: Ecology, Democracy and Nationalism', in Stephen Hussey and Paul Thompson, *The Roots of Environmental Consciousness*, Routledge: New York, 2000, pp. 139–59.

Efegil, Ertan, 'Turkish AK Party's Central Asia and Caucasus Policies: Critiques and Suggestions', *Caucasian Review of International Affairs*, vol. 2, no. 3, 2008, pp. 166–72, http://www.cria-online.org4_6.html

Erkinov, Aftandil, 'Manuscripts of the Works by Classical Persian Authors (Hafiz, Jami, Bidil): Quantitative Analysis of 17th–19th c. Central Asian Copies', in *Iran: Questions et connaissances. Actes du IVe Congrès Européen des études iraniennes organisés par la Societas Iranologica Europeana, Paris, 6–10 September 1999*, Vol. II, *Périodes médiévale et moderne*. [Cahiers de Studia Iranica 26], M. Szuppe, Association pour l'avancement des études iraniennes-Peeters Press: Paris and Leiden, 2002, pp. 213–28.

Ernst, Carl, and Bruce Lawrence, *Sufi Martyrs of Love: The Chisti Order in South Asia and Beyond*, Palgrave Macmillan: New York, 2002, pp. 65–83.

Esposito, John, *The Iranian Revolution: Its Global Impact*, University of Florida: Gainesville, FL, 1990.

Faroqhi, Suraiya, *Pilgrims and Sultans: The Hajj under the Ottomans*, I. B. Tauris: London, 2014.

Faruqi, Ziya ul Hasan, 'The Tablighi Jama'at', in S. T. Likandwala (ed.), *Islam and Contemporary India*, Indian Institute of Advanced Study: Simla, 1971, p. 60.

Filanovic, Margarita, and Zamira Usmanova, 'Les frontières occidentales de la diffusion du bouddhisme en Asie centrale', *Cahiers d'Asie centrale*, nos. 1–2, 1996, pp. 185–201.

Finkel, Caroline, *Osman's Dream: The Story of the Ottoman Empire 1300–1923*, John Murray: London, 2006.

Foltz, Richard, 'Cultural Contacts between Central Asia and Mughal India', *Central Asiatic Journal*, vol. 42, no. 1, 1998, pp. 44–65.

BIBLIOGRAPHY

Fourniau, Vincent, 'Les Arabes d'Asie central soviétique: maintenance et mutation de l'identité ethnique', *Revue du monde musulman et de la Méditerranée*, no. 59–60, 1991, pp. 83–100, http://www.persee.fr/web/revues/home/prescript/article/remmm_0997-1327_1991_num_59_1_1493

Fragner, Berg, 'Soviet Nationalism: An Ideological Legacy to the Independent Republics of Central Asia', in Willem van Schendel and Erik J. Zürcher, *Identity Politics in Central Asia and the Muslim World*, I. B. Tauris: London, 2001, pp. 13–34.

Frappi, Carlo, *Central Asia's Place in Turkey's Foreign Policy*, Instituto per Gli Studi di Politica Internazionale (ISP), no. 225, 2013, http://www.ispionline.it/sites/default/files/pubblicazioni/analysis_225_2013.pdf

Friedmann, Yohannan, *Shaikh Ahmad Sirhindi: An Outline of his Thought and a Study of his Image in the Eyes of Posterity*, Oxford University Press: New Delhi, 2000.

Fumagalli, Matteo, 'Ethnicity, State Formation and Foreign Policy: Uzbekistan and "Uzbeks Abroad"', *Central Asian Survey*, vol. 26, no. 1, 2007, pp. 105–22.

———, 'Framing Ethnic Minority Mobilisation in Central Asia: The Case of Uzbeks in Kyrgyzstan and Tajikistan', *Europe-Asia Studies*, vol. 59, no. 4, 2007, pp. 567–90.

Gaborieau, Marc, 'The Transformation of Tablighi Jama'at into a Transnational Movement', in Muhammad Khalid Masud, *Travellers in Faith: Studies of the Tablighi Jama'at as a Transnational Movement for Faith Renewal*, Brill: Leiden, 2010, pp. 121–38.

———, 'What is Left of Sufism in Tablighi Jama'at?', *Archives de sciences sociales des religions*, no. 135, 2006, pp. 53–72.

Gayer, Laurent, 'From the Oxus to the Indus: Looking Back at India—Central Asia Connections in the Early Modern Age', in Marlène Laruelle, Sébastien Peyrouse, Jean-François Huchet and Bayram Balci, *China and India in Central Asia. A New "Great Game"?*, Palgrave Macmillian: New York, 2010.

Gaziyev, Jamshid, *Ethnonationalism in Central Asia: Inter-Ethnic Conflicts and Institutional Ethnicity in the Land of Eternal Friendship and Brotherly Nations*, LAP LAMBERT Academic Publishing: Sarrbrücken, 2010.

Ginat, Rami, *The Soviet Union and Egypt, 1945–1958*, Frank Cass: London, 1993.

Golan, Galia, *Soviet Policies in the Middle East*, Cambridge University Press: Cambridge, 1990.

Goyushov, Altay, and Elçin Eskerov, 'Islam and Islamic Education in Soviet and Independent Azerbaijan', in Michael Kemper, Raoul Motika and Stefan Reichmuth, *Islamic Education in the Soviet Union and its Successor States*, Routledge: Abingdon, 2000, pp. 168–222.

BIBLIOGRAPHY

———, 'Islamic Revival in Azerbaijan', *Current Trends in Islamic Ideology*, vol. 7, November 2008, pp. 66–81.

Gozaydin, Istar, *Diyanet, Türkiye Cumhuriyetinde Dinin Tanzimi*, Iletisim Yayinlari: Istanbul, 2009.

———, 'Diyanet and Politics', *The Muslim World*, vol. 98, nos. 2–3, pp. 216–27, April 2008, http://onlinelibrary.wiley.com/doi/10.1111/j.1478-1913.2008.00220.x/abstract

Gril, Denis, 'De l'usage sanctifiant des biens en islam', *Revue de l'histoire des religions*, vol. 215, no. 1, 1998, pp. 59–89.

Gross, Jo-Ann, 'The Naqshibandiyya Connection from Central Asia to India and Back (16th-19th centuries)', in Scott Levi, *India and Central Asia: Commerce and Culture, 1500–1800*, Oxford University Press: Delhi, 2007, pp. 233–59.

Gülen, Fethullah, *Terror and Suicide Attacks: An Islamic Perspective*, The Light: New Jersey, 2004.

Haahr, Kathryn, 'Spanish Police Arrest Jamaat al-Tabligh Members in Bomb Threat', Jamestown, ND, February 2008, http://www.jamestown.org/single/?tx_ttnews%5Btt_news%5D=4722&no_cache=1#.VrbrbljhDIU

Hagan, Jacqueline, and Helen Rose-Ebaugh, 'Calling upon the Sacred: Migrants' Use of Religion in the Migration Process', *International Migration Review*, vol. 37, no. 4, 2003, pp. 1145–62.

Haidar, Mansura, *Central Asia in the Sixteenth Century*, Manohar: New Delhi, 2002.

Hall, Stuart, 'Cultural Identity and Diaspora', in Jonathan Rutherford (ed.), *Identity: Community, Culture, Difference*, Lawrence and Wishart: London, 1990, pp. 222–37.

Heathershaw, John, and David W. Montgomery, *The Myth of Post-Soviet Muslim Radicalization in the Central Asian Republics*, Royal Institute of International Affairs, Chatham House: London, November 2015, https://www.chathamhouse.org/sites/files/chathamhouse/field/field_document/20141111PostSovietRadicalizationHeathershawMontgomery.pdf

Hendrick, Joshua, *Gülen: The Ambiguous Politics of Market Islam in Turkey and the World*, New York University Press: New York, 2013.

Herzig, Edmund, *Iran and the Former Soviet South*, Royal Institute of International Affairs: London, 1995.

Hiro, Dilip, *Inside Central Asia: A Political and Cultural History of Uzbekistan, Turkmenistan, Kazakhstan, Kyrgyzstan, Tajikistan, Turkey and Iran*, Overlook Press: New York, 2009.

Hisao, Komatsu, 'The Andijan Uprising Reconsidered', in Sato Tsugitaka, *Muslim Societies: Historical and Comparative Perspectives*, Routledge: Abingdon, 2004.

BIBLIOGRAPHY

Horn, Robert, *Soviet-Indian Relations: Issues and Influences*, Praeger: New York, 1982.

Hunter, Shireen, *Iran's Foreign Policy in the Post-Soviet Era: Resisting the New International Order*, ABC-CLIO/Greenwood: Westport, CT, 2010, pp. 169–85.

———, 'Security and Environment in the Caspian Sea', in William Ascher and Natalia Mirovitskaya, *The Caspian Sea: A Quest for Environmental Security*, Kluwer Academic Publishers: Dordrecht, 2000, pp. 117–24.

———, 'Iran and the Transcaucasus in the Post-Soviet Era', in David Menashri, *Central Asia Meets the Middle East*, Frank Cass: London 1998, pp. 98–125.

———, 'Greater Azerbaijan: Myth or Reality', in Mohammad Reza-Djalili, *Le Caucase post-soviétique. La transition dans le conflit*, Bruylant: Brussels, 1995, pp. 115–42.

Hurgronje, Christiaan Snouck, 'Notes sur le mouvement du pèlerinage de la Mecque aux Indes Néerlandaises', *Revue du Monde Musulman*, no. 15, 1911, pp. 397–413.

Huskey, Eugene, 'National Identity from Scratch: Defining Kyrgyzstan's Role in World Affairs', *Journal of Communist Studies and Transition Politics*, vol. 19, no. 3, 2003, pp. 111–38.

Ishakova, Hege, and Khadia Akhmedova, 'Les migrations des Ouïgours vers l'Asie centrale ex-soviétique', *Cahiers d'Études sur la Méditerranée Orientale et le monde Turco-Iranien*, no. 25, 1998, http://cemoti.revues.org/59

Ismailbekova, Aksana, and Emil Nasritdinov, 'Transnational Social Networks in Central Asia: Structure, Travel, and Culture of Krygyz Tablighi Jama'at', *Transnational Social Review*, vol. 2, no. 2, 2012, pp. 177–95.

Jackson, Peter, *The Delhi Sultanate: A Political and Military History*, Cambridge University Press: Cambridge 1999.

Jaffrelot, Christophe, *The Hindu Nationalist Movement and Indian Politics, 1925 to the 1990s*, Hurst: London, 1996.

———, 'Le syncrétisme stratégique et la construction de l'identité nationaliste hindoue', *Revue française de science politique*, vol. 42, no. 4, 1992, pp. 594–617.

Jalali, Ali A., 'Iran–Central Asia: Reminiscing the Past and Looking to the Future', *Journal of Iranian Research and Analysis*, vol. 16, no. 2, 2000, pp. 72–8.

Janson, Marloes, 'Roaming about for God's Sake: The Upsurge of the Tabligh Jama'at in Gambia', *Journal of Religions in Africa*, vol. 35, no. 4, 2005, pp. 450–81.

Jeangène Vilmer, Jean-Baptiste, *Turkménistan*, CNRS Éditions: Paris, 2010.

Jones Luong, Pauline, *Islam, Society, and Politics in Central Asia, Central Eurasia in Context*, University of Pittsburgh Press: Pittsburgh, PA, 2017.

BIBLIOGRAPHY

Jonker, Gerdien, *The Ahmadiyya Quest for Religious Progress: Missionizing Europe 1900–1965*, Brill: Leiden 2009.

Jonson, Lena, *Tajikistan in the New Central Asia: Geopolitics, Great Power Rivalry and Radical Islam*, I. B. Tauris: London, 2006, p. 25.

Kakachia, Kornely K., 'Iran and Georgia: Genuine Partnership or Marriage of Convenience?', *PONARIS, Eurasia Policy Memo*, no. 186, September 2011, http://www.gwu.edu/~ieresgwu/assets/docs/ponars/pepm_186.pdf

Kane, Eileen, *Odessa as a Hajj Hub: 1880's to 1910's*, National Council for Eurasian and East European Research, March 2011.

———, *Russian Hajj: Empire and Pilgrimage to Mecca*, Cornell University Press: Ithaca, NY, 2015.

Kappeler, Andreas, Gerhard Simon and Georg Brunner, *Muslim Communities Reemerge: Historical Perspectives on Nationality, Politics, and Opposition in the Former Soviet Union and Yugoslavia*, Duke University Press: Durham, NC, 1994.

Karagiannis, Emmanuel, *Political Islam in Central Asia: The Challenge of Hizb ut-Tahrir*, Routledge: New York, 2011.

Kehl-Bodrogi, Krisztina, *'Religion is not so strong here': Muslim Religious Life in Khorezm after Socialism*, Halle Studies in the Anthropology of Eurasia, Lit Verlag: Berlin, no. 18, 2008.

Kehren, Lucien, *Tamerlan: l'empire du seigneur de fer*, La Braconnière: Neuchâtel, 1978.

Keller, Shoshana, *To Moscow, Not Mecca: The Soviet Campaign against Islam in Central Asia 1917–1941*, Praeger: Westport, CT, 2001.

Kemper, Michael, Raoul Motika and Stefan Reichmuth, *Islamic Education in the Soviet Union and its Successor States*, Routledge: Abingdon, 2000.

Kemper, Michael, Anke von Kügelgen and Dmitruy Yermankov, *Muslim Culture in Russia and Central Asia from the 18th to the Early 20th Century*, vol. 1, Berlin, 1999.

Kepel, Gilles, '*Foi et pratique*: Tablighi Jama'at in France', in Muhammad Khalid Masud, *Travelers in Faith: Studies of the Tablighi Jama'at as a Transnational Movement for Faith Renewal*, Brill: Leiden, 2010, pp. 188–205.

Kervran, Monique, 'Entre l'Inde et l'Asie centrale: les mausolées islamiques du Sind et du sud Penjab', *Cahiers d'Asie centrale*, no. 1–2, 1996, pp. 133–71.

Khalaji, Mehdi, 'The Last Marja: Sistani and the End of Traditional Religious Authority in Shiism', *Washington Institute for Near Eastern Policy*, September 2006, http://www.washingtoninstitute.org/uploads/Documents/pubs/PolicyFocus59final.pdf

Khalid, Adeeb, *Islam after Communism*, University of California Press: Oakland, CA, 2014.

———, 'Ulama and the State in Uzbekistan', *Asian Journal of Social Science*, vol. 42, no. 5, 2014, pp. 517–35.

BIBLIOGRAPHY

———, *The Politics of Muslim Cultural Reform: Jadidism in Central Asia*, University of California Press: Oakland, CA, 2007.

Kirimli, Hakan, *National Movements and National Identity among the Crimean Tatars (1905–1916)*, Brill: Leiden, 1996.

Korkut, Şenol, 'The Diyanet of Turkey and its Activities in Eurasia after the Cold War', *Acta Slavica Iaponica*, vol. 28, pp. 117–39, http://src-hokudai-ac.jp/publictn/acta/28/06Korkut.pdf

Laçiner, Sedat, 'Turgut Özal Period in Turkish Foreign Policy: Özalism', *Journal of Turkish Weekly*, 9 March 2009, http://www.turkishweekly.net/print.asp?type=2&id=333

Lal, Rollie, *Central Asia and its Asian Neighbors: Security and Commerce at the Crossroads*, Rand Corporation: Santa Monica, 2006, p. 11.

Landau, Jacob, and Barbara Kellner-Heinkele, *Language Politics in Contemporary Central Asia: National and Ethnic Identity and the Soviet Legacy*, I. B. Tauris: London, 2012.

Laruelle, Marlène, and Sébastien Peyrouse, *Globalizing Central Asia: Geopolitics and the Challenges of Economic Development*, Routledge: Abingdon, 2013.

Le Berre, Marc, and Gérard Fussman, 'Monuments bouddhiques de la region de Caboul, 1, Le monastère de Gul Dara', *Mémoires de la Délégation Archéologique Française en Afghanistan*, Vol. XXII, Diffusion de Boccard: Paris, 1976.

Lemercier-Quelquejay, Chantal, 'Islam and Identity in Azerbaijan', *Central Asian Survey*, vol. 3, no. 2, 1984, pp. 29–55.

Leverrier, Ignace, 'L'Arabie saoudite, le pèlerinage et l'Iran', *Cahiers d'Études sur la Méditerranée Orientale et le monde Turco-Iranien*, no. 22, 1996, http://cemoti.revues.org/137

Levi, Scott, *Indian Merchants on the Silk Road*, Penguin/Allen Lane: London, 2015.

Levi, Scott, and Muzaffar Alam, *India and Central Asia: Commerce and Culture, 1500–1800*, Oxford University Press: New Delhi, 2007, pp. 1–37.

Liberman, Sherri, *A Historical Atlas of Azerbaijan*, Rosen Publishing Group: New York, 2004.

Lisnyyansky, Dina, 'Tashaya (Conversion to Shiism) in Central Asia and Russia', *Current Trends in Islamist Ideology*, vol. 8, 2009, pp. 108–17.

Louër, Laurence, 'Déconstruire le croissant chiite', *Revue internationale et stratégique*, no. 76, 2009, pp. 45–54.

Louw, Maria Elisabeth, *Everyday Islam in Post-Soviet Central Asia*, Routledge: New York, 2007, pp. 52–4.

Low, Michael Christopher, *Empire of the Hajj: Pilgrims, Plagues, and Pan Islam under British Surveillance, 1865–1926*, History Thesis, University of Georgia: Athens, OH, 2007, http://scholarworks.gsu.edu/cgi/viewcontent.cgi?article=1021&context=history_theses

BIBLIOGRAPHY

Lukonin, Vladimir, and Anatoli Ivanov, *Central Asian Arts*, Parkstone International: London, 2012.

Madelung, W., *Māturīdiyya. Encyclopédie de l'Islam*, Brill Online, 2015, http://referenceworks.brillonline.com/entries/encyclopedie-de-l-islam/ma-turi-diyya-SIM_5046

Mardin, Serif, *Religion and Social Change in Modern Turkey: The Case of Bediuzzaman Said Nursi*, State University of New York Press: New York, 1989.

Massicard, Elise, 'L'organisation des rapports entre État et religion en Turquie', *CRDF*, no. 4, 2005, pp. 119–28, http://www.unicaen.fr/puc/ecrire/revues/crdf/crdf4/crdf0411breuillard.pdf

Mastibekov, Otambek, *Leadership and Authority in Central Asia: The Ismaili Community in Tajikistan*, Routledge: New York, 2014, pp. 83–112, 127–48.

Masud, Muhammad Khalid Masud, *Travellers in Faith: Studies of the Tablighi Jama'at as a Transnational Movement for Faith Renewal*, Brill: Leiden, 2010.

———, 'Ideology and Legitimacy', in Masud, *Travellers in Faith*, Brill: Leiden, 2010, pp. 3–44.

McChesney, Robert D., 'Central Asia's Place in the Middle East—Some Historical Considerations', in David Menashri, *Central Asia Meets the Middle East*, Frank Cass: London, 1998, pp. 25–51.

Melvin, Neil J., *Uzbekistan: Transition to Authoritarianism on the Silk Road*, Taylor and Francis Library, 2005, p. 42.

Mervin, Sabrina, *Les Mondes chiites et l'Iran*, Karthala/IFPO: Paris and Beirut, 2007.

———, 'Les autorités religieuses dans le chiisme duodécimain contemporain', *Archives de sciences sociales des religions*, no. 125, January–March 2004, http://assr.revues.org/index1033.html

———, *Histoire de l'Islam, fondements et doctrines*, Flammarion: Paris 2000.

Metcalf, Barbara, *Islamic Revival in British India: Deoband, 1860–1900*, Princeton University Press: Princeton, NJ, 2005.

Minkel, Elizabeth, 'The magazine that almost changed the world', *New Yorker*, 26 May 2011, http://www.newyorker.com/books/page-turner/the-magazine-that-almost-changed-the-world

Mirzoyan, Alla, *Armenia, the Regional Powers, and the West: Between History and Geopolitics*, Palgrave Macmillan: Basingstoke, 2010.

Mkrtchyan, Tatevik, 'Shi'a Politics, "Strategic Culture" and Iran's Relations with the South Caucasus', in Alexander Agadjanian, Ansgar Jödicke and Evert van der Zweerde (eds), *Religion, Nation and Democracy in the South Caucasus*, Brill: Leiden, 2014, pp. 221–37.

Moazami, Behrooz, *State, Religion, and Revolution in Iran, 1796 to the Present*, Palgrave Macmillan: Basingstoke, 2013, pp. 93–117.

BIBLIOGRAPHY

Moojan, Momen, *An Introduction to Shi'i Islam: The History and Doctrines of Twelver Shiism*, Yale University Press: New Haven, CT, 1985.

Morton, A.H., 'The Early Years of Shah Ismail in the Afzal al tavarikh and Elsewhere', in Charles Melville, *Safavid Persia: The History and Politics of an Islamic Society*, I. B. Tauris: London, 1999.

Motika, Raoul, 'Islam in Post-Soviet Azerbaijan', *Archives de sciences sociales des religions*, no. 115, July–September 2001, http://assr.revues.org/18423; DOI: 10.4000/assr.18423

Mukminova, Razia, 'Les routes caravanières entre villes de l'Inde et de l'Asie centrale: déplacements des artisans et circulation des articles artisanaux', *Cahiers d'Asie centrale*, no. 1–2, 1996, pp. 85–90.

Muminov, Achirbek, Uygun Gafurov and Rinat Shigabidinov, 'Islamic Education in Soviet and Post-Soviet Uzbekistan', in Michael Kemper Raoul Motika and Stefan Reichmuth, *Islamic Education in the Soviet Union and its Successor States*, Routledge: Abingdon, 2000.

Naby, Eden, 'The Uzbeks of Afghanistan', *Central Asian Survey*, vol. 3, no. 1, 1984, pp. 1–21.

Najafizadeh, Mehrangiz, 'Gender and Ideology: Social Change and Islam in Post-Soviet Azerbaijan', *Journal of Third World Studies*, vol. 29, no. 1, 2012, pp. 81–107.

Natufe, O. Igho, *Soviet Policy in Africa from Lenin to Brezhnev*, Bloomington University Press: Bloomington, MD, 2011.

Naumkin, Vitaly V., 'Militant Islam in Central Asia: The Case of the Islamic Movement of Uzbekistan', *Berkeley Program in Soviet and Post-Soviet Studies— Working Papers Series*, Spring 2003, pp. 44–8, http://iseees.berkeley.edu/bps/publications/2003_06-naum.pdf

Niblock, Tim, *Saudi Arabia: Power, Legitimacy and Survival*, Routledge: New York, 2006.

Niyozov, Sarfaroz, 'Evolution of the Shi'a Ismaili Tradition in Central Asia', Institute of Ismaili Studies, *The Ismaili UK*, March 2002, http://www.iis.ac.uk/SiteAssets/pdf/evolution_central_asia.pdf

O'Dell, Emily, 'The Teaching, Practice and Political Role of Sufism in Dushanbe', NCEEER Working Paper, 2011, URL: https://www.ucis.pitt.edu/nceeer/2011_825–01h_O'Dell.pdf

Oka Natsuko, 'A Note on Ethnic Migration Policy in Kazakhstan: Changing Priority and a Growing Dilemma', Institute of Developing Economies: Tokyo, March 2013, https://ir.ide.go.jp/dspace/bitstream/2344/1218/1/ARRIDE_Discussion_No. 394_oka.pdf

Oran, Baskýn, 'Occidentalisation, nationalisme et "synthèse turco-islamique"', *Cahiers d'Études sur la Méditerranée Orientale et le monde Turco-Iranien*, no. 10, 1990, http://cemoti.revues.org/417

BIBLIOGRAPHY

Özgür, Iren, *Islamic Schools in Modern Turkey: Faith, Politics and Education*, Cambridge University Press: Cambridge, 2012.

Özkan, Mehmet, 'Turkey's Religious and Socio-Political Depth in Africa', *London School of Economics*, http://www.lse.ac.uk/IDEAS/publications/reports/pdf/SR016/SR-016-Ozkan.pdf

Pearson, M. N., 'Mughals and the Hajj', *Journal of Oriental Society of Australia*, vol. 18–19, 1986–7, pp. 164–79.

Pelkmans, Mathijs, Realigning Religion and Power in Central Asia: Islam, Nation-State and (Post)socialism', *Europe-Asia Studies*, vol. 61, no. 9, 2009, pp. 1517–41.

Petric, Boris, 'Les Ironis en Ouzbékistan post-soviétique ou les vertus de la dissimulation mentale (taqiyya) dans un contexte de sunnitisation de la société', in Mervin, *Les Mondes chiites et l'Iran*, pp. 189–210.

Peyrouse, Sébastien, 'Iran's Growing Role in Central Asia? Geopolitical, Economic and Political Profit and Loss Account', *Al Jazeera*, 2014, http://studies.aljazeera.net/en/dossiers/2014/04/2014416940377354.html

Peyrouse, Sébastien, and Sadykzhan Ibraimov, 'Iran's Central Asia Temptations', *Current Trends in Islamist Ideology*, vol. 10, 2010, pp. 87–101.

Peyrouse, Sébastien, *Turkménistan. Un destin au carrefour des empires*, Belin: Paris, 2007.

Philippon, Alix, *Soufisme et politique au Pakistan. Le mouvement barelwi à l'heure de la 'guerre contre terrorisme'*, Khartala: Paris, 2011.

Pieri, Zakarias, *Tablighi Jamaat and the Quest for the London Mega Mosque: Continuity and Change*, Palgrave: Basingstoke, 2015.

Polonskaya, Ludmila and Alexei Malashenko, *Islam in Central Asia*, Ithaca Press: Reading, 1994.

Poujol, Catherine, *L'Islam en Asie centrale: vers la nouvelle donne*, Ellipse: Paris, 2001.

Prasad, Conor, *Georgia's Muslim Community: A Self-Fulfilling Prophecy?*, European Center for Minority Issues, Working Paper no. 58, 2012, http://www.ecmi.de/uploads/tx_Ifpubdb/Working_Paper_58_En.pdf

Purtas, Firat, 'Kültürel Diplomasi ve TÜRKSOY', http://mekam.org/mekam/kulturel-diplomasi-ve-turksoy

Putz, Catherine, "Turkish Targeting of Gülen Movement Reaches into Central Asia", *The Diplomat*, 25 July 2016, http://thediplomat.com/2016/07/turkish-targeting-of-gulen-movement-reaches-into-central-asia/

Rahmonova-Schwarz, Delia, 'Migrations during the Soviet Period and in the Early Years of the USSR's Dissolution: A Focus on Central Asia', *Revue européenne des migrations internationales*, vol. 26, no. 3, 2010, http://remi.revues.org/5196

Raine, Fernande, 'Stalin and the Creation of the Azerbaijan Democratic Party in Iran, 1945', *Cold War History*, vol. 2, no. 1, 2001, pp. 1–38.

BIBLIOGRAPHY

Rasanayagam, Johan, 'Morality, Self and Power: The Idea of Mahalla in Uzbekistan', in Monica Heintz, *The Anthropology of Moralities*, Berghahn Books: Oxford, 2009, pp. 102–17.

Reynolds, Michael A., 'Damaging Democracy: The U.S., Fethullah Gülen, and Turkey's Upheaval', Foreign Policy Research Institute, September 2016, http://www.fpri.org/article/2016/09/damaging-democracy-u-s-fethullah-gulen-turkeys-upheaval/

Reza Djalili, Mohammad, 'L'Iran et la Turquie face à l'Asie centrale', *Journal for International and Strategic Studies*, no. 1, 2008, pp. 13–19.

———, 'Iran and the Caucasus: Maintaining Some Pragmatism', *Quarterly Journal*, no. 3, September 2002, pp. 49–57.

———, and Thierry Kellner, *Géopolitique de la nouvelle Asie centrale, de la fin de l'URSS à l'après-11 septembre*, Graduate Institute Publications: Geneva, 2001, ch. 5, pp. 185–278.

———, 'L'Iran face aux développements en Transcaucasie et en Asie Centrale', *Cahiers d'Etudes sur la Méditerranée Orientale et le monde Turco-Iranien*, no. 16, 1993, http://cemoti.revues.org/313

Ro'I, Yaacov, *Islam in the Soviet Union: From the Second World War to Perestroika*, Columbia University Press: New York, 2000.

Rosskeen Gibb, Sir Hamilton Alexander, *The Arab Conquests in Central Asia*, Royal Asiatic Society: London, 1923, https://archive.org/details/arabconquestssince00gibbuoft

Rotar, Igor, 'Uzbekistan: Tight Restrictions on Shia Muslim Minority', Forum 18, April 2004, http://www.forum18.org/archive.php?article_id=307&07&pdf=Y

Roy, Olivier, *Généalogie de l'islamisme*, Pluriel: Paris, 2002.

———, *L'Islam mondialisé*, Seuil: Paris, 2002.

———, 'Islam et politique en Asie centrale', *Archives de sciences sociales des religions*, no. 115, 2001, pp. 49–61.

———, *La nouvelle Asie centrale ou la fabrication des nations*, Seuil: Paris, 1997.

———, 'En Asie centrale: kolkhozien et entreprenants', in Jean-François Bayart, *La Réinvention du capitalisme*, Karthala: Paris, 1994, pp. 73–86.

———, 'Ethnies et politique en Asia centrale', *Revue du monde musulman et de la Méditerranée*, nos. 59/60, 1992, pp. 17–37, http://remmm.revues.org/persee-178997

Rtveladze, Edvard, 'The Great Indian Road: India—Central Asia—Transcaucasia', in Anita Sengupta and Mirzhoid Rakhimov (eds), *Insight and Communities: South and Central and South*, KW Publishers: New Delhi, 2015, pp. 59–74.

Sadegh-Zadeh, Kaweh, 'Iran's Strategy in the South Caucasus', *Caucasian Review of International Affairs*, vol. 2, no. 1, Winter 2008, pp. 1–7.

BIBLIOGRAPHY

Sadowsky, Yahya, 'For the Tablighi Islam is not Totalitarian', *Brookings Review*, vol. 14, no. 3, Summer 1996.

Sattarov, Rufat, 'Islamic Revival and Islamic Activism in Post-Soviet Azerbaijan', in Galina Yemelianova (ed.), *Islamic Radicalism in the Former Soviet Union*, Routledge: New York, 2011, pp. 146–211.

Saunders, Robert, 'A Forgotten Core? Mapping the Globality of Central Asia', *Globality Studies Journal*, 2010, http://www.oalib.com/paper/2178855#.U81fl1d5Bqw

Savory, Roger, *Iran under the Safavids*, Cambridge University Press: Cambridge, 1980.

Serrano, Silvia, 'L'Eglise orthodoxe géorgienne, un référent identitaire ambigu', in Bayram Balci and Raoul Motika, *Religion et politique dans le Caucase post soviétique*, Maisonneuve et Larose: Paris, 2007, pp. 251–76.

Shalinski, Audrey, 'Islam and Ethnicity: The Northern Afghan Perspective', *Central Asian Survey*, vol. 1, nos. 2–3, 1982, pp. 71–84.

Shanahan, Rodger, 'Iranian Foreign Policy under Rouhani', Lowy Institute for International Policy: Sydney, February 2015.

Shelala II, Robert M., Nori Kasting and Anthony H. Cordesman, 'US and Iranian Strategic Competition: Afghanistan, Pakistan, India, and Central Asia', Center for Strategic and International Studies: Washington, DC, 2013, http://csis.org/files/publication/130626_AfPak_Asia.pdf

Sikand, Yoginder, 'Plane "Plot": Media Targets Tablighi Jamaat', *Milli Gazette Online*, 19 August 2006, http://www.milligazette.com/dailyupdate/2006/20060819_Tablighi-Jamaat_terrorism.htm

———, 'The Tabligh Jama'at and Politics: A Critical Re-Appraisal', *Muslim World*, vol. 96, no. 1, pp. 175–95, January 2006.

Souleimanov, Emil and Maya Ehremann, 'The Rise of Militant Salafism in Azerbaijan and its Regional Implications', *Middle East Policy Council*, vol. 20, no. 3, 2013, http://www.readcube.com/articles/10.1111/mepo.12037

Starr, Frederick, *Lost Enlightenment: Central Asia's Golden Age from the Arab Conquest to Tamerlane*, Princeton University Press: Princeton, NJ, 2013.

Suvorova, Anna, *Muslim Saints of South Asia: The Eleventh to Fifteenth Centuries*, Routledge: London, 2004, pp. 59–80.

Swietochowski, Tadeusz, *Russia and Azerbaijan: A Borderland in Transition*, Columbia University Press: New York, 1995.

———, *Russian Azerbaijan, 1905–1920: The Shaping of a National Identity in a Muslim Community*, Cambridge University Press: Cambridge, 1985.

Tamm, Eric Enno, *The Horse That Leaps through Clouds: A Tale of Espionage, the Silk Road and the Rise of Modern China*, Douglas & McIntyre: Vancouver, 2010.

Thackston, W. M. Jr, *The Baburnama: Memoirs of Babur, Prince and Emperor*, Modern Library: New York, 2002.

BIBLIOGRAPHY

Tittensor, David, *The House of Service: The Gülen Movement and Islam's Third Way*, Oxford University Press: Oxford, 2014.

Togliacozzo, Eric, *The Longest Journey: Southeast Asians and the Pilgrimage to Mecca*, Oxford University Press: Oxford, 2013.

Toktogulova, Mukaram, 'The Localization of the Transnational Tablighi Jama'at in Kyrgyzstan: Structures, Concepts, Practices and Metaphors', *Crossroads Asia: Conflict, Migration, Development*, March 2014, Bonn.

Tozy, Mohamed, 'Sequences of a Quest: Tablighi Jama'at in Morocco', in Muhammad Khalid Masud, *Travellers in Faith: Studies of the Tablighi Jama'at as a Transnational Movement for Faith Renewal*, Brill: Leiden, 2010, pp. 161–73.

Trimingham, Spencer, *The Sufi Orders in Islam*, Oxford University Press: Oxford, 1971.

Troll, Christian, 'Two Conceptions of Da'wa in India: Jama'at-i Islami and Tablighi Jama'at', *Archives de sciences sociales des religions*, no. 87, July–September 1994, pp. 115–33.

Tursunbaeva, Kanykei, 'Central Asia's Rulers View Turkish "Soap Power" with Suspicion', *Global Voices*, 7 August 2014, http://globalvoicesonline.org/2014/08/07/central-asias-rulers-view-turkish-soap-power-with-suspicion

Ulrich, Rudolph, *Al-Maturidi and the Development of Sunni Theology in Samarquand*, Brill: Leiden, 2014.

van der Heide, Nienke, *The Manas Epic and Society in Kyrgyzstan*, Rozenberg Publishers: Amsterdam, 2008.

Warikoo, K., 'Trade Relations between Central Asia and Kashmir Himalayas during the Dogra Period (1846–1947)', *Cahiers d'Asie Centrale*, no. 1–2, 1996, pp. 113–24.

Wastnidge, Edward, 'Pragmatic Politics: Iran, Central Asia and the Cultural Foreign Policy', *Central Asia and the Caucasus*, vol. 15, no. 4, 2014, http://www.ca-c.org/online/2014/journal_eng/cac-04/11.shtml

Weismann, Itzchak, *The Naqshbandiyya: Orthodoxy and Activism in a Worldwide Sufi Tradition*, Routledge: New York, 2007.

Winrow, Gareth, *Turkey's Energy Aspirations: Pipe Dream or Real Projects?*, Brookings Institute Policy Paper no. 4, April 2014, http://www.brookings.edu/~/media/research/files/papers/2014/04/realization%20turkeys%20energy%20aspirations%20winrow/turkeys%20energy%20aspirations.pdf

Yanik, Lerna, 'The Politics of Education Exchange: Turkish Education in Eurasia', *Europe-Asia Studies*, vol. 56, no. 2, 2004, pp. 293–307.

Yemelianova, Galina, 'Islam, National Identity and Politics in Contemporary Kazakhstan', *Asian Ethnicity*, vol. 15, no. 3, 2014, pp. 286–301, http://pureoai.bham.ac.uk/ws/files/17507783/Yemelianova_Islam_national_identity_politics_contemporary_Kazakhstan_Asian_Ethnicity_2014.pdf

BIBLIOGRAPHY

Yodfat, Aryeh Y., *The Soviet Union and the Arabian Peninsula: Soviet Policy towards the Persian Gulf and Arabia*, Routledge: New York, 1983, pp. 1–32.

Yörük, Zafer and Pantelis Vatikiotis, 'Izmir University of Economics: Soft Power or Illusion of Hegemony', *International Journal of Communication*, vol. 7, 2013, pp. 2361–85.

Zarcone, Thierry, 'Pilgrimage to the "Second Mecca" and Ka'bas's of Central Asia', in Alexandre Papas, Thomas Welsford and Thierry Zarcone, *Hajj Routes and Pious Visits between Central Asia and the Hijaz*, Islamkundliche Untersuchungen Band 308, Klaus Schwarz Verlag: Berlin, 2011, pp. 251–77.

———, *Le Soufisme. Voie mystique de l'islam*, Gallimard: Paris, 2009.

———, 'Ahmad Yasavï héros des nouvelles républiques centrasiatiques', *Revues des mondes musulmans et de la Méditerranée*, no. 89–90, July 2000, http://remmm.revues.org/284

———, 'Une route de sainteté islamique entre l'Asie centrale et l'Inde: la voie Ush-Kashghar-Srinagar', *Cahiers d'Asie centrale*, nos. 1–2, 1996, pp. 227–54.

———, 'Réseaux confrériques et guides charismatiques dans les relations turco-arabes (héritage de l'histoire et situation actuelle)', *Anatolia Moderna*, IV (IFEA): Istanbul, 1992.

Zeghidour, Slimane, *La Vie quotidienne à La Mecque, de Mahomet à nos jours*, Hachette: Paris, 1989.

Zevaco, Ariane, 'From Old to New Matcha: Mass Resettlement and the New Redefinition of Islamic Practice between Tajikistan's Upper Valleys and Cotton Lowlands', in Stéphane A. Dudoignon (2014), pp. 148–201.

Zevaco reference and on the line after that please insert Reports and Websites.

'Samarkand Resident Sentenced for Propagating Sh'ite Islam', Radio Free Europe, Radio Liberty, 2013, http://www.referl.org/content/uzbek-propagating-islam/25175284.html.

'2014 Annual report', United States Commission on International Religious Freedom, http://www.uscirf.gov/reports-briefs/annual-report/2014-annual-report

'Georgia's Armenian and Azeri Minorities', International Crisis Group, Europe Report no. 178, 2006, https://www.files.ethz.ch/isn/26285/178_georgias_armenian_and_azeri_minorities.pdf

'Kazakhstan: Wave of Prosecutions Against 'Extremist' Muslims', *Eurasia Review*, http://www.eurasiareview.com/09102015-kazakhstan-wave-of-prosecutions-against-extremist-muslims

'Tajikistan: Why are around 93 Muslims being detained?', Forum 18, http:www.forum18.org/archive.php?article_id=1297

INDEX

Ablai Khan 161
Abu Bakr mosque (Azerbaijan) 172
Abu Hanifah 185
Abul Khair 161
Academies of Science 86, 91;
   Soviet Academy of Sciences 26
Adjara 51, 98
Adolat 169
Afghanistan ix, 9, 32–3, 37, 82,
   88, 107, 116–17, 118, 119–20,
   140, 149, 169, 170, 187, 188
Afghans 82
Africa 55, 111, 142
Afsana 13
Agha Khan Shah Karim Hussaini IV
   85–6
Ahlu Bay 99
Ahmadinejad, Mahmud 82
Ahmadiyya 139, 179
Ahmed Yassawi University 40, 162
Ahrar, Khwaja Ubaydullah 135,
   163
Akbar 133
Akhundov, Mirza Fatali 19, 98
AKP (Justice and Development
   Party) 5, 42, 60–63, 100
Al Azhar 103, 106, 108
al Hoda bookshops 86–7

Albania 139
Algeria 106
Al-Haramain Foundation 123
Al-Hila 137
Ali 89, 162
Aliyev, Haji Alikram 93, 172
Aliyev, Heydar 25, 162
Aliyev, Ilham 94
Allahyar, Haji Habibullah 136
Alloma, Rahmatullah 30
Almaty 86
Al-Qaeda 166, 170
Alu Bayt 99
Amman 37
Amu Darya 14
ANAP (Motherland Party) 44
Andijan 17, 79, 133, 164, 201
   (endnote)
Ankara 47
Ansari, Murtada al- 96
Aqtau 86
Arab countries (general) 29, 37,
   chapter 4, 171, 182, 187, 188
Arab League 109
Arabic language 51, 104, 106, 108
Arabic-Persian alphabet ix
Arabs (general) 12, 104, 108–9,
   113

239

INDEX

Aral Sea 31
ARAMCO 107
Aras 15, 88, 101
Armenia 16, 21, 29, 72, 75–6, 88–9
Arya Samaj 139
Ashgabat 40, 47, 48
Ashura 89, 91, 99
Assad, Bashar al- 101, 106
Assad, Hafez al- 106
Astana 40, 86, 109
Astrakhan 112, 168
Avicenna (Abu Ali al-Hasan Ibn Abdullah Ibn-Sina) 13, 73, 78, 105
Ayni, Sadriddin 19
Azad, Abu Kalam 137
Azerbaijan 16, 17, 18, 21, 22, 25, 30, 31, 32, 36, 46, 47, 50, 51, 57, 60, 61, 63, 66, 70, 72, 73, 74–6, 77, 78, 79, 80, 81, 83, 84–5, 88–95, 97–101, 115, 125, 145, 157, 162, 171–4, 176–9, 178, 187
Azeris 18, 20, 35, 37, 39, 72, 80, 83, 84–5, 88–90, 97, 98, 145, 158
Aziz Mahmud Hudayi Vakfi 50

Babajanov, Bahtiyar 175
Babur 133, 134
Badakshan 14
Baha'is 179
Bahili, Rabiah al- 15
Bakhchisaray 18
Bakikhanov, Abbasgulu 18
Baku Tbilisi Ceyhan (BTC) pipeline 40, 73, 75, 77
Baku vii, 18, 24, 27, 38, 46, 47, 50, 79, 87, 90, 92, 93, 98, 109, 171, 177, 184
Balkans 44, 54

Bangladesh 8, 132, 142, 147, 154
Baptists 179
Barda 15
Bashkirs 99
Bashkortostan 60
Basmachi 119, 208 (endnote)
Berdimuhammedov, Kurbanguli 147
Bibi Heybat 27, 31, 162
Bidil, Abdul Qadir 133
Bihzad 133, 134
Billah, Baqi 135
Birlik 31
Bishkek 51, 85, 86, 87
Blue Mosque 46
Bolshevik revolution 20–22, 98, 137
Bouygues 40
BP 79
Brezhnev, Leonid 24, 27
Britain 21, 71, 75, 105, 111, 112, 136, 142
Buddhism 12, 133
Bukhara 12, 13, 14, 16, 17, 18, 19, 20–21, 26, 49, 73, 77, 78, 83, 110, 113, 119, 133, 136, 137, 140, 163, 173, 177
Bukhari Institute 173
Bukhari, Muhammad ibn Ismail al- 12, 105, 120
Bulgaria 50

Cairo 18, 105
Calik, Ahmet 60
Caliphate 170
Caspian Sea 69, 72–3, 75, 77, 78–9, 85, 86, 88
Catherine II 16
cemaat 6, 58–62
Chaghatay ix
Chechens 16, 172
Chicago 142

INDEX

China 76, 117–18, 124, 133
Chisti 142, 143
Christianity 12, 15, 20, 55, 60, 76, 111, 140, 141, 159, 179
Circassians ix, 37
COMECON 33
Communism 22–3, 25, 37–8, 48, 74, 89, 107, 114, 122
cotton 25
Council of Europe 75
Council of Religious Affairs (Tajikistan) 178
Crimea 18
Cyprus 45
Cyrillic alphabet ix, 41

Dagestan 15, 16, 30, 89, 172
Damascus 105, 112
Darul Uloom 140
Datka, Kurjuman 151, 162
Delhi 105, 133, 134, 135, 145
Deoband School 138, 140, 148
Derbent 15, 104
Dhahran 107
Dhaka 154
Directorate of Spiritual Affairs (Azerbaijan) 100, 177
Directorate of Spiritual Affairs (Kyrgystan) 152–3
Directorate of Spiritual Affairs (Uzbekistan) 115, 178
Directorates of Spiritual Affairs 4, 149
Diyanet Işleri Başkanlığı 42, 43–8, 64–6, 155
Dmanisi 98
Dushanbe 133

Ebdul, Haji 171
education 4–5, 18–19, 24, 40–41, 46–8, 56–67, 85, 86–7, 95, 100, 101, 108–9, 173–7, 181

Egypt 71, 103, 106, 107–9, 123, 124, 137, 176
Elçibey, Ebulfeyz 31, 76, 92
elechek 150–51
Enver Pasha 37
Eratov, Rawshan 152
Erdoğan, Recep Tayyip 5–6, 57, 60, 62–3, 186, 187
Ergenekon affair 61, 197–8 (endnote)
Erkin party 87
Eurasian Islamic Council 45
European Union 187

Farabi, Abu Nasr al- 12, 73, 78, 105
Fazail-e-Amaal 153
Fergana 77, 122, 169, 170
Fethullaci, *see* Gülen
Fitrat, Abdulrauf 19–20, 21, 137
Foi et Pratique 142
Forum 180
France vii-viii, 40, 44, 71, 128
Furqat 137

Gadhafi, Muammar al- 106
Gamber, Isa 171
Gambia, The 142
Gangohi, Rashid Ahmed 143
Gasprinski (Gaspirali), Ismail 18, 35, 41
Georgia 16, 21, 29, 51, 75, 76, 89, 98–9, 145, 158
Germany 23–3, 44
Ghazni, Mahmud 134
Ghulam Ahmad, Mirza 139
Göktepe, Battle of 111, 136
Gorbachev, Mikhail 30–31, 114
Gori 98
Gülen, Fethullah, and Gülenists (Fethullaci) 6, 49, 51–65, 181

hajj 7–8, 104, 109–16, 123, 161

241

INDEX

Halk Cephesi (Popular Front) (Azerbaijan) 31, 92
Hamada 13
Hanafi school 28, 36, 43, 47, 49, 67, 84, 148, 174
Hanbali 167
*hawza*s 95
Hejaz 110, 112
Herat 133, 135
Hezbollah 90, 93, 101
Hikmet, Nazim 41
Hind Ixtilolchilari 137
Hindus 139, 141, 145
Hindustani, Domullah 30, 127, 138, 167
Hizb ut-Tahrir 127, 149, 170, 181
hizmet 6, 58–9
Homs 37
Hudoysizlar 23
Hujjabiyya madrasa 97
Human Rights Watch 180
Hurgronje, Christiaan Snouck 112, 128–9
Hussain 89

Ibn al Sa'ud 167
ibn Muslim, Habib 15
Ibn Taymiyya 14
Ibn-Sina, Abu Ali al-Hasan Ibn Abdullah (Avicenna) 13, 73, 78, 105
Ibrahimoglu, Haji Ilgar 93–4, 171, 180
Imam Hatip Okullari 47
Imam Khomeini University 87
imamzade 162
India 8, 18, 30, 52, 117–18, 127–8, 131–42, 145, 147, 154, 155, 166, 187, 188
Indonesia 128
International Islamic Relief Organization 123

International Religious Liberty Association 94
International Turkmen-Turkish University 60
Iran 6, 13–14, 16, 29, 32, 38, chapter 3, 110–11, 115, 135, 137, 171, 172, 182, 186, 187, 188
Iraq 70, 71, 82, 88, 90, 96, 100, 101, 108, 168
IRCICA (Research Center for Islamic History, Art and Culture) 109
Ironis 83–4, 85
ISESCO (Islamic International Educational, Cultural and Scientific Organization) 109
Islam Sesi 173
Islamic education 4–5, 24, 46–8, 51, 56–67, 85, 87, 95, 100, 101, 108–9, 173–7
Islamic inheritance and background 2–5, 11–35
Islamic Movement of Uzbekistan (IMU) 125, 149, 166, 166, 169–70
Islamic Party of Azerbaijan 100, 172
Islamic revival (general) 29–34
'Islamic State' 188
Islamic University, Azerbaijan 30, 177
Islamism, *see also* Jihadism; radical Islam 20, 49, 57–8, 61, 70, 122, 148, 165–73, 181
Isma'ilis 85–6
Ismail, Shah 13
Istanbul 18, 19, 47, 105, 110
Ivan the Terrible 15
Ivanishvili, Ibidza 76
Izmir 54

Jadids 18–23, 105, 137, 164, 165

INDEX

Jafari school 83
Jalalabad 51
Jama'at i Islam 144
Jamiat-e-Islami 155
Java 111, 128
Jawna 105
Jeddah 111, 120, 126
Jehovah's Witnesses 179
jellaba 149, 150
Jeltoksan 31
Jesuits 55, 64
Jews, Judaism 55
Jihadism, see also Islamism; radical Islam 9, 32–3, 122, 125, 128–9, 132, 145, 156, 166, 170, 172, 187–8
Jordan 37, 170
Jurabekov, Ismail 84, 88

Kabiri, Muhiddin 168
Kabul 135
kamis 149, 150
Kandhlawi, Muhammad Ilyas 52, 141–4
Kaplanci 55
Kara Balya 47
Karabekir, Kazim 46
Karakhanids 73
Karbala 95, 96, 100, 110, 115
Karimov, Islam 80, 84, 122, 125–6, 160–64, 169
Karshi 105
Kasansay 77
Kashgar 118, 136
Kaufman, General Von 17
Kazakhs 16, 18, 20, 31, 35, 150–51, 154
Kazakhstan viii, 27, 31, 40, 46, 51, 57, 61, 63, 65, 72, 77, 78, 79, 80, 86, 109, 118, 123, 125, 147–8, 149, 155, 157, 161–2, 175, 176, 179

Kazan 17
Kemal Atatürk 5, 36–7, 43–4, 52, 55
KGB 162
Khamenei, Ali 71, 97, 101
Khatami, Mohammad 82
Khiva 14, 16, 73, 77, 119
Khomeini, Ayatollah 71, 82, 97
khoms 96, 98
Khorasani, Vahdi 97
Khrushchev, Nikita 24
Kirkinci, Mehmet 53
Kists 98
Kokand 14, 16, 73, 77, 119
Kolbin, Gennady 31
kolkhoz and sovkhoz 3, 28, 30
Konye-Urgench 162
Koran 19, 51, 52, 53, 113, 124, 147, 174, 180
Krishna 135
Kubra, Najmuddin 162
Kubraviyah 162
Kunaev, Dinmukhamed 31
kurtan 150
Kutkular, Mehmet 53
Kyrgyz 9, 31, 35, 150–51, 154, 159
Kyrgyzstan 9, 40, 46, 51, 57, 61, 63, 65, 77, 84, 88, 115, 118, 123, 126, 139, 145, 148, 149, 150–56, 162, 170, 174, 176, 179, 187

Lahore school of Ahmadiyya 139
Lahore 154
Latin alphabet ix, 41
Lebanon 82, 90, 96, 101
Lenkeran 177
Lenkerani, Fazil 97
Libya 33, 106
Lucknow 148
Lycée Turgut Özal 60

243

INDEX

maarifçilik 106
Madali, Muhammad Ali (Dukchi Islam) 17, 163–4
Madrasa Imam Khomeiny 95, 97
Madrasat ul-Hujjatiyya 95
mahallahs 162
Mahtumkuli 78
Manas epic 153, 162
Manas University 40
Marghiloni, Maqsud 125
marifat ve manaviyat 176
marja' al taqlid 96, 97–8, 99, 110
marjaiyya 95–8
Marmara, University of 47
Marneuli 98
Mashhad 85, 87, 92, 93, 95, 100, 101, 110, 115
Maturidi, Abu Mansar al- 174, 185
Maturidiyyah 84
mausoleums 4, 113, 143, 162
Mawdudi, Abu Ala al- 52
Mecca and Medina 103, 106, 107, 108, 120, 123, 161
Medina University 108, 172
Merv 12, 85
Mesopotamia 14
Mewat 141
migration ix, 7, 37, 44, 48, 55, 99, 107, 116–26, 151, 208 (endnote)
Mir-i Arab madrasa 173
Mirzoev, Abduvali Qari 30
Molla Nasraddin 98
Mongols 13, 15, 162
Morocco 109, 142
mosques 23, 46, 85, 122, 124, 128, 147, 165, 171, 172, 179
Mubarak, Hosni 176
Mughals 8, 110, 133–6
Muhammad, Prophet 117, 120, 127, 167
Mujaddid, Sheikh Muhammad Sulfikar Naqshbandi 140

Mujaddidiyya 167
Muminov, Achirbek 175
Musa al-Kazim 32, 162, 172
Musavat 171
Musavvir, Mir 133
Mushfiq 133
Muslim Brotherhood 166, 175
Muslim summits 45
Muslim World League/Rabita 7, 118, 123–4, 127, 128

Nabhani, Taqiuddin al- 170
Nagorno-Karabakh 46, 69, 72, 75, 88, 90, 99
Najad, Ahmad Ojak 90–91
Najaf 95, 96, 100
Nakhchivan 46
Namangan 169
Namangani, Juma 32–3, 125, 169
Naqshbandi, Bahauddin 27, 31, 113, 135, 163
Naqshbandiyya 16, 17, 36, 49–50, 59, 134, 135–6, 139, 163, 185
Nardaran 31, 92, 97, 172
Narin 51
Nasritdinov, Emil 153
Nasser, Gamal Abdel 108, 124
National Action Party 37–8
National Library, Kazakhstan 86
Navoi, Mir Alisher 13, 134
Navruz 27
Nazarbayev, Nursultan 161, 175
Nejat, Seyyid Ali Akbar Ocaq 97
Nestorians 12
Netherlands 111, 112, 128
Nevada Semipalatinsk 31
New Delhi 145, 154
New York 142
Niyazov (Turkmenbashi), President Sapar Murad 60, 147, 176
Nizami 73, 78

INDEX

Nizamuddin Markaz 143, 145, 148, 154
North Caucasus peoples, *see also* Dagestan 15–16, 17, 37, 99, 172
North Yemen 106
nurcu movement 53
Nuri, Sayid Abdullah 168
Nur-Mubarak university 109, 176
Nursi, Said 49, 51–3, 58

Och 176
Odessa 112
oil and gas 40, 73, 75, 78–9, 80
Olympic Games 115–16
Organization of Islamic Cooperation 109
Oriental Studies institutes 86
Osh 47, 51, 151
Ottoman Empire 15–16, 36, 49, 51, 82, 110–11, 137, 174
Özal, Turgut 38, 44, 49, 56

Pakistan ix, 8, 132, 138–40, 142, 145, 147, 149, 150, 154, 155, 170, 187, 188
Palestine 94
pan-Islamism 112
Pankisi Gorge 98
pan-Turkism 42, 48–9, 60, 76, 93
Paris 142
Party of Islamic Renaissance 81, 87, 148, 157, 166, 168
Pashazadeh, Allah Shukur 100, 171, 177
Pentecostalism 179
Persian culture and language 13, 18, 27, 36, 70, 73, 77–8, 80, 86–7, 95, 97, 103–7, 133–5
pilgrimage 7–8, 17, 84, 90, 104, 109–16, 123, 126, 128–9, 143, 154–5, 161
Polatov, Abdurrahman 31

Popular Front/*Halk Cephesi* (Azerbaijan) 31, 92
Protestants 139

Qadiani 139
Qadimists 19–20, 21
Qadiriyya 16
Qajars 74, 81–2, 88
Qanun al Tibb 13
Qasr-i Hinduvan 135
Qatar 109
Qazvin 93
Qom 85, 92, 93, 95, 96, 97, 100, 101
Qori, Munnavar 19
Qutayba ibn Muslim 12

radical Islam, *see also* Islamism; Jihadism 5, 87, 125, 138, 168
Rafsanjani, Hashemi 82
Rahim Hanim 32, 92, 172
Raiwind 154
Rashidov, Sharof 25
Red Sea 112
refugees 72, 90, 99, 116–17
Republican People's Party 55
ribats 121
Risale-i Nur 52, 53, 95, 96
Rouhani, Hassan 82
Rudaki 73, 77
Ruhnama 147, 176
Russia, post-1991 ix, 40, 60, 71, 72, 73, 76, 79, 88, 89, 98, 99, 145, 173, 187
Russia, Tsarist 2–3, 13–14, 105–6, 111–13, 126, 136–7, 162, 163–4, 188
Russian language 154
Russians 154
Ruzbihan, Fazlullah 14, 17

Saakashvili, Mikhail 76

245

INDEX

Sabir, Haji 177
Sadat, Anwar al- 108
Saddam Hussein 71
SADUM (Spiritual Administration of the Muslims of Central Asia) 24, 29, 158, 178
Safavids 13, 16, 81, 82, 88, 92, 110, 133
Saidazimabev, Said 112
Salafism ix, 45, 71, 122, 124, 127, 129, 138, 165, 166, 167, 172, 174–5
Samadov, Movsum 93
Samanids 77
Samarkand 12, 13, 14, 26, 73, 77, 78, 83, 133, 135, 136
Samarqandi, Maulana 133
Sanskrit 134
Sarajevo 45
Sassanids 73
Saudi Arabia 7–8, 37, 38, 45, 71, 86, 123–9, 139, 167, 186
Seljuk Turks 15
September 11 attacks 57–8
Shahid, Ahmad 144
Shamil, Imam 16
Sharia 14, 22
Shaybanids 13, 14
Shaykh al-Islam (Azerbaijan) 93, 98–9
Sheki 50, 174, 177
Shi'a Islam 13–15, 31, 32, 36, 47, 70–71, 76, 80, 81–5, 87–102, 106, 110–11, 115, 176, 177, 180, 186
Shirazi, Mekarim 97
Shymkent 176
Silk Road 14, 105, 132, 136
Sirhindi, Ahmad 135
Sistani, Ali 97, 99
Slav University, Kyrgyzstan 86
Sodiq, Muhammad Yusuf Muhammad 160
South Africa 142
Soviet Union viii, 3–5, 20–34, 36–8, 58, 69–70, 71, 74, 79, 91, 92, 98, 106–8, 113–16, 118–20, 124, 126, 137–8, 149, 151, 153, 154, 157–61, 162, 165, 167, 171, 172, 176–7, 178, 180, 182, 183, 188
Spain 145
Spiritual Directorate (Baku) 158
Spiritual Directorate (Kyrgyzstan) 65
Srinagar 136
Stalin 24, 25, 108, 113, 119
State Committee for Religious Affairs (Kyrgyzstan) 152
State Committee for Religious Affairs (Uzbekistan) 178, 179
State Committee for Working with Religious Bodies (Azerbaijan) 178–9
Sufism 110, 135, 142–3, 165, 185, 186
Suhrawardiyya 143
Suleimanov, Ganet 172, 180
Suleimenov, Olzhas 31
Suleymanci 51
Suluk al-muluk 14, 17
Sungur, Mustafa 53
Sunni Islam 13, 15, 36, 67, 80, 82, 84, 87, 91, 98, 106, 174, 176, 177, 180, 186
Syr Daria 14
Syria ix, 9, 33, 37, 90, 94, 101, 106, 137

Ta'if 120
Tablighi Jamaat 9, 131–2, 138, 140–55, 166
Tabriz 133
Tabrizi, Jevad 97
Tahmasp 133

INDEX

Tajikistan 27, 57, 61, 63, 69, 70, 71, 73, 77, 78, 80, 81, 85–6, 87, 123, 133, 148, 149, 164, 168, 169, 176, 178
Tajiks 20, 26, 31, 36, 77, 84, 85–7, 154
Talas, Battle of 104
Taliban 140, 166, 170, 187
Talish and Talishis 73
Tashkent vii, 18, 24, 27, 38, 48, 85, 86, 109, 112, 138, 158, 169, 173, 175, 183; Islamic University 175–6
Tatars 18, 99, 154, 168
Tatarstan 60, 173
Tbilisi 98
Tehran 18, 73, 93, 105
temsil 58–9
Terjuman 18
Termez 73, 133
Timur 13, 160
Timurids 13–14, 73, 133, 124, 135
Tirmidhi, Abu Isa Muhammad al- 12
Toktomushov, Maksat 155
Topbaş, Osman Nuri 50, 59
Tövbe 171
Trans-Caspian Railway 113
Tunahan, Süleyman Hilmi 50, 59, 65
Turajanzade, Akbar 87
Turajanzade, Eshoni 87
Türkeş, Alparslan 38
Turkestan (city) 162
Turkestan 16–17, 37, 117, 118, 119, 120, 133, 137
Turkey 5, 6, 29, chapter 2, 70, 71, 76, 77, 79, 91, 100, 101, 118, 121, 146, 155, 162, 171, 176, 177, 181, 182, 186–7, 188
Turkish and Turkic peoples, culture and languages 15, 18, 27, 35–41, 61, 73, 77–8, 84, 103, 105–6, 129, 133, 135
Turkish International Cooperation and Development Agency 39
Turkistani, Rahmatullah 118
Turkmenbashi (Niyazov), President Sapar Murad 60, 147, 176
Turkmenbashi/Krasnovodsk 85
Turkmenchay, Treaty of 14, 16, 74, 88, 111
Turkmenistan 35, 40, 46, 51, 60, 66, 72, 73, 77, 78, 79, 80, 83, 84, 111, 146–7, 157, 162, 178, 179, 176, 187
Turkmens 20, 35, 80, 116–17
Turkophone summits 39
TURKSOY (International Organization of Turkish Culture) 41–2
Turpan 118
Twelver Shia 14, 32, 36, 83, 84, 110

Ubaidullah Khan 14
Uighur National Congress 118
Uighurs 7–8, 104, 117–18, 124
ulama 14, 19, 110
Ulugh Beg 13
Ummayad Caliphate 12
United Arab Emirates 109
University of Human Sciences, Kyrgyzstan 86
Urdu 154
US Commission on International Religious Freedom 180–81
USA 39, 53, 71, 75, 76, 77, 79, 86, 88, 107, 108, 138, 142, 175, 187
Ush 136
Üsküdar 110
Uttar Pradesh 138
Uulu, Tursunbai Bakir 87–8
Uzbekistan 8, 12, 22, 23, 25, 26,

247

INDEX

27, 31, 39, 41, 45, 46, 50, 51, 53, 57, 58, 60, 66, 70, 71, 73, 77, 78, 79, 80, 83, 84, 86, 88, 114–15, 118–22, 124–6, 127, 128, 133, 140, 145, 149, 155, 156, 159–66, 168, 169–70, 174–7, 178–9, 181, 185, 187
Uzbeks 7–8, 18, 20, 26, 31, 35, 37, 78, 82, 84, 104, 105, 110, 116–17, 118–29

veil 150–51

Wahhab, Muhammad Abud 167
Wahhabism 7–8, 45, 71, 122, 123, 124, 125, 127, 129, 165, 167–8, 174
Wali, Mahmud Amir 133
Waliullah, Shah 144
Warsaw Pact 33
Washington University 175
World Vision 55, 60
World War, First 46, 52
World War, Second 23–4

Xin Jiang 116–17

Yanbu' 120
Yarkant 118
Yassawi, Ahmad 27, 113, 161–2
Yemen 106, 107
Yeni Asya 53
Yeni Musavat 94
Yoldashev, Tahir 125, 169
Young Bukharians 19, 105
Young Ottomans 19, 105
Yovqochev, Shuhrat 175
Yusuf, Muhammad Sadik Muhammad 146

Zahedan 87
zakat 96, 118
Zakatala 50, 177
Zaman 54
Zengi Ata 27
zikr 143
Zir-Ulugbek 133
ziyarat 113–14
Zoroastrianism 12, 15